CHARIS: Christianity and
Renewal—Interdisciplinary Studies

Wolfgang Vondey and Amos Yong, *Editors*

Wolfgang Vondey (PhD, Marquette University) is associate professor of systematic theology and director of the Center for Renewal Studies at the School of Divinity of Regent University in Virginia Beach, Virginia. He is the author and editor of several books and publications on themes of the global renewal movements, including aspects of pentecostalism and pentecostal theology, ecumenical theology, ecclesiology, pneumatology, and the intersection of theology and science. He is organizer of the annual conference in Renewal Theology.

Amos Yong (PhD, Boston University) is professor of theology and mission, and director of the Center for Missiological Research at Fuller Theological Seminary in Pasadena, California. He is author and editor of more than 30 books and has published in diverse fields of study, including widely on themes related to Christianity and renewal, pentecostalism, hermeneutics, pneumatology, interfaith dialogue, disability studies, and the intersection of theology and science. He is coeditor of the Pentecostal Manifestos series and Studies in Religion, Theology, and Disability series.

Christianity and Renewal—Interdisciplinary Studies provides a forum for scholars from a variety of disciplinary perspectives, various global locations, and a range of Christian ecumenical and religious traditions to explore issues at the intersection of the pentecostal, charismatic, and other renewal movements and related phenomena, including:

- the transforming and renewing work of the Holy Spirit in Christian traditions, cultures, and creation;
- the traditions, beliefs, interpretation of sacred texts, and scholarship of the renewal movements;
- the religious life, including the spirituality, ethics, history, and liturgical and other practices, and spirituality of the renewal movements;
- the social, economic, political, transnational, and global implications of renewal movements;
- methodological, analytical, and theoretical concerns at the intersection of Christianity and renewal;
- intra-Christian and interreligious comparative studies of renewal and revitalization movements; and
- other topics connecting to the theme of Christianity and renewal.

Authors are encouraged to examine the broad scope of religious phenomena and their interpretation through the methodological, hermeneutical, and historiographical lens of renewal in contemporary Christianity.

Under the general topic of thoughtful reflection on Christianity and renewal, the series includes two different kinds of books: (1) monographs that allow for in-depth pursuit, carefully argued, and meticulously documented research on a particular topic that explores issues in Christianity and renewal and (2) edited collections that allow scholars from a variety of disciplines to interact under a broad theme related to Christianity and renewal. In both kinds, the series encourages discussion of traditional pentecostal and charismatic studies, reexamination of established religious doctrine and practice, and explorations into new fields of study related to renewal movements. Interdisciplinarity will feature in the series both in terms of two or more disciplinary approaches deployed in any single volume and in terms of a wide range of disciplinary perspectives found cumulatively in the series.

PUBLISHED

Wolfgang Vondey (ed.), *The Holy Spirit and the Christian Life: Historical, Interdisciplinary, and Renewal Perspectives* (2014).

Nimi Wariboko, *The Charismatic City and the Public Resurgence of Religion: A Pentecostal Social Ethics of Cosmopolitan Urban Life* (2014).

Leah Payne, *Gender and Pentecostal Revivalism: Making a Female Ministry in the Early Twentieth Century* (2015).

GENDER AND PENTECOSTAL REVIVALISM

MAKING A FEMALE MINISTRY IN THE EARLY TWENTIETH CENTURY

Leah Payne

palgrave
macmillan

The following are reprinted with permission: "Reflections on the Potential of Gender Theory for Pentecostal History" by Leah Payne, *Pneuma: The Journal of the Society for Pentecostal Studies* © 2014; and "Pants Don't Make Preachers: Fashion and Gender Construction in Late Nineteen- and Early Twentieth-Century American Revivalism" by Leah Payne, *Fashion Theory: The Journal of Body, Dress and Culture* © 2014.

Copyright protected images are used by express consent of the International Church of the Foursquare Gospel and the Flower Pentecostal Heritage Center.

First published in 2015 by
PALGRAVE MACMILLAN®
in the United States—a division of St. Martin's Press LLC,
175 Fifth Avenue, New York, NY 10010.

Where this book is distributed in the UK, Europe and the rest of the world, this is by Palgrave Macmillan, a division of Macmillan Publishers Limited, registered in England, company number 785998, of Houndmills, Basingstoke, Hampshire RG21 6XS.

Palgrave Macmillan is the global academic imprint of the above companies and has companies and representatives throughout the world.

Palgrave® and Macmillan® are registered trademarks in the United States, the United Kingdom, Europe and other countries.

ISBN: 978–1–137–49469–6

Library of Congress Cataloging-in-Publication Data

Payne, Leah.
    Gender and pentecostal revivalism : making a female ministry in the early twentieth century / Leah Payne.
        pages cm.—(CHARIS : Christianity and renewal—interdisciplinary studies)
    Includes bibliographical references and index.
    ISBN 978–1–137–49469–6 (alk. paper)
    1. Women clergy—United States—History—20th century. 2. Women evangelists—United States—History—20th century. 3. McPherson, Aimee Semple, 1890–1944. 4. Woodworth-Etter, Maria Beulah, 1844–1924. 5. Pentecostalism—United States—History—20th century. 6. United States—Church history—20th century. I. Title.

BV676.P39 2015
262'.14082—dc23   2014032487

A catalogue record of the book is available from the British Library.

Design by Newgen Knowledge Works (P) Ltd., Chennai, India.

First edition: February 2015

10 9 8 7 6 5 4 3 2 1

For Thomas

CONTENTS

Figures and Tables

Figures

Tables

Acknowledgments

I am indebted to many for their support of this book. I must first thank Professors Kathleen Flake and Amy-Jill Levine for their advice, critiques, encouragement, compassion, and good humor over the years. I cannot adequately express my appreciation for their contributions to my life as woman and as an academic. In addition, I am very thankful for the time and attention that Professors Jay Geller and Dennis Dickerson gave to me during this project and throughout my graduate career.

Much of my work was made possible by generous grants and fellowships from Vanderbilt University's Graduate School, the Carpenter Program in Religion, Gender, and Sexuality, the Center for the Study of Religion and Culture, and the Vanderbilt University Women and Gender Studies Program. In addition, I am very grateful to the Louisville Institute for their current support of my ongoing research. I am also indebted to Steve Zeleny, Jackie Miller, and Janet Simonsen at the Foursquare Heritage Center, the Foursquare Church, and Glenn Gohr and the Flower Pentecostal Heritage Center. In addition, Vanderbilt University and George Fox University's library and staff contributed greatly to this study.

I am thankful for the supportive and loyal friends that I made as I wrote this book. My friends from Vanderbilt's Graduate Department of Religion were especially helpful to me as I wrote and researched. In particular, I am grateful for the support of Jimmy Barker and Katy Attanasi, Meredith Hammons, Lydia Willsky, Keri Day, Klem-Mari Cajigas, Tamura Lomax, Maria Mayo, Mika and Christina Edmondson, Devan Stahl, Derek Axelson, Andrew C. Smith, Noel Schoonmaker, Carolyn Davis, Kelly Williams, and all of my friends in the 2006 PhD cohort.

I was inspired, encouraged, and critiqued at the annual meetings for the American Academy of Religion, the American Society of Church History, the Society for Pentecostal Studies, and the Wesleyan Theological Society. In addition, my work has flourished with encouragement from scholars of Pentecostalism including Linda Ambrose,

Amos Yong, Dave Roebuck, Estrelda Alexander, Kim Alexander, Pam Holmes, Michael McClymond, Steve Overman, as well as my fellow students of Pentecostalism at the Society for Pentecostal Studies.

I wish to thank my friends (new and old) at George Fox Evangelical Seminary and George Fox University, including (but not limited to!): Paul Anderson, Phil Smith, Sarita Gallagher, Roger Nam, Dan Brunner, Loren Kerns, Nell Becker Sweeden, Paula Hampton, MaryKate Morse, Jenny Matheny, Trisha Welstad, and Cliff Berger. I also appreciate my students at Vanderbilt Divinity School, George Fox Evangelical Seminary, and George Fox University, from whom I learned much in our classes together.

I owe my family a lifetime of gratitude. My mother April encouraged me in every way and took me to the library throughout my childhood, where I developed an enduring interest in late-nineteenth- and early-twentieth-century female pioneers. My father Lowell gave me the gift of his confidence in my intellect and my first Aimee Semple McPherson autobiography. My siblings Mike, Annie, and Amber are my closest friends and biggest fans. My parents-in-law Tom and Tammy are kind enough to be proud of me. And Moxie the dog provided loyalty and companionship during the long days of writing.

Finally, and most dearly, my spouse Thomas gave me endless friendship, sympathy, humor, inspiration, prayers, proofreading, and cups of coffee during the writing process. There are not enough words with which to acknowledge his contribution to my life and work.

INTRODUCTION

In the late nineteenth and early twentieth centuries, Americans delighted in many things: industrialization, a closed Western frontier, new methods of social engineering, science and technology, mass media, and all manner of modern innovations. If there was one group that did *not* delight most Americans, it was female ministers. "There is in most of us," wrote "a Discontented Man" in an 1895 editorial in the popular periodical *The Review of Reviews*, "an inwardness of instinct against setting up a female in the prominence of the pulpit to lecture on their sins to a mixed congregation of men and women."[1] "Women should," he recommend further, "eschew such employments as involve (1) much public association or juxtaposition with men on common terms, (2) the addressing of large mixed public audiences, (3) an attitude of effrontery or undue self-assertiveness, (4) a *métier* ignoring in any way the essential distinctions of sex, (5) the exercise of much muscular strength or nerve."[2]

Pentecostal celebrity ministers Maria Woodworth-Etter (1844–1924) and Aimee Semple McPherson (1890–1944) thoroughly and cheerfully disregarded the Discontented Man's advice. They had regular public association with men (and often told them what to do). They spoke to large, mixed gender audiences, were often assertive, and displayed a good deal of nerve. Most of all, their *métier* of choice was a vocation that threatened to blur the seemingly, "essential distinctions of sex," in the 1890s–1920s.[3]

The Discontented Man's turn-of-the-century editorial raises the central questions of this book. How did women become powerful female revivalist ministers during the 1890s–1920s—an era in which public leadership was seen as naturally, "instinctively" male? More specifically, this project asks how two Pentecostal women—Woodworth-Etter and McPherson—overcame not only their gender, but also the taints of divorce, single motherhood, and public scandal to become authoritative revivalist pastors. In addition, this project aims to investigate what it is about Pentecostalism that allowed for such talented (albeit scandalous) women to rise so remarkably within the movement.

I will argue that Woodworth-Etter and McPherson became authoritative celebrity ministers by co-opting versions of ideal womanhood in service to their ministerial identities, and by displaying those identities through classic Pentecostal revivalist methods. In other words, the Pentecostal movement, which they helped to shape, and were being shaped by, included instincts, tastes, and sensibilities that created a space for their careers. The women utilized Pentecostal biblical narratives, manipulated their public images, capitalized on revivalist worship spaces, and adopted preaching styles to perform versions of themselves that were womanly (according to the standards of their day) and authoritative for their Pentecostal followers.

In this introductory chapter, I will discuss the methodological approach I have chosen for this book and the anticipated outcomes of the study. Before I discuss methodology and outcomes, however, I will first introduce Woodworth-Etter and McPherson as female pastors. When it comes to women as famous (and infamous) as Woodworth-Etter and McPherson, there are many ways that their lives and careers could be framed. I am studying them in their capacity as pastors, however, and while much more could be said about them, these women's biographies are selective; they show their exceptional ascent to powerful female Pentecostal revivalist ministry.

MARIA WOODWORTH-ETTER

Maria Woodworth-Etter was born on July 22, 1844 to indigent farmers Samuel and Matilda Underwood in New Lisbon, Ohio. Her father, an abusive alcoholic, was unable to provide for his family.[4] When he died from sunstroke in 1856, Matilda Underwood struggled to feed and clothe her children.[5] Woodworth-Etter and her older sisters dropped out of school and worked in order to support their mother and younger siblings.[6]

At the age of 13, Woodworth-Etter attended a Disciples of Christ church service. When the minister gave the altar call, Woodworth-Etter was the first down the aisle, and the next day she was baptized. "While I was going into the water," she wrote, "a light came over me, and I was converted."[7] From that moment, she dreamed of working as a revivalist pastor's wife or missionary.[8]

During the Civil War, however, 19-year-old Woodworth-Etter met and married injured veteran Philo Harris (P. H.) Woodworth. P. H. Woodworth had no interest in his wife's revivalist passion. Rather, he wanted to make a living in agriculture, and he and his new wife moved to the country where they set out to become farmers and have children. In both enterprises, they had little success. Woodworth's war injuries brought the man mental and physical frailties that made him a poor candidate for the manual labor of farming.[9] Woodworth-Etter had difficult pregnancies, and all but her eldest daughter Lizzie died in childhood.

She fell ill from grief after each child's death. "From the time of the sad occurrences," she wrote, "my health was very poor, and in many times I was brought near the brink of the grave. I seemed to be hovering between life and death."[10] Adding to her distress, in the country she could not attend regular church meetings. "I was away from all Christian influence," Woodworth-Etter wrote, "Often when hearing the church bells ringing, which had been the signal for me to repair to the house of worship, and knowing that I could not go, I would cry myself to sleep."[11]

When her son Willie died in 1880 and only her daughter Lizzie and P. H. remained, 35-year-old Woodworth-Etter began her career as an itinerant holiness minister and church planter. Since P. H. Woodworth insisted that she stay close to home, she remained within a seven mile radius, riding to a town, preaching a few times, and then riding back to her family. After a few spectacular revival successes, she became a sought-after preacher in her region. The resulting financial resources enabled Woodworth-Etter, Lizzie, and a reluctant P. H. to travel on the Midwest revival circuit.

Together, the Woodworths ran a traveling holiness revival that featured preaching, altar calls, and prayers for healing. Woodworth-Etter and Lizze thrived, but P. H. Woodworth was not well-suited for life as a minister's spouse. He was accused of profiteering (because he sold refreshments at his wife's meetings), using crass language, and making inappropriate remarks to reporters; rumors were rampant that he had propositioned Woodworth-Etter's female disciples.[12] Reporters noticed that the Woodworths often spent their evenings in different sleeping quarters.[13] Eventually, P. H. Woodworth left his wife and returned to Ohio. Woodworth-Etter filed for divorce. It was finalized in 1891.

Without P. H. Woodworth's embarrassing behavior, Woodworth-Etter's career relaunched in the 1890s. She toured with a small entourage that included her daughter, a few women assistants, and their husbands whom Woodworth-Etter referred to as her "praying lieutenants."[14] Within the next few years she had appeared in Oakland, California and South Framingham, Massachusetts and dozens of major cities (as well as numerous small towns) in between. She planted churches and appointed (mostly male) ministers along the way.[15]

She published and sold thousands of autobiographies detailing her calling to the ministry. She also included in these books snippets from the hundreds of pieces of fan mail she received. She developed a national reputation as a healer who put on a spectacular one-woman preaching show.

At the turn of the twentieth century, the middle-aged Maria B. Woodworth was a well-established celebrity holiness pastor. In many ways her career was just beginning. In 1902, at the age of 58, Woodworth-Etter met and married Samuel Etter. Their marriage was a boon for the minister. Etter was a much more suitable partner who supported his new wife financially and emotionally.

Woodworth-Etter also joined the Pentecostal movement. She initially resisted becoming a Pentecostal because she was skeptical of the movement's more flamboyant characters. Early in her career she wrote that holy rollers had a tendency toward excess such that the "Holy Ghost was driven away,"[16] but the Pentecostals were sure she belonged with them. They imitated her preaching style and liked her teachings. Many came to her revivals even before she joined their movement. Finally, after 1904 (when she was dismissed from the Church of God), Woodworth-Etter began to identify as a member of the movement. By 1912 she was considered one of its most powerful leaders.[17]

By 1918, Woodworth-Etter had been an itinerant minister and ad hoc bishop for over three decades. Firmly ensconced as a living legend in the Pentecostal revivalist movement, she built a large permanent church in Indianapolis, Indiana. In 1918, she unwittingly passed the torch of Pentecostal revivalist celebrity when she received a visit from an eager young woman named Aimee Semple McPherson.

AIMEE SEMPLE MCPHERSON

Aimee Elizabeth Kennedy was born on a farm near Ingersoll, Ontario to a lower middleclass Methodist farmer and his young Salvation Army wife on October 9, 1890. McPherson remembered her early years as an idyllic, pastoral upbringing complete with cow milking, a beloved family horse named "Flossie," and down home cooking.[18] In December of 1907, Robert Semple, an Irish preacher, held a revival meeting at the local mission hall; that meeting introduced McPherson to Pentecostal revivalism.[19] Semple preached about the baptism of the Holy Spirit and speaking in tongues.[20] "To me," Aimee Kennedy recalled, "this Spirit-prompted utterance was like the voice of God."[21]

Robert Semple and his young convert shared romance as well as a desire to spread the good news. In the summer of 1908, they married and began to work together in his evangelistic efforts.[22] That August, they accepted a call to the mission field in China. Soon after arriving, a pregnant McPherson contracted malaria. Semple also became ill, and he died of dysentery in the fall of 1910. McPherson was left in China alone. She bore a daughter, named her Roberta named after her father, borrowed money from her mother, and returned home.

Upon her return, McPherson traveled between New York where her mother worked for the Salvation Army, Chicago where Robert Semple's Pentecostal friends remembered her, and her childhood home in Canada. She was determined to "take up Robert's task of evangelism," but McPherson felt alone in big cities and restless in the small town of Ingersoll.[23] She also worried about providing for her infant daughter; without a husband to bring in income, the future was dim.[24]

McPherson's loneliness did not last long. Harold McPherson, a young hotel manager, soon fell in love with Robert Semple's pretty widow. They married and quickly conceived a son named Rolf. "By all the laws of domestic arrangement," wrote McPherson of her time as a stay-at-home mother, "I should have been happy."[25] The only obstacle to marital bliss was that "a voice kept hammering at my [McPherson's] heart. It shouted, 'Preach the Word! Do the work of an evangelist!'"[26] McPherson thus felt torn between the belief that she was called to preach and her responsibilities as a wife. She eventually gave in to the call.

An innovator from the beginning, she had an idea to travel the country in a "Gospel Car." By 1916, she was touring the United States in a motor vehicle with the following slogan emblazoned on its side: "JESUS IS COMING SOON—GET READY." She published a nationally distributed periodical called *The Bridal Call*, which she used to keep her audience informed about her ministry and to spread her revivalist message. In 1918, she drove to Woodworth-Etter's church in Indianapolis. "We rejoiced and praised the Lord together," she wrote of her encounter with Woodworth-Etter, "the power of God fell."[27]

At first, Harold McPherson decided to follow his wife into itinerant ministry. He even preached occasionally, but he quickly grew tired of being known as the preacher's husband. Citing spousal abandonment, he filed for divorce; their marriage officially ended in 1921.[28]

After her divorce, McPherson's career profited immensely. In January of 1923, she opened a 5,300-seat auditorium in Los Angeles.

In February of 1924, she purchased a radio station (KFSG, Kall Foursquare Gospel) and began broadcasting. She created the Echo Park Evangelistic and Missionary Training Institute in 1923, which became the Lighthouse of International Foursquare Evangelism (L.I.F.E.) in 1926. In 1927, she founded her own denomination, the International Church of the Foursquare Gospel (Foursquare). No revivalist minister rivaled McPherson for power, fame, and influence in the 1920s and early 1930s.

A FAMOUS FEMALE MINISTER

There are many reasons why Woodworth-Etter and McPherson's power, popularity, and influence are surprising. First, the women had few conventional qualifications to recommend them to the ministry. They lacked seminary education that revivalists like Christian Missionary Alliance Albert Benjamin "A. B." Simpson had, recognition from a denominational governing body like Presbyterian J. Frank Norris enjoyed, or any claim to the apostolic succession that Methodist revivalists claimed.[29] Woodworth-Etter had an elementary-level education, and McPherson had a high school diploma. Both were largely self-taught in the theory and methods of ministry. They also had spotty track records when it came to ordination. Woodworth-Etter held ordination briefly with the Church of God, but the denomination revoked her license.[30] She was embraced by holiness congregations and Pentecostals, but had no official ordination in either circle. At different points during her career, Baptist, Assemblies of God, and Methodist Episcopal Church bodies ordained McPherson, but she did not remain with any denomination but her own for very long.[31] Therefore, the women's authorization to lead, perform rites, discern and interpret the divine, and instruct congregants was in question perpetually.

In addition to lacking traditional ministerial markers, there were few 1890s–1920s American ministers as scandalous as Woodworth-Etter and McPherson. National newspapers branded the women as quacks for their controversial practice of divine healing.[32] They were criticized for their association with African American people and practices.[33] Their sanity was questioned.[34] They had regular run-ins with the law. Woodworth-Etter was accused of disturbing the public peace and embezzlement. She was arrested and tried for obtaining money under false pretenses in 1913. In 1926, at the height of her fame, McPherson was tried for criminal conspiracy and perjury. Her trial garnered international news coverage and solidified McPherson's status as one of the most famous women in the world and one of the biggest celebrities in American Protestantism. She also weathered numerous other scandals, lawsuits, a third marriage,[35] and a second divorce.[36] In short, the women were as notorious as they were admired.

Finally, the women eschewed the institution closely associated with late-nineteenth- and early-twentieth-century era womanliness, and instead participated in an institution thought to be reserved for men. As divorcees, the women withdrew from the "central act" of womanhood: marriage.[37] Instead, they participated in the male *métier* of the ministry. The Discontented Man voiced the opinion of many others who believed that women were not meant to pursue public vocations like the ministry.[38] In spite of their unconventional qualifications, notorious lives, and status as females, Woodworth-Etter and McPherson proved themselves more than able to overcome the "inwardness of instinct," of their fellow revivalists. As such, they are useful subjects for the study of gender, the ministry, and revivalism in the late nineteenth and early twentieth centuries.

GOALS OF THIS STUDY

This study has several objectives. One is to understand, through the women's stories, more about the tumultuous era in which they ministered. I hope that analysis of their efforts to gain authority in a male institution will show the reader how gender construction worked during this era as well as how it was changing. Thus, I attempt to situate Woodworth-Etter and McPherson's work in relationship to male celebrity revivalists and Pentecostal discourse of the era.

A second goal of this study is to illuminate how Pentecostalism was being formed as a movement distinct from its holiness roots. There has been (and most likely will always be) overlap among Pentecostal and holiness/Wesleyan groups such as the Nazarenes, Wesleyans, or Free Methodists, but the movements have very distinct theological and sociological sensibilities and instincts. By examining these two foundational figures, I hope to show that even in the early generations of the movement, Pentecostal theologies about the relationship between the practitioner and the world were under construction. I will argue that these changes set the movements on different trajectories that produced the communities in existence today.

I also hope that this study will show readers how authority was constructed and maintained in revivalism in general and in Pentecostalism in particular. I believe that examining how Woodworth-Etter and McPherson utilized authoritative resources such as the Bible to argue for female ministry will show how Pentecostalism was distinct from both liberal mainline Protestantism and fundamentalism. And, by explaining what worked and what did not work for these women, I hope to show how Pentecostals were utilizing theology, biblical narrative, mass media, and architecture in ways that are still employed in the movement today.

Finally, my aim is to take the work of Woodworth-Etter and McPherson seriously. Each of these pastors had extraordinary careers and extraordinarily colorful lives. The temptation with such scandalous women is to concentrate on the most sensational aspects of their work, particularly aspects of their sexuality. This can have the unfortunate consequence of reducing McPherson's success, for example, to sex appeal (although sex appeal certainly did play a pivotal role in her work). The same might be said for Woodworth-Etter, whose philandering husband took the spotlight during much of her ministry. In this study, I deliberately focus my energies on the strategies these women employed that made them famous enough to direct public attention toward their sex lives. The scandals, I argue, were just as much a result of, as well as a vehicle for their female authority. I hope to show the pragmatism, energy, and creativity that went in to making Woodworth-Etter and McPherson powerful ministers.

HISTORIOGRAPHY

Woodworth-Etter and McPherson are well known to students of gender and American Protestantism, although the historiography of gender, revivalism (Pentecostal or otherwise), and the ministry in the late nineteenth and early twentieth centuries is relatively limited.[39] Turn-of-the-century gender studies focus primarily on how women were permitted or denied access to the pulpit. Examples include: Susan Hill Lindley's *You Have Stepped Out of Your Place: a History of Women and Religion in America*,[40] *Women and Twentieth-Century Protestantism*,[41] edited by Margaret Bendroth and Virginia Lieson Brereton, Catherine Wessinger's edited volume *Religious Institutions and Women's Leadership: New Roles inside the Mainstream*,[42] and Mark Chaves' *Ordaining Women: Culture and Conflict in Religious Organizations*.[43] Works specifically dedicated to the study of gender and revivalist ministers also analyze ways in which women were allowed or disallowed ordination. Margaret Bendroth and Betty DeBerg examine how fundamentalist revivalists harbored anxieties about women entering leadership roles in society and in particular the church.[44] Grant Wacker discusses the access women had to Pentecostal leadership posts compared to their conservative evangelical counterparts.[45] Catherine Wessinger's *Women's Leadership in Marginal Religions* analyzes the ways in which female revivalists were admitted to the pulpit.[46]

These studies examine how women entered the ministry, recover the "experiences of women who did gain the title and office of minister,"[47] and uncover the social and cultural shifts that made the ordination of women possible or impossible. They do not, however, seek to reveal how women, once ordained, established authoritative ministries. This is a worthwhile avenue of research because studies have repeatedly demonstrated that simply having access to ordination did not (and does not) guarantee female power from the pulpit.[48]

For example, Mark Chaves points out that denominations that ordain women do not necessarily have women "banging on denominational doors," and usually have few in influential pulpits or in upper-level organizational leadership.[49] Conversely, denominations that do not allow women access to ordination often have women in prominent leadership roles such as leading missions or women's organizations.[50] Late-nineteenth- and early-twentieth-century female ordination, Chaves concludes, had more to do with the public message that female ordination sent to the outside world than about empowering female church leaders.[51] Ordination therefore granted access to the office, but did not necessarily grant authority upon female ministers. This project seeks to fill this gap in scholarship by identifying the strategies (beyond ordination) that two popular women used to catapult themselves into the upper echelon of American ministerial celebrity.

Although famous and powerful in her own day, analysis of Maria Woodworth-Etter's revivalist influence and legacy is generally limited to short entries in women's history encyclopedias. Roberts Liardon compiled a volume of her teachings and several newspaper articles written about her.[52] Wayne Warner's biography *The Woman Evangelist: the Life and Times of Charismatic Evangelist Maria B. Woodworth-Etter* provides a valuable description of the minister's life and work. Warner's work, however, stops short of providing analysis of the minister's methods and their efficacy. In-depth scholarly investigation into her ministerial authority has not yet been done.

Aimee Semple McPherson, in contrast, is the subject of several insightful biographies. McPherson-centric literature largely explores her appeal, but it does not delve into how she developed and wielded power. Daniel Epstein's sympathetic portrayal of McPherson in *Sister Aimee: The Life of Aimee Semple McPherson* allows the pastor's storytelling to characterize his portrait of the revivalist and does not analyze what sorts of strategies she employed to gain authority.[53] Edith Blumhofer's *Aimee Semple McPherson: Everybody's Sister* argues that McPherson attracted followers because of her simple message, practical methods, and her all-American persona.[54] Matthew Sutton's *Aimee Semple McPherson and the Resurrection of Christian America* argues that McPherson's appeal came in part from her ability to tap into proto-religious right sensibilities with patriotic sermons and calls for America to return to its Christian roots.[55] While Sutton is correct in noting McPherson's turn toward the patriotic (particularly during World War II), he does not provide a direct family tree between her teachings and the political activism of later generations. In addition, the connection between McPherson's teachings and late-twentieth-century religious right revivalists is less noteworthy when compared with her much more politically active celebrity revivalist contemporaries like William "Billy" Sunday and J. Frank Norris. In his chapter on Aimee Semple McPherson from *Western Lives: A Biographical History of the American West*, Richard E. Etulain claims that "thousands found solace and a sense of community" from her "charisma and presence," but does not explain what it was about her presence that provided solace and community, or how her charisma authorized her to lead.[56] Peter Gardella analyzes McPherson's work psychosexually and argues that her ecstatic relationship with God gave her power to heal and overcome her "sex role."[57] He does not, however, explain how her intimacy with God translated to power over people.[58] The question of how McPherson wielded power over her followers, therefore, has not been satisfactorily addressed.

This project seeks to fill these lacunae and to contextualize the women's success firmly within the Pentecostal setting in which they established their ministries. In other words, this study is not only a study of female ministry in the late nineteenth and early twentieth centuries. It is also a study of how Pentecostalism shaped (and was shaped by) two powerful female leaders. Studies have discussed Pentecostal theological development in the early years of the movement, but few have shown how Pentecostal women helped create the theologies that made a place for them to minister. I hope to show that Pentecostalism both facilitated and restricted the women's development as leaders, and that the women themselves accommodated and resisted Pentecostal theological and practical norms in their ministries.

Theory and Method

The primary methodology employed in this book is historical, but this project is by design interdisciplinary. The quest for authority for female ministers was an extraordinarily complex task and the women who managed to attain legitimate power over their followers used diverse strategies. Thus, in order to give these women their due, and to interrogate their ministries robustly, I will employ multiple theoretical lenses and methodologies.

In this project I study Woodworth-Etter and McPherson as Pentecostal revivalists. Historians typically classify Woodworth-Etter as a holiness person turned Pentecostal[59] and McPherson as a Pentecostal or charismatic fundamentalist who became evangelical and then went back to Pentecostalism.[60] Pentecostals, fundamentalists, and evangelicals are most often identified according to their theological leanings. For example, fundamentalists are distinguished by their doctrine of the inerrancy of scripture, evangelicals are set apart by their crucicentrism, and Pentecostals are distinct because of their pneumatology.[61]

Framing these women in this way and studying them in a primarily theological manner is problematic because the women's doctrinal commitments were notoriously malleable. Although they themselves argued that theology had no place in their work, Woodworth-Etter and McPherson created theological amalgams of various kinds. Woodworth-Etter counted the holiness movement and Methodism among her theological influences.[62] Aimee Semple McPherson drew upon her Salvation Army and Methodist roots, as well as A. B. Simpson's Christian Missionary Alliance to construct her denomination's fourfold gospel.[63]

It is likewise unfruitful to classify the women by the doctrines of their many denominational affiliations (Salvation Army, Church of God, Assemblies of God, Baptist, etc.). Both Woodworth-Etter and McPherson changed movements several times (sometimes voluntarily, sometimes involuntarily) and attracted followers from diverse denominational backgrounds. Therefore, classifying them by affiliation does provide a meaningful context in which to study them.

This project examines the women first by their practices as revivalists rather than by their doctrines or denominations. Revivalists are Protestants known primarily for their distinctive practices. Historians typically trace the act of reviving or "awakening" American Protestantism to the eighteenth century during a period known as the "Great Awakening."[64] Revivalists sought to breathe life into what they saw as ailing American Christianity.[65] Revivalist practitioners, whether in the North or South, Calvinist or Arminian, Baptist or Pentecostal, shared several common practices, including public individual conversions (often displayed during an "altar call"), enthusiasm and other "scandalous practices"[66] (e.g., crying, laughing, shouting, wailing, fainting, dancing, lifting hands, etc.), holy living (refraining from dancing, drinking, going to movies, playing cards, etc., and embracing Bible reading, evangelism, caring for the poor, etc.), and what Charles Finney called "social religious meetings," or what historians usually refer to as "revivals."[67]

Pentecostals were certainly not the only American Protestants to embrace emotive worship and to shun drinking and dancing. Indeed, many Nazarenes, Free Methodists, and holiness people behaved similarly. Pentecostals at the turn of the twentieth century were distinguished from their holiness and Wesleyan counterparts by typical (although not exclusive) Pentecostal revivalist practices. The most commonly cited practice was glossolalia, or speaking in tongues, but Pentecostals were well known for other practices, including faith healings and prophetic utterances.

Revivalist ministers were ordained in several different ways. Revivalists from mainline denominations like Presbyterians A. B. Simpson and Mark Matthews attended seminary and were ordained by presbyteries.[68] Others, like 1910s' Methodist Martin Wells Knapp or 1920s' Presbyterian-turned-Baptist Billy Sunday, were self-educated and then ordained by a bishop or presbytery.[69] Some from the so-called low-church traditions like Baptists or holiness people received ordination from individual congregations, and many claimed to have been self-ordained.[70]

The most critical component of revivalist ordination could not be bestowed by any denominational governing body. Revivalist ministers were authorized primarily by "the call."[71] The call, or an ecstatic experience (or series of experiences) providing a sense of "mission to the lost and service to God,"[72] was part of any revivalist pastor's ordination. In many ways the call superseded all other forms of authorization. Denominations, seminaries, or congregations might affirm a pastor's suitability to the ministry, but revivalists believed that the call came directly from the Divine.[73] "If God really gives men a special call to this special work," wrote turn-of-the-century revivalist Henry Trawick, "then all argument is at an end."[74]

Most Pentecostals considered "the call" to be *the* authorizing component to the ministry. Whether it be to "Darkest Africa" or to New York City, Pentecostals recounted (and reprinted) accounts of both male and female callings to the ministry. For example, Pentecostal minister Charles Price included the following prayer that God would call ministers to missions work in Venezuela: "Yea; a Macedonian call, 'Come over and help us', is heard far and near and we can only pray that as these lines are read of the Lord of the Harvest may speak to some heart and life, calling him or her to this land, and that there will come the call to prayer for others."[75]

Many scholars of revivalism argue that because of this emphasis on calling, women like Woodworth-Etter and McPherson had more access to the ministry and more authority as ministers than their Protestant counterparts.[76] It is certainly true that the call gave revivalist women a way around traditional avenues to the pulpit such as seminary education or denominational ordination. The revivalist call then did function to give women more access to the institution, and Woodworth-Etter and McPherson reported typical revivalist calls. Woodworth-Etter claimed to have received an intense calling experience, which she and her followers considered to be sufficient for her to be considered a minister.[77] McPherson likewise relayed to her followers her ecstatic call experience that she believed gave her permission to minister.[78]

Access, however, did not guarantee authority. Grant Wacker, Edith Blumhofer, Lisa Stephenson, and Elaine Lawless demonstrate that women in Pentecostal revivalist communities faced many of the same institutional barriers to the ministry that other Protestant female ministers faced.[79] Even with a compelling call, female revivalist ministers were often relegated to small churches, prohibited from making doctrine or policy, and absent from positions of power in denominational leadership.[80]

In addition to their lack of upward institutional mobility, female revivalist ministers often failed by what was perhaps the most enduring measure of authority for any revivalist minister: attendance.[81] Accounts of late-nineteenth- and early-twentieth-century revivalist meetings usually began or ended with a notation of the number of the faithful in attendance. Revivalists maintained that one of the first signs of "vigorous preaching" was a minister's ability to "call a crowd."[82] The larger the meeting, the logic went, the more powerful the minister and his or her message. The scarcity of female ministers with large congregations further demonstrates that attaining authority in revivalist communities, as in any other Protestant group, was a much more complex process than simply gaining ordination or receiving and relaying a call.

Authority has a plethora of meanings,[83] and it remains undefined in many texts that explore gender and American revivalism.[84] Historians' use of the term typically reflects a Weberian understanding: authority is "a species of power, the kind of power one person exercises over another when he invokes a principle of legitimation which the person subject to domination himself views as a binding norm."[85] For Weber, an authoritative leader led without the use of coercion or force because she or he had power that was based in legitimacy and as such was "considered binding" by followers.[86]

Weber famously identified three principles of authority from which leaders exercise legitimate power: traditional, rational-legal, and charismatic.[87] Traditional authority is maintained through "an established belief in the sanctity of immemorial traditions and the legitimacy of the status of those exercising authority under them."[88] Rational-legal authority is power to make binding prescriptions legitimized through "a belief in the 'legality' of patterns of normative rules and the right of those elevated to authority under such rules to issue commands."[89] Charismatic authority is legitimized through devotion to the "exceptional sanctity, heroism, or exemplary character of an individual person and of the normative patterns or order revealed or ordained by him."[90]

Even though Weber recognized that authoritative leaders rarely appealed to only one form of legitimization,[91] historians of American revivalism often classify ecclesial leaders as one type or another. Thus, authority given to and exercised by mainline ministers is classified as traditional because of their participation in an ancient office, or rational-legal authority because they complied with the regulations enacted by their respective denominations.[92] Charismatic authority is often used as a catchall category for those who receive power from nonmainstream sources. Historians typically cite charismatic authority as the primary means by which nonwhite, nonmiddleclass, nonmale persons attain public power.[93]

Because of their emphasis on an extra-denominational call experience and because of their affinity for public displays of "scandalous practices" outside mainstream Protestantism, scholars typically argue that revivalist ministers are legitimated through charismatic authority.[94] Pentecostal female ministers in particular, who were often marginalized by their gender, education, class, etc., but who established popular ministries without the traditional markers of denominational authority, are frequently noted as examples of charismatic authority in action.[95]

This categorization has limited explanatory power, however, because any celebrity minister was authorized to a certain degree through charisma. Woodworth-Etter and McPherson were not the only popular and powerful pastors whose followers responded to their display of sanctity, heroism, or exemplary character from the pulpit. For example, mainline educated professional minister Harry Fosdick was authorized through traditional means (ordination, church appointment), but he was also hailed as an exemplary liberal Protestant man known for his "electric" pulpit presence.[96] Similarly, revivalist ministers like A. B. Simpson and Billy Sunday were legitimized through traditional and legal rational means of denominational affiliation (Christian Missionary Alliance and Presbyterian) as well as through charismatic authority.

This project therefore does not seek to categorize the women in Weberian terms and instead analyzes the women's authority through their interaction with their congregations. Rather than arguing that power is acquired through accessing types of authority, Catherine Bell claims that it is ritualized acts that are "strategic schemes for power relationships—schemes that hierarchize, integrate, define, or obscure."[97] In this sense, power is created and managed through the relationship between leaders and followers during the performance of ritualized acts.

Amy Hollywood links Judith Butler's notion of the performative, that speech acts constitute that to which they refer, with Bell's articulation of ritualization by arguing that bodily practices signify as do speech acts.[98] And, Hollywood claims that performative acts, just like speech acts, are subject to "misfirings."[99] These misfirings, or acts that are not performed conventionally or appropriately by all involved, have "room for improvisation and resistance within the very authoritarian structures (e.g., of child rearing, education, and religion) in which subjects are constituted."[100] Thus, although outside the boundaries of convention and propriety, theoretically, one could create, through ritualized acts, an identity of authoritative, female, ministry.

I will show that the key to Woodworth-Etter and McPherson's authority was their ability to create female ministry through misfirings of male revivalist practice. This project examines Woodworth-Etter and McPherson at the height of their popularity from the apex of Woodworth-Etter's career in the 1890s–1910s to the pinnacle of McPherson's ministry in the 1920s and early 1930s.[101] Chapter 1 begins by examining how gender (specifically maleness), beyond a call or official ordination, authorized revivalist ministers from the 1890s to the early 1930s.

Gender is a highly theorized term.[102] The study of gender, according to Daniel Boyarin, is a study of the "praxis and process by which people are interpellated into a two (or for some cultures more) sex system that is made to seem as if it were nature, that is, something that always existed."[103] Joan Scott, in her influential monograph, *Gender and the Politics of History*, writes that "gender…is a primary way of signifying relationships of power" and "a constitutive element of social relationships based on perceived differences between the sexes [male and female]."[104] Gender history, therefore, is the study of how the practices and processes that create this two-sex system of power relations change over time.

American gender has been understood as part of a binary system inherited from the Enlightenment[105] wherein the world is divided into two discrete brackets. In a world gendered according to the binaries established in Table I.1, maleness, manliness, and masculinity were attached to any persons, places, things, and acts associated with the public world of science, rationality, and society. Femaleness, womanliness, and femininity referred to the private, sacred, nonrational realm. This binary also produced a sense of "normative sexuality."[106] Men and women who performed acts that identified their bodies within the heterosexual framework of dominant gender binaries (e.g., men showing their attraction for and attractivity to women and vice versa) performed normative sexuality.

Table I.1   Enlightenment gender binaries[107]

Male	Female
Public	Private
Society	Individual
Science	Religion
Secular	Sacred
Rational	Irrational/nonrational

Chapter 1 uses prominent newspapers and monographs of the era to outline 1890s–1920s articulations of gender binaries and the idealized forms of womanhood and manhood that these binaries beget. Then, this chapter employs advice literature, newspaper articles, and editorials written by and for revivalist pastors to show how, for revivalists of the era, the ideal minister was gendered as an ideal man. Thus, the ideal woman and ideal minister inhabited mutually exclusive gendered categories. Chapter 1 then outlines the (generally unsuccessful) strategies employed by women who found that their womanliness kept them from the pastorate.

Gender was not the only obstacle facing female revivalists. Chapter 2 shows how the women overcame the biblical prescriptions used to deter women from the ministry. This chapter uses 1890s–1920s literature discussing women, the ministry, and the Bible to argue that while other female ministers and their proponents claimed that biblical passages used to restrict the office to men should be reinterpreted, Woodworth-Etter and McPherson forwent this strategy. They circumvented the problem of the Bible by using biblical arguments as an engine for identity creation. Chapter 2 argues that Woodworth-Etter and McPherson constructed classic Pentecostal biblical narratives that incorporated aspects of popular womanhood with their status as ministers. Their efforts brought the women's seemingly incoherent biographical details and ministerial impulses into one consistent, biblically authoritative identity.

Chapter 3 moves beyond written accounts and analyzes the women's attire. The goal of this chapter is to demonstrate how the women provided their followers with corresponding images for their narrative identities. The body was (and is) an enduring instrument of representation,[108] and for late-nineteenth- and early-twentieth-century revivalists, the body of the ideal revivalist minister was a fit, conservatively groomed, suited white male. Female ministers were tasked therefore with providing followers with an image of a minister without a male body or the male professional garb of a suit. Using photographic evidence and first-hand accounts, chapter 3 shows that Woodworth-Etter and McPherson solved this problem by constructing visual representations of their biblical identities as mother and bride rather than wearing traditional ministerial garb.

Bodies were not the only instruments through which revivalist leaders constructed their identities. Chapter 4 investigates how the women used the sacred space of their revivalist meeting places, in addition to their bodies, to communicate their status as female ministers. This chapter outlines the close relationship revivalist ministers had with their meeting places, and the ways in which revivalist sacred space communicated the masculinity and power of celebrity ministers. Chapter 4 then shows how Woodworth-Etter and McPherson constructed meeting places to display their power as ministers and their status as womanly women.

It is one thing to give followers narratives and images of authority, but it is another thing to exercise authority over followers. Chapter 5 examines how the women realized their authority over their followers during their worship services. Chapter 5 analyzes 1890s–1920s Pentecostal revivalist preaching as a ritualized act. This chapter argues that male ministers repeated preaching acts that gave the minister the masculine role of the initiating aggressor, and their congregation the feminine role of submitting receiver. Woodworth-Etter and McPherson repeated acts that were a "misfiring" of conventional revivalist preaching performance. They maintained their womanly biblical identities, while simultaneously performing in ways that evoked submission from their audiences. Using insider testimony and outsider accounts of revivalist services, chapter 5 shows how the women's performances and performance venues signified ideal notions of femininity and ministerial authority.

During the preaching moment maleness was a critical concern for late-nineteenth- and early-twentieth-century revivalists, but race and class also played a part. Pentecostal revivalists, with their interracial meetings and reputation for widespread appeal in working class and indigent circles, wrestled with how to convey middleclass white respectability from the pulpit. Chapter 5 analyzes how Woodworth-Etter and McPherson performed their gender, race, and class, and how their performance shaped their mainstream revivalist authority.

In spite of their authoritative revivalist meetings, chapter 6 shows how the boundaries surrounding the discrete categories of woman and minister were policed in the ministries of Woodworth-Etter and McPherson. Chapter 6 compares the public response to Woodworth-Etter and McPherson to the coverage that scandalous male revivalists received and concludes that ridicule heaped upon female ministers for comparable (and in the case of McPherson lesser) crimes was more severe than for their male counterparts. The women's criminal trials—how they were tried and how they were covered in the media—illustrate why many believed the women were not legitimate, authoritative ministers.

In the conclusion, I assess the extent of each woman's ministerial and theological impact. I do this by examining and evaluating the women's legacies in the Pentecostal movement. I also compare the women's approaches to ministry, gender, and sexuality. Finally, I discuss what their ministries illuminate about the study of revivalism and gender in the 1890s–1920s.

1

"Truly Manly": The Ideal American Minister

This chapter explores the gendered nature of the ideal American minister in the 1890s–1920s.[1] Like all else at the turn of the twentieth century, ideals of Christian ministry were informed by regnant notions of what women and men ought to be. Chapter 1 argues that the institution of the ministry was gendered male during the 1890s–1920s according to the era's standards of masculinity. Revivalists in particular expressed this masculinity through rhetoric and displays of late-nineteenth- and early-twentieth-century manliness. Strategies that female revivalists employed to lead in an institution that was ideally masculine had limited success.

That the minister was gendered male in late-nineteenth- and early-twentieth-century American life is hardly a surprise. It is an office that, from its inception, has been considered male.[2] Female ministers throughout the formation of the Christian tradition were members of a very small, usually derided, and often persecuted group.[3] But, in the late nineteenth and early twentieth centuries, many advocates for female ministers saw in the era's progressive spirit an opportunity for change.[4] In this age of first-wave feminism,[5] late-nineteenth- and early-twentieth-century feminist activists Susan B. Anthony, Elizabeth Cady Stanton, and their colleagues encouraged women to enter institutions of higher learning at greater rates than ever before.[6] Once they graduated, these women entered into professional life at unprecedented rates and began careers in traditionally male vocations such as the law, medicine, and the academy.[7] They also created new so-called female professions such as social work and public health nursing.[8] In addition, women of the era mobilized to effect change in many aspects of American public life: health care and welfare reform, the temperance movement, and suffrage.[9]

This shift in the place and presence of women in noneclesial profes-sions put pressure on the country's oldest institution to follow suit.[10] Many denominations responded to progressive trends by chang-ing their policies on female ministers. For example, between 1890 and 1930, the Methodist Episcopal Church, the African American Episcopal Zion Church, the Church of the Nazarene, the Mennonite Church, and many others opened ordination to women.[11] Thus, the number of denominations giving women access to ordination in the 1890s and 1920s was unprecedented.

Proponents of female ministers expressed optimism in light of their accomplishments. "In five or ten years," said Methodist Rev. M. Madeline Southard, "all denominations will grant ecclesiastical equality to women."[12] Southard's prediction proved to be optimistic. In spite of the influx of women into the profession, for Protestants from fundamentalism to the mainline, the ministry, in its most ideal form, remained male.[13]

The trend toward female ministers was followed by swift and intense backlash against female ministers and their supporters. The fundamentalists, a group born (in part) out of frustration with shift-ing gender roles in the nineteenth century, produced some of the best-documented and most virulent responses to female ministers.[14] Fundamentalists were opposed to women in church leadership of any sort,[15] and they peppered their rhetoric with accusations of female theological shallowness and moral feebleness.[16] "Woman," wrote fundamentalist H. B. Taylor, "is too easily beguiled to be a leader."[17] Whereas women ministers were depicted as too weak and gull-ible for the ministry, fundamentalists portrayed men as the natural defenders of orthodoxy and the hope for the future of American Christianity.[18]

Fundamentalists provided some of the more extreme instances of retaliation, but they were not alone in their disapproval of female min-isters. Evangelical and mainline Protestants alike were uncomfortable with the idea of women entering the ministry.[19] Protestants in denom-inations with both permissive and restrictive policies regarding female ministers strongly preferred male ministers.[20] For example, well-known progressive ministers and theologians Walter Rauschenbush and Harry Fosdick promoted male ministers as the ideal form of the pastorate.[21] Christian-themed novels such as Charles Monroe Sheldon's *In His Steps* regularly gendered the nature of the ministry by reiterating the importance of a Christian home—wherein men were the public figures who spread the manly good news to the world, and women took care of religious education for children in the domicile.[22]

Some revivalists in the 1890s–1920s had a long history of empowering women to teach, preach, testify, and prophesy publicly, but that
did not exempt them from preferring men in the office of the ministry.[23]
Even individuals and groups who heartily affirmed female access to
the pulpit often expressed ambivalence toward women ministers.[24]
Famed turn-of-the-century revivalist A. B. Simpson, who allowed
for female pastors, encouraged male ministers to lead followers "into
all the fullness of the mature manhood of Christ."[25] In 1915, Billy
Sunday aggressively called for more men to lead the church in its mission. "We need men," he wrote, "men that will fight."[26]

Thus, even as women entered professional ministry in increasingly
greater numbers, most American Protestants, and revivalists in particular, called for male ministers. Not just any male, however, would
do. Americans had a specific kind of man in mind. They wanted a
minister who was gendered according to 1890s and 1920s standards
of manliness.

MAKING MANLY MEN

There were many qualities that made a manly late-nineteenth- and
early-twentieth-century man. First and foremost, the manly man
was gendered by what he did not possess: effeminacy.[27] Effeminacy,
"having the qualities of a woman; womanish; soft and delicate in an
unmanly degree; destitute of manly qualities,"[28] was the result of a
man taking on womanly behaviors and sensibilities. As such, it was
a condition that could only afflict men. "Effeminacy is not being
female," according to one observer, but "being less masculine."[29]
Therefore, femininity, while a positive quality in a woman, became
the undesirable quality of effeminacy when practiced by a man.[30]

Many worried that the "effeminacy of American youth"[31] was
at an all time high at the turn of the century, and pundits of the
era placed the blame for the supposed effeminacy of their generation firmly upon their Victorian ancestors.[32] The man that turn-
of-the-century Americans inherited—the "archetypal buttoned-down
Victorian gentleman" whose manners, reserve, and manful purity of
heart and body had once been celebrated as a cornerstone of American
civilization—was no longer seen as the kind of man who could lead
Americans into the modern era.[33] The customs and mannerisms that
had been considered manly, refined, and poised in the nineteenth
century became "overcivilized," "pussyfooted," and "sissy," in the
1890s–1920s.[34] According to early-twentieth-century Americans,
the "weakling" Victorian man possessed none of the self-starting,

independent powers that men needed to survive in the modern world; he was lazy, submissive, and had a fondness for luxury and leisure.[35] Therefore, the ideal man of the late nineteenth and early twentieth centuries was further defined as not Victorian.

Instead of being a pussyfooted Victorian, the ideal man was modern, which meant that he welcomed the scientific advancements, technological changes, and intellectual challenges that Americans faced at the turn of the twentieth century. The post-Victorian era was a time when Americans were at the latter stage of a "hump of transition" from eighteenth-century republic to "complex industrial and urban life."[36] Americans faced vast changes both in "physical landscape" and in "psychic circumstances" as immigration increased, higher criticism reigned in universities, and technology advanced at exponential rates.[37]

Not everyone handled these changes well. "Weakling" Victorian men living in the modern age who were unable to face the "increased pace and technological advancement of modern civilization"[38] risked catching "neurasthenia." Neurasthenia "expressed the *cultural* weakness of civilized, manly [Victorian] self-restraint in *medical* terms."[39] Defined as a mental disorder caused by a "deficiency or lack of nerve,"[40] neurasthenia was considered to be a plague among men who were unprepared for the physical and psychic changes in American culture. Neurasthenics were weak, ineffectual, mediocre, and, most terrifying for turn-of-the-century Americans, effeminate. Ideal men had the strength and education to withstand neurasthenia. They were those who took President Woodrow Wilson's 1909 advice and were prepared to "adapt themselves to modern life," so as not to risk "passing out of existence."[41]

Part of that adaptation meant becoming middleclass professionals. Between 1870 and 1910, the number of white collar jobs in established fields like the law and medicine as well as in new careers such as engineering grew by eight times until 20 percent of male workers counted themselves as part of the professional middleclass.[42] Ideas about the consummate turn-of-the-century man followed this trend. The exemplary man was identified as having middle-class qualities such as cleanliness, integrity, and honor, and by his employment in middle-class professions like medicine or the law.[43]

Thanks in part to the growth of the American middle class and American industry, and post-World War I economic development, prosperity also became a marker of American manliness in the following decade.[44] The truly masculine man of the 1920s was an independent breadwinner. He was man enough to provide for his wife and children, and he had sufficient financial resources to enjoy the Jazz Age.[45] Films during this period portrayed men as wealthy and heroic with the brawn and the means to rescue damsels in distress.[46] The "young, vibrant, avowedly consumerist masculinity" of the period required an independent man who basked in his self-made wealth.[47] Jay, "the Great" Gatsby, was a fictional version of this kind of manliness. Although possessing a sketchy, lower class past, Gatsby manufactured an identity for himself as an ideal man of self-made wealth. Powerful banker and philanthropist Henry Pomeroy Davidson was another example of ideal self-made manhood. When he died suddenly in 1922, the *New York Times* eulogized him as a paragon of Roaring Twenties manliness: "He knew finance and business and many other subjects as few men did," the *Times* reported, "and was an example of that honored citizen the self-made man."[48]

The exemplary man of the 1890s–1920s was middleclass, but he did not use his financial gain to become "soft" or domesticated.[49] In addition to modern philosophies and innovations, as well as economic prosperity, Americans in the 1890s–1920s inherited a newly closed Western frontier and a rapidly industrializing nation.[50] In order to tame the American West[51] as well as the new frontier of American industry, the ideal man needed toughness and aggression.[52] He needed what quintessential turn-of-the-century American outdoorsman Teddy Roosevelt called "rugged courage."[53] He did not wait for permission. He was the ultimate initiator. He may have worked as an accountant or a salesman, but internally the truly manly man was raw, and primitive.[54] He was a cowboy. Thus, in the late nineteenth and early twentieth centuries, terms such as strenuous, vigorous, virile, and strong became watchwords for all things manly.[55]

This emphasis on a man of strength (mental and physical) brought the male body to the forefront of notions of manliness.[56] The ideal man exhibited his strength through robust activities. Men like Teddy Roosevelt, YMCA founder Luther Gulick, and minister Josiah Strong were touted as models of men who "stressed action rather than reflection and aggression rather than gentility."[57] Throughout the 1890s–1920s, muscle development was considered to be an outer indication of inner manhood, and American men invested in making their bodies into specimens of virility through activities like sports and bodybuilding.[58] Competitive sports became venues to display manly physical prowess[59] and men's magazines like *Esquire* included extensive coverage of professional sports such as boxing and baseball.[60] "Whatever vigor there is in the original protoplasm of your person and your ancestry," wrote Dr. Leonard Keene Hirshberg of

Johns Hopkins University about the connection between muscularity and manliness, "will be found ready to be developed by your physical culture and training in your muscles."[61]

If there was anything that threatened the virility and power of the "original protoplasm" of the modern American man, it was ancestry. Americans of "native-born white, presumably going back generations,"[62] descent were proud of their accomplishments and credited America's "estimable Anglo-Saxon ancestors," with their success.[63] Many feared that Chinese, Japanese, Italian, Jewish, Austro-Hungarian, Russian, Polish, and Irish male immigrants were "servile immigrant men," who would only produce more of the same, rather than the virile Anglo-Saxons who had thus far brought the country into the industrial era.[64] Immigrants from predominately Roman Catholic nations were a special worry because they brought with them beliefs and practices that Protestants believed threatened to undermine the supposedly sturdy form of Christianity that made America, America.[65]

Many white Americans believed that American manhood and womanhood had domestic as well as foreign racial threats. Prominent immigration activist Prescott Hall warned that African-American men were cursed with inferior masculinity and a lack of self-control.[66] According to Hall, their propagation with "morally deviant" but fertile African-American women as well as "unsuspecting" white women posed a threat to modern American manhood.[67] The model American man was a man whose gene pool was tainted neither by longstanding nor by new non-Anglo American flaws.[68] A real man was the white[69] Protestant who shunned Catholicism and the "effeminate traits of southeastern European races."[70]

New immigrants, newly freed African Americans, and the children they produced created anxiety among many white Americans that their supposedly strong white civilization was in danger.[71] To preserve the future of the white American man and prevent this so-called race suicide, white American men were called to put their virility to very practical use and keep up with the birth rates of immigrants and African-Americans by producing children.[72] Therefore, in a departure from Victorian predecessors, the ideal American man embraced his sex drive as a public service.[73] The capacity to appear sexually attractive to fertile white women in order to produce more vigorous Americans became a laudatory quality for turn-of-the-century men.

Thus, 1890s–1920s Americans added their culturally specific binaries to established Enlightenment categories.

Table 1.1   1890s–1920s gender binaries

Masculine	Feminine
War	Peace
Aggression	Passivity
Initiation	Reception
Dominance	Submission
Virility	Fertility
Professional	Domestic
Strength	Weakness
Christian (Protestant)	Non-Christian (including Roman Catholic)
White	Nonwhite

As Table 1.1 illustrates, the future of men, and indeed public American life, according to 1890s–1920s Americans, was "red-blooded,"[74] virile, and manly. Any kind of civic concern, be it politics, work, economics, foreign policy, or science, was thought to be best executed by a manly man.[75] Politicians sought to portray themselves as masculine men ready to fight (literally or figuratively) their opponents.[76] Newspapers argued for the "maintenance of the manhood of our men" and carried appeals for manly men on topics including war, fiscal policy, politics, employment, recreation, and physical fitness.[77] Advertisers promised increased manhood and masculinity in everything from cures for alcoholism to digestion aids to "Urethral Vigoral Pads" and "electrotherapy" to increase male sexual performance.[78] Countless clubs, fraternal orders, and lodges sprang up with promises to produce adult manly specimens.[79] Organizations like the Boy Scouts were created to teach manliness to young boys.[80] Manliness was touted as the "most valuable asset of citizenship," capable of bringing out the "Godlike in the sons of God."[81]

THE MANLY MINISTER

For the most part, American ministers did not resist the manliness movement.[82] Many were among its most enthusiastic supporters. Protestant interest in a manly minister was first and most popularly voiced in the muscular Christianity movement.[83] A British import, muscular Christianity took root in the fertile ground of mid- to late-nineteenth-century American culture. The movement was in full bloom at the turn of the century, and it maintained a strong presence in American Protestantism throughout the 1920s, particularly in revivalist circles.

The archetypal muscular Christian minister was a virile, white Protestant professional man of keen intellect and physical prowess, who stood firm against the dangers that accompanied industrialization, immigration, and other aspects of modern American life.[84] Like most Americans of the era, Protestant ministers and their congregations believed they were facing a masculine scientific era and encroaching secularism armed with nothing but the hopelessly effeminate brand of Victorian Christianity inherited from the previous generation.[85] Motivated by a fear that the faith of their Victorian forefathers could not stand up to the rough modern era, muscular Christianity proponents got to work creating a strenuous faith and a strenuous minister for the strenuous life.[86]

American churchgoers were, according to one Presbyterian minister, "infallible judges of manliness, and, above all things, they believe in a manly minister."[87] In accordance with 1890s–1920s standards of manliness, muscular Christians evaluated their ministers by their physically fitness. In a Progressive era survey concerning the ideal American minister, respondents listed "manliness" and "strength" as one of the most important qualities exhibited by an ideal minister.[88] These abstract notions of manliness and strength were accompanied by concrete physical details: "he must be tall, stately, six feet, strong to look at, well proportioned, etc.," with a "finely proportioned body, well developed chest, broad shoulders."[89]

This consummate masculine minister possessed sex appeal. Revivalists were particularly noted for their combination of preaching and sexuality. "The revivalists," wrote historian and Vassar professor Woodbridge Riley in 1928, "account as nothing else can do for those twin obsessions of the national mind – salvation and sex."[90] For example, Billy Sunday's manly persona was popular with men, but the enthusiastic response he received from attendees at women-only meetings revealed his status as a sex symbol for female revivalists.[91]

Revivalist preachers were supposed to use their appeal, according to Congregational revivalist Charles Reynolds Brown, to cultivate an intimate connection between the minister and the congregation. Brown compared the relationship between preacher and congregant to a romantic seduction. "When a man is declaring his affection for a certain young woman and asking her to marry him, he does not get off twenty or thirty feet away and call it out to her in loud tones," wrote Brown. "You are wooing these people to a Christian life and to more active Christian service."[92]

Not all pastors embodied this "red-blooded" masculinity, but that did not deter muscular Christianity enthusiasts. "Manly ministers are made as well as born," one Baptist minister philosophized.[93] Those who were not born with "manliness" were advised to be about the work of "cultivating of manly characteristics of the Christian minister."[94] Instructional literature for ministers was full of advice for increasing manliness. Characteristics such as courage, energy, and a "vigorous" mind could help a minister develop from a "frail body into manly vigor."[95] Working with deacons and elders with virile bodies and minds helped as well.[96] "Men want a fellow man for a minister," opined one homiletician. "They want him to be a man before he is a minister."[97]

There was perhaps no group more enthusiastically supportive of muscular male church leadership than the revivalists.[98] They consistently sought ministers with the "supernaturally imparted vitality," of manliness.[99] "God Almighty's business in this world," wrote revivalist F. W. Gunsaulus in 1908, "is the making of manhood."[100] "'Each tool is ordained of God for the reenforcement [sic] of manhood,'" wrote revivalist minister William Bell Riley. "'Every time a river is enslaved a thousand men are set free. Every time an iron wheel is mastered, a thousand muscles are emancipated.' Beloved, the machinery in the church of God ought to mean the same thing."[101]

Revivalist celebrity ministers were noted examples of "rugged manhood."[102] For example, turn-of-the-century Congregationalist revivalist minister R. A. Torrey embodied turn-of-the-century manliness. He was a white, professional minister with a degree from Yale Divinity School. In addition, he had served under Dwight L. Moody, whose influential Victorian era ministry ushered the muscular Christian movement into the late nineteenth and early twentieth centuries. Torrey devoted much of his ministerial life to promoting Christianity's "truly manly"[103] nature; his books supporting that goal included *Talks to Men about the Bible and the Christ of the Bible* published in 1904.[104] Billy Sunday, who carried the manliness torch into the 1910s and 1920s was the kind of self-made man adored by muscular Christians: he grew up in obscurity and poverty, became a professional athlete, dramatically converted, and went on the road as a minister.[105] Sunday celebrated his own masculinity and encouraged others to reject "spineless, effeminate, ossified" liberal expressions of manhood and faith in favor of his more manly conservative Christianity.[106] "It takes manhood to live for Christ," said Sunday, and he regularly preached the virtue of the manly Jesus.[107] The ideal muscular revivalist minister was a paragon of late-nineteenth- and early-twentieth-century "red-blooded manhood."[108]

Given the masculinity of revivalist ministry, the question becomes: how did women minister with authority in a field that was ideally masculine? The first step in proposing a response is to consider the gender confusion inherent in early-twentieth-century ideals of ministry. Though professionals in a historically male office, American ministers were called upon to exhibit traits outside the boundaries of late-nineteenth- and early-twentieth-century constructions of masculinity. Whereas manly men were aggressive, bold, and rugged, ministers were required to nurture, soothe, and sympathize with their congregants.[109] Like physicians, ministers were often called to visit congregation members in their homes. Unlike doctors, ministers did not dispense masculine medical or scientific expertise. Instead, they brought emotional and spiritual care to the family.[110] Whereas the manly man was a figure of public authority, ministers spent many hours in the privacy of the home.[111] In addition to being a bold and aggressive defender of the faith like Torrey or Sunday, a minister was called upon to receive from God and teach others to do the same. Male revivalists attempted to masculinize the supposedly feminine revivalist practice of receiving and accepting, as chapter 5 will demonstrate. In spite of these efforts, however, there was no denying that in many ways the duties of a minister aligned more closely with ideal models of late-nineteenth- and early-twentieth-century womanliness rather than manliness.

THE WOMANLY WOMAN

Manhood was not the only gender construct being redesigned during the late nineteenth and early twentieth centuries. The ideal woman was also a work in progress. Like the consummate masculine man, the quintessential turn-of-the-century woman was constructed against a caricature of her Victorian predecessor. The consensus among opinion-makers of the day was that the "adorably weak"[112] Victorian woman was just as ill-equipped to survive and thrive in the scientific age as her male counterpart. Late-nineteenth- and early-twentieth-century Americans worried that women, exposed to the "more demanding mental activity"[113] of the modern era, ran the risk of becoming neurasthenics as well as men. Thus, the supposedly demure, placid Victorian woman of "unquestioning unintelligence"[114] was discarded for a more suitable complement to the modern man.

The ideal woman was modern, which meant that she was educated and embraced intellectual life.[115] The corseted woman had stepped off the "pedestal of homebound domesticity and female purity" and was given unprecedented access to education and professional opportunities.[116] Unlike the supposedly overly mannered Victorian woman, the educated "New" modern woman was committed to "willing, thinking, and doing," in the world beyond domestic confines.[117]

There were, however, limits to what an exemplary woman willed, thought, and did outside the home. For example, she was not a feminist.[118] That is, she did not take on the male duty of professional life and therefore she rejected "non-motherhood, free love, easy divorce, economic independence," and other sorts of "destructive theories," first-wave feminists adopted.[119] A truly womanly woman knew that her modern powers were best exercised within the home.[120] Thus, the ideal woman of the 1890s–1920s was founded on two enduring models of domestic womanhood: motherhood and wifedom.[121]

The womanly woman of the late nineteenth and early twentieth centuries was portrayed, more often than not, as a mother. Proponents of motherhood as the epitome of womanhood were careful to distinguish between the mother of the Victorian era and the modern mother.[122] The Victorian mother was a standard of domestic purity, but modern mother was an "educated mother."[123]

An educated mother (or an "efficient mother" as she was also known)[124] used the latest scientific expertise and technology to raise her children and manage her household.[125] She was encouraged to "become scientific" and acquire "knowledge of hygiene and cleanliness" in order to provide her household with the latest medical and technological innovations.[126] She was to learn the latest "fastidious and painstaking mothering practices."[127] Educated mothering became so popular that schools dedicated to the art and science of "mothercrafting" with the purpose of assisting women in the development of modern mothering skills opened during the early twentieth century.[128] Publishers also produced manuals such as *Mothercraft* and *The Mothercraft Manual* to teach women the latest mothering skills.[129] Classifying mothering as a craft gave women a kind of professional skill that was exclusively practiced in the home. As craftswomen, they belonged to a domestic guild that corresponded to the male public professional but did not put them in competition with men for male professions.

Mothercrafting included a number of skills. One of the most important skills was teaching and so the educated mother was herself an educator. Her classroom was her home and her students were her children.[130] She was responsible for the "mental life" of her children that included their religious (Protestant) and moral development.[131] To many, the most imporant act of motherhood was to "teach religion" to the children.[132] Thus, the educated mothers' first educational duty was to "make God real in the hearts and lives of their children."[133]

A true educated mother, according to one 1910 essayist, "recognizes the value of obedience and insists upon her children being obedient to authority."[134] In order to have authority over her growing obedient, vigorous, healthy Americans, an educated mother herself had to be strong and in good health.[135] One of the surest ways to reach that goal was for her to strengthen her body through exercise. Magazines, advertisements, and other literature encouraged women to develop vigorous physiques, and women's colleges like Vassar, Wellesley, and Smith (and an increasing number of coeducational institutions)[136] promoted gymnastics, basketball, and physical education to make scientifically improved mothers.[137]

The goal of educated mothering was to "produce the healthiest, best educated, and most honorable citizens."[138] Just as the virility needing for impregnating white women was part of the turn-of-the-century ideal consruction of masculinity, birthing children from a "quality" (white) American gene pool was another responsibility of an educated mother.[139] White women of marriageable age were encouraged to choose a mate with whom they would be likely to produce healthy, intelligent, attractive children of Anglo-Saxon descent.[140]

The standard of the educated mother ideal was often impossible to achieve. One reason for this was because it was based upon several factors that were outside the control of female practitioners. For example, it depended upon a specific version of whiteness, the ability to conceive, and access to education.

It also depended upon money. The educated mother, like her vigorous male counterpart, was middleclass.[141] Supported by a prosperous professional husband, she was a fastidious mothercrafter, but she did not work for pay. The educated mother dedicated her life to the welfare of her children and the efficiency of her home, and she had time to donate to making other homes models of modern competency and economy. Educated mothers energetically worked to make sure the food, education, and health of their children (and other Americans' children) were safe.[142] Mother-activist Elizabeth MacFarlane Chesser argued that mothering led naturally to activism:

> The ideal of motherhood cannot be restricted to the care of one's own children. The mother spirit must go out to every child who needs us and who we can serve. The joy of motherhood must find expression in the desire to help those mothers to whom maternity means only suffering and sorrow. What a power in social reform might not we have in intelegent mother love awakened, eager to serve![143]

Thus, the ideal mother of the turn of the century had "mother love," and financial resources that freed up her volunteer time, and middle-class sensiblities to apply to a variety of health, education, and labor reforms.

The boundaries around the educated mother were strictly maintained. Women whose sexual practices were outside the married, heterosexual norm were classified as "bad girls" in need of intervention and reform.[144] Those who did not marry earned the unflattering name of "spinster," were pitied for their inability to acquire a husband, feared for their unnatural sense of independence, and often suspected of lesbianism.[145] Those who failed to uphold the motherhood ideal because their economic status prevented them from doing so, or those whose racial or religious identity placed them outside the Protestant white American ideal were accused of being "mentally inferior," pitied for their ignorance, and criticized for their supposed irresponsibility.[146]

The reward for fulfilling the ideal was great. Educated mothers were celebrated. They were praised for bringing up hearty young Americans. They were congratulated for raising the socioeconomic status of their families. They were admired for uplifting the entire human race, and for being an all around "superior woman."[147]

Educated motherhood was the dominant way of performing womanliness properly, but it was not the only popular model of womanhood. The "companionate wife" joined the educated mother as an ideal form of mainstream womanliness in the 1910s–1920s.[148] The companionate wife was in many ways similar to the educated mother: she was white; middleclass which meant she was supported by her husband; and educated, which meant that she could engage her husband with conversation as well as rear their children.[149]

While the primary domestic relationship of the educated mother was from mother to child, the primary relationship for the companionate wife was between the husband and the wife. A companionate wife was one of a two-member partnership.[150] She was devoted to her husband's wellbeing (and he to hers) in a marriage whose goal was that "each partner would develop his or her separate talents and interests to the fullest while enjoying lifelong intimacy and companionship."[151]

American women's books, magazines, and advertising heavily propagated the companionate wife model. Literature analyzing the culture, such as *The Trend of the Race: A Study of Present Tendencies in the Biological Development of Mankind*, included lengthy discussions of the "requirements of an ideal wife," such as health, "looks," dress, housekeeping ability, education, maternity, etc.[152] Magazines like *Good Housekeeping* promoted women who embodied "ideal wife" qualities. For example, in his article, "The Superwoman," *Good Housekeeping* writer Arthur Crabb told the story of a woman who took advantage of "these new days of freedom and equal rights," not by getting a profession, but by throwing off tradition and proposing marriage to her husband.[153] Crabb approved of this use of female freedom. In his view, the advances in women's educational and vocational opportunities were best put to use in the marital relationship. "I'll make him a good wife," wrote "The Superwoman," heroine in a pledge to conform to this domestic ideal, "the very best wife I know how."[154]

The idea of a mutually satisfying marriage was hardly new, but the 1910s and 1920s version took on qualities specific to the culture.[155] The first was the notion that the marriage relationship was *the* location for fulfillment of all desires, dreams, and relational needs.[156] While in earlier generations a woman had an intimate same-sex friend with whom to confide (as did her spouse), the companionate wife's one and only "best friend" was her husband.[157]

The marital relationship was built not only upon friendship but also upon passionate sexual intimacy.[158] This was a change from the previous generation's notion of womanliness. In the 1890s–1910s, according to popular literature, "bad *girls*" enjoyed sex and displayed sexuality.[159] "Good" *women* of the era, very much like their Victorian predecessors, kept their sexual urges firmly under control. Their bodies, like their households, were "clean," which meant free from dirt and disease as well as sexual behaviors outside of procreation.[160]

In contrast to her predecessor, while expected to be chaste for the general public, the ideal woman of the 1920s was encouraged to "abandon herself fully to the sexual embrace," of her husband.[161] The American film industry quickly became one of the leading purveyors of this ideal womanliness.[162] Films, such as *Why Change Your Wife* (1920), *Too Wise Wives* (1921), and *What Do Men Want* (1922), promoted wives who encouraged their husband in their careers and provided them with sexual satisfaction along with friendship.

The companionate wife's celebration of friendship and sexual satisfaction did have limitations. First, ideal women were supposed to express sexual interest in their husbands only.[163] Although the sexually adventurous flapper was a memorable model of womanhood during the 1920s, she was by no means the ideal woman of the day. Flappers were received with ambivalence.[164] Some celebrated their healthy enjoyment of sex and sexuality,[165] but they were most often scolded for flaunting their bodies outside the bonds of marriage.[166]

In addition, a companionate wife was supposed to pursue her own happiness but not if that happiness led her away from "life-enriching domesticity."[167] Her career came second to her primary duty to "achieve in the world without giving up feminine graces."[168] Feminine graces referred in this case to a life that centered on caring for her husband and bearing and raising children.

As with the educated mother, the companionate wife was a model that was heavily policed. To step outside the ideal was to step into a hazardous world. Advertisements and magazine covers portrayed the woman who had the protection of neither parents nor spouse as a woman who lived a life, "fraught with physical danger and reputation-tarnishing temptation."[169] Unmarried women were blamed for threatening the foundations of society. "The unmarried woman," wrote the University of Georgia's 1920 *Studies in Citizenship*, "presents a problem both in industry and in the professions. Our present institution, the home, is founded upon the principle of a married man and a married woman, father and mother, living together and rearing a family of children. All of home life is centered around this plan of economy."[170]

Unmarried mothers had a particularly hard life. Not only did they lack marriage, the "predominant measure of women's success and normalcy in life,"[171] they faced limited marriage prospects and (in the case of children born outside of wedlock) humiliation for their sexual indiscretions.[172] They also had to take on the masculine role of breadwinner for their children and the majority of single mothers were faced with problems ranging from economic woes, housing shortages, and labor discrimination.[173]

Thus, in order for a woman to embody the ideal of the 1920s, she needed to be a mother and a wife. She was welcome to pursue her own satisfaction, so long as her primary satisfaction was found in the home. For both the educated mother and the companionate wife, therefore, ideal womanliness remained domestic.

A FEMALE MINISTRY

Given the ministry's emphasis on nurture, education, and its domestic associations, female ministers saw an opportunity to reconcile the seemingly discordant identities of "woman" and "minister" in the gender confusion of the ministry. Unitarian Anna Garlin Spencer, Universalist Olympia Brown, Methodist Protestant Anna Howard Shaw, United

Brethren minister Ella Niswonger, and Presbyterian Louisa Woosley could argue that their status as seminary-educated professionals qualified them to minister.[174] But more often than not women ministers argued that it was their status as ideal women—as educated mothers and/or companionate wives—that qualified them to pastor.[175]

For the most part, female revivalist ministers sought authority in the ministry through motherhood and wifedom. Turn-of-the-century married female revivalists such as National Baptist Virginia Broughton and Northern Baptist Helen Barrett Montgomery, who led congregations and held denominational leadership in their Baptist Conventions,[176] argued that American religious wellbeing fell under their purview as mothers.[177] Like other mother activists, female revivalist ministers believed they were specially qualified to minister based on their role as mothers to their congregations.[178] They argued that as mothers of congregations they had authority to oversee the mental, spiritual, and physical needs of their spiritual children. In turn, their spiritual children entrusted their development to their watchful mothercrafting. Proponents argued that this mother minister was not just beneficial for one individual church but the entire community in which she lived. "It's the woman pastor," wrote itinerant Methodist minister Madeline Southard in 1923, "who mothers the town."[179]

Other revivalist women used the model of a companionate wife to make a bid for pastoral legitimacy. Married women ministers often argued that as long as they were dutiful wives with happy husbands and home lives, they were entitled to minister: their responsibilities to the men in their lives were fulfilled, and their free time could be invested in a pastorate. For example, Pentecostal revivalist Emma Cotton proclaimed her legitimacy based upon fulfilling her wifely duties to her spouse and their felicitous union.[180] Carrie Judd Montgomery made a point of repeatedly mentioning her husband's status as her "helpmeet" which placed him in the feminine role as Eve from Genesis 2:18.[181] She downplayed his feminization, however, by emphasizing her dependence upon him, even though his assistance was primarily behind the scenes.[182] Some widowed ministers inherited their ministries from their deceased husbands and claimed ministerial authority based upon their previous work as companionate wives. For example, Jennie Seymour, widow of Azusa Street revivalist William Seymour, continued her husband's legacy by teaching, preaching, and mentoring younger pastors.[183]

Other women ministers forsook models of ideal womanhood and claimed that their decision to abstain from motherhood, marriage, and even womanhood altogether qualified them to minister. Salvation Army General Evangeline Booth eschewed marriage for the sake of the ministry and portrayed herself as a chaste pastor who forsook relationships with men in order to serve the church.[184] Pentecostal Uldine Utely ministered as a virginal girl committed to preaching rather than a husband, but after she matured into a woman and married, her preaching career ended.[185] African-American minister Mary Evans, pastor of Cosmopolitan Community Church in Chicago, wore men's clerical clothing in the pulpit and observers believed Evans's pulpit gestures, dress, and hairstyles were "sexually ambiguous."[186] European American Methodist minister Anna Howard Shaw wore traditional black robes in the pulpit and at the beginning of her career in the late nineteenth century wore her hair cropped short.[187] After facing criticism for appearing too manly, however, she made a conscious effort to take on traditionally feminine attire, to wear her hair long, and to appear more womanly when not preaching.[188]

Thus, female ministers in the 1890s–1920s used diverse means to make a case for their authority as ministers. A few tried to make a way outside the popular domestic roles for women. But most, recognizing the gender ambiguity of the office of the ministry and attempting to capitalize on that fact, chose to make their case as mothers and wives.

A Profession in Peril

Had the institution of the ministry been thriving during this period, as was the case for the law or medicine, these arguments may have become widely accepted. Instead, Protestants of the era believed that the profession of ministry was in jeopardy and they placed the blame for its decline firmly upon the gendered confusion of the institution.[189] In many ways this fear was justified. Once *the* profession of American society, the crown jewel of the academy, and the most powerful institution in any given American village, the office of the ministry was a shadow of its early republican self at the turn of the century.[190] Whereas the late nineteenth and early twentieth centuries were a golden age for classic professions such as the law and medicine and new professions like psychology and engineering,[191] American ministers were floundering.[192] Ministers saw their salaries decrease, and their voice in public policy diminish.[193] "He [the minister] must not now interfere in politics," wrote British historian James Bryce on his perception of the state of American ministers and public life; "he must not speak on any secular subject *ex cathedra*."[194] Ministers also saw their status as pillars of society wane. Sinclair Lewis's *Elmer Gantry* popularized the image of a corrupt and greedy twentieth-century minister rather than a knowledgeable, competent professional.[195] Indeed from the perspective of many early-twentieth-century ministers, the period was an "American Religious Depression."[196] Church attendance declined, the liberal-fundamentalist controversy raged, and ministers worried about both the future of American Christianity and the clergy's future in American society.[197]

Ministry as an institution faced an uncertain future as funding to seminaries disappeared, fewer talented young people sought to enter the profession, and Americans expressed little confidence in the ability of the office to help them cope with industrial life.[198] "The great reason why young men are not going into the ministry," wrote one culture critic, "is that when children, they didn't hear father say that the ministry was much of a profession. Father was talking mostly about making big money in real estate and oil wells. Father was too busy running after the dollar to have family prayers."[199]

For 1890s–1920s Protestants, the perceived femininity of the ministry was cited as a (if not *the*) reason for the institution's decline. Ministers themselves recognized that the practices associated with the vocation, such as home visits and pastoral care, contributed to the notion that the ministry was a feminine profession.[200] "It is said that religion breeds effeminacy," wrote frustrated Methodist minister and theologian Edgar Sheffield Brightman, "that it appeals to women and children, but that it lacks masculinity."[201]

The solution to the problem of a supposedly effeminate profession was to purge the church of leftover Victorian femaleness and masculinize it. "Might it not be well to consider," asked *The Christian Advocate*, "the importance of a more manly type of Gospel, a Gospel in which young men will see the qualities that directly appeal to them—virility, force, independence, power? Can we not manage in some way to make our young men feel that religion gives them fiber, stamina, character, and purpose and that in it they have the noblest preparation for the strife and turmoil which lie before them?"[202] Female ministers, along with the "perfumed pastors of doting parishes" were out of fashion and "men with red blood" were the future of the ministry.[203] The most ideal minister of the 1890s and 1920s, therefore, was a man who displayed the modern, red-blooded, muscular qualities so treasured by late-nineteenth- and early-twentieth-century Americans.

CONCLUSION

In conclusion, the institution of the ministry was informed to a significant degree by gender binaries of the 1890s–1920s. In addition to being ideally white and middleclass, the ministry was supposed to be male. In every era of the church, maleness was an enduring qualification for ministering, but for Protestants of the late nineteenth and early twentieth centuries, and for revivalists in particular, manliness had critical value. A manly minister and his vigorous, manly church were qualified to face the anxieties that modernity brought to the American church. In addition, manly ministers, it was hoped, would attract more energetic young men to an institution that was seemingly in decline. The ideal revivalist minister, therefore, was a man who could use his muscular body and manly rhetoric and gestures to inspire a "rise in manhood" as well as "the cause of our Christ."[204]

Strategies that female revivalists employed to lead in an institution that was ideally masculine, therefore, had limited success. Women tried diverse ways of circumventing the notion that the ministry was male. Although many used their status as ideal wives and mothers as proof that they were qualified to lead in the church, few were convinced by their efforts. Thus, during the 1890s–1920s, while their female colleagues in the law, medicine, and other professions made significant advancements in their institutions, for most, the idea of an authoritative female minister seemed as far away as it had ever been.

2

"WALKING BIBLES": NARRATING FEMALE PENTECOSTAL MINISTRY

The manner in which the ministry was gendered male was not the only impediment for women entering the pastorate. The inconsonance between the identities of woman and minister was compounded by the legal prescriptions in the New Testament used to ward off ministers. Therefore, the aim of this chapter is to show how Maria Woodworth-Etter and Aimee Semple McPherson used Pentecostal readings of the Bible to authorize their ministry. First, the chapter discusses the set of scriptures that most American Protestants used to argue for or against female pastors. Then, it outlines the passages that Woodworth-Etter and McPherson used to authorize their ministries. Their approaches show early Pentecostal hermeneutics at work and demonstrate how their biblical interpretations allowed the women to circumvent fundamentalist-modernist arguments about the Bible while supporting pastoral identities built on biblical prototypes.

The most powerful source of authority for American Protestants (revivalist or otherwise) was the Bible.[1] It therefore followed that in order for any individual to achieve ministerial authority, biblical endorsement was essential.[2] Unfortunately for women ministers, several biblical passages have been used to preclude female pastors.[3] These include: I Timothy 2:12, "But I [Paul] suffer not a woman to teach, nor to usurp authority over the man, but to be in silence"; I Corinthians 14:34, "Let your women keep silence in the churches: for it is not permitted unto them to speak; but they are commanded to be under obedience as also saith the law"; I Corinthians 11:3, "But I [Paul] would have you know, that the head of every man is Christ; and the head of the woman is the man; and the head of Christ is God"; and Ephesians 5:22–23, "Wives, submit yourselves unto your own husbands, as unto the Lord. For the husband is the head of the wife, even as Christ is the head of the church: and he is the saviour of the body."[4] Most churches insisted that women needed to follow the Pauline model for husband–wife/man–woman relationships and so excluded women from exercising authority over men in the church as well as in the home.[5]

The issue of female ministers and the Bible was contended hotly in all segments of Protestantism during the 1890s–1920s. For hundreds of years the minister's inherent maleness had not been a question for most Protestants. By the late nineteenth century, the academic science of biblical study, known as "higher criticism," had trickled down from German-influenced seminaries into American ministerial circles.[6] Higher critical approaches to the Bible led some Protestants to question church positions on passages related to the prohibition of female pastors.[7] This, coupled with the influx of women into professions like the ministry, brought the Bible and its relationship to female ministers to the fore of public discourse.[8]

Protestant rhetoric arguing about whether the Bible permitted women to minister was sharp. Many in favor of female ministers argued that the so-called prohibitive passages had been misinterpreted, and when read in the light of higher critical scholarship were not in fact bans on all female pastors.[9] The historical critical principle of investigating the context in which passages were written led pro-female ministry advocates to argue that the world in which prohibitive passages were written was so different from modern American life, that Pauline restrictions no longer applied to late-nineteenth- and early twentieth-century Christians. For example, Presbyterian Louisa Woolsey wrote that in the modern era, "only poor, stereotyped dark age theologians" would think of keeping women called to the ministry from the pulpit.[10] Journalist W. T. Stead echoed this sentiment and gave thanks that modern female ministers were no longer in "bondage to Corinthian standards."[11]

Opponents to female ministers remained unmoved.[12] "Is this a translation," asked one irked biblical scholar of a Salvation Army translation of I Timothy 2:11–14 who retranslated the King James Version of the passage in such a way that removed the ban on women from "usurping authority over the man," "or a travesty?"[13] Those against women ministers argued that using modern approaches to overturn the ban against female ministers would lead to all manner of debauchery. "If we have the right to interpret [I Corinthians 14:34] thus [as invalid for modern times]," wrote Lutheran minister Juergen Ludwig Neve, "and so get rid of something that does not suit the taste of our age, what then can we answer if, for instance, a champion of 'free love' attacks the institution of marriage, saying that such requirements of the Bible do not hold for our day?"[14]

In general, revivalists were leery of higher critical methods.[15] They worried that such approaches would undermine biblical authority in the church and would ultimately stymie revivalism.[16] "We have never seen, nor have we ever heard of a preacher who was a higher critic and believed this infidel doctrine (for it is nothing else)," wrote revivalist J. Walter Malone, "that held revivals or had souls born into the kingdom under his ministry."[17] Those who were opposed to female ministers blamed their increase in part on higher critics and their "modernist" theories about the Bible.[18]

Revivalists who advocated for female ministers eschewed appeals to modern interpretations and instead used time-tested arguments to make their case.[19] The story of Deborah (Judges 4–5), the judge and prophet who led Israel, was a popular passage for revivalists promoting women in ministry.[20] Revivalists asked their critics, if women church leaders were prohibited by God, then "why did God send Deborah to show Barak his duty and not Barak to show Deborah?"[21]

Another scripture touted by early-twentieth-century revivalists was Joel 2:28–29 (and the Apostle Peter's sermon quoting it in Acts 2:17–18), "And it shall come to pass afterward, that I will pour out my spirit upon all flesh; and your sons and your daughters shall prophesy, your old men shall dream dreams, your young men shall see visions: And also upon the servants and upon the handmaids in those days will I pour out my spirit."[22] Revivalist ministers such as Carrie Judd Montgomery and Alma White argued that they were the prophetic daughters of Joel 2 whom Peter identified in Acts 2, and that the passage "forever settles the question as to woman's ministry."[23] Those in favor and those opposed to female involvement in the clergy argued repeatedly with one another throughout the first few decades of the twentieth century.[24] Rarely did they convince one another to change positions.

For those women ministers who did succeed in their quest to overcome traditional biblical prohibitions, permission to join the guild did not equal authority from the pulpit. Even those who, through argumentation and bureaucratic measures, won the right to be ordained, struggled to gain ministerial appointments or to exercise authority over congregants. Their struggle was due in part to late-nineteenth- and early-twentieth-century muscular Christians who believed that the manly gospel of the scriptures naturally bestowed such power to lead upon male ministers.[25] Many revivalists took for granted the idea that the authority of the scriptures was interwoven with masculinity.

"The Gospel of Christ is a manly Gospel," wrote revivalist Frederick Taylor, who warned that without a manly preacher, the message of the Bible would become "anemic in character."[26] "Nobody can read the Bible thoughtfully," observed Billy Sunday, "and not be impressed with the way it upholds the manhood of a man."[27] Revivalist Grant Stroh summed up revivalist sentiment on the subject in the *Moody Bible Institute Monthly* periodical. "A pastor is one who has authority of a church," he wrote, "and there is nothing recorded in the Bible of that [female] kind. We admit that it is difficult to interpret Paul's words to the Corinthians and to Timothy on this subject in light of experience [with women ministers], but you will agree that on general principles it is safer to stand on the Word of God than on human experience."[28]

Maria Woodworth-Etter and Aimee Semple McPherson were able to circumvent these biblical prohibitions to female ministry. One way that they overcame the biblical barrier to ministering was by simply changing the subject away from the fiery arguments over scripture that were blazing through mainstream Protestantism in the form of the fundamentalist-modernist controversy. While their counterparts argued based on restrictive texts, Woodworth-Etter and McPherson went around them.

In the late nineteenth and early twentieth centuries, it was common for women ministers like Madeline Southard to host conventions, rallies, and give newspaper interviews arguing that the Bible endorsed "ecclesiastical."[29] Woodworth-Etter showed little interest in arguments for overturning the historic ban on female pastors. Of the hundreds of pages of her surviving written materials—her autobiography, sermons, and other writings—Woodworth-Etter published very little about female access to the ministry.[30] What she said in one sermon on the topic was in line with other revivalists. Concerning female pastors, she cited "Miriam, Deborah, Hannah, Hulda, Anna, Phoebe, Narcissus, Tryphena, Persis, Julia, and the Marys, and the sisters who were co-workers with Paul in the gospel whose names were in the Book of Life, and many other women whose labors are mentioned with praise," as evidence of a woman's right to minister.[31]

Like Woodworth-Etter, McPherson was not particularly interested in the debates about whether or not the Bible allowed for women ministers. And, like her predecessor, what she did say was in line with conventional revivalist rhetoric. In her autobiography, McPherson placed arguments against female ministers in the Bible in the mouth of her mother, Minnie Kennedy, and then recollected her own response.

> "Mother, do women ever preach the gospel?" I asked one night over the ironing board. "No, dear." "Why?" "Oh you and your whys! Well, Eve the mother of all living was the first transgressor."
>
> Gathering up my algebra, trigonometry, and physiology books, I retired to my room and got out my Bible and concordance. "Women. . .women. . .women," I queried aloud. "Why are they prevented from Christianizing the world?" I found that Deborah, a woman, led forth her gleaming armies beneath the flaming banners under the sunshine of God's smile. The woman at the well preached the first salvation sermon and led an entire city to Christ, having chosen as her text, "Come, see the man that told me all I ever did." Moreover, a woman had delivered the first Easter message and none other than the Master had commissioned her.[32]

McPherson then recounted her reaction to what her father, the head of her household, suggested:

> "Why wasn't a man dispatched with that first all-important message?" I mused audibly.
>
> "Because the men were all in bed and sound asleep, I presume," replied my father, who had appeared unexpectedly in the doorway.
>
> Sheepishly, I leaped up and faced him. "How long have you been standing there?"
>
> "Just a moment. Why?"
>
> "Why are there no women preachers, dad?" I demanded.
>
> "There's Evangeline Booth."
>
> "But her work is mostly that of a commander. She doesn't pastor a church."
>
> "But Paul was taught by a man and his wife, Priscilla and Aquila. He tells of one man who had seven daughters and another who had nine that prophesied."[33]

In this conversation between her father and herself, McPherson created an extra-biblical narrative. While Acts records Paul working and ministering alongside Priscilla and Aquila (Acts 18:2, 18) Apollos, not Paul was their theological mentee (Acts 18:26). The writer of Luke-Acts (and not Paul) mentions Philip the Evangelist's four (not seven or nine) prophesying daughters in Acts 21:8–9. McPherson's extra-biblical story served her well. It gave her discussion of biblical women in prominent positions additional clout because it came with Paul's apostolic authority, and it quadrupled the number of prophesying daughters.

McPherson most likely invented Minnie Kennedy's position to give voice to the argument against female ministers. Kennedy was raised Salvation Army, a denomination that ordained women, and for much of McPherson's career she was one of her staunchest supporters. Placing a discussion of Paul's supposed female mentor and prophesying daughters in her father's mouth had strategic value. To have the man of the house, not the woman, speak the rhetoric that McPherson used as permission to pastor carried with it additional gendered authority.

Other than this childhood vignette, McPherson did not write or speak extensively on the issue of whether women should or could pastor. In her autobiography, *This is That*, she referred to Joel 2:28 although not in order to defend her right to preach, but to encourage her congregation's ecstatic worship.[34] Elsewhere, she offered occasional exclamations such as "Oh, don't you ever tell me that a woman cannot be called to preach the Gospel!"[35]

Woodworth-Etter and McPherson's relative lack of engagement with scripturally based arguments about female ministers did not mean that they devalued the Bible. Rather than offer their own interpretations of the scriptures being analyzed and reanalyzed by higher critics, fundamentalists, and evangelicals, Woodworth-Etter and McPherson did something arguably more powerful than address legal prescriptions. They used the Bible to make an identity. "God wants us to be walking Bibles,"[36] claimed Woodworth-Etter, and the narratives that each woman created made them just that. Like the fictional early-twentieth-century figure Jay Gatsby, the women created their own identities, but unlike Gatsby, they were not self-made heroes. The identities that they created came from biblical models that highlighted aspects of their ministries that repeated 1890s–1920s womanly ideals, obscured events that undermined their respectable womanliness, and emphasized aspects of Pentecostal biblical theology that authorized them to lead.

THE WARRING MOTHER

Woodworth-Etter had many disparate identities: mother, minister, publisher, divorcee, and defendant. The overarching plot of her story as a minister, as recounted in her autobiographies, sermons, tracts, and occasional newspaper interviews, was that of a mother protecting her children both biological and spiritual. Woodworth-Etter told her followers that she resisted her initial call to the ministry because she wanted to fulfill her duties as a mother. "Oh Lord!" she wrote of her struggle both to minister and to parent her son Willie, "I cannot take Willie with me, nor can I leave him behind."[37] "If I were a man I would love to work for Jesus," she wrote.[38] She found her inspiration to mother a congregation through her vision of her five dead children "shining in dazzling beauty around God's Throne."[39] "If mothers could see their children as I saw them," she wrote, "they would never weep for them, but would leave all and follow Jesus."[40]

As she grieved the loss of her children and read her Bible, Woodworth-Etter came to understand her identity as a warring mother minister. She claimed,

> The dear Savior stood by me one night in a vision and talked face to face with me, and asked what I was doing on earth.
>
> I felt condemned, and said, 'Lord, I am going to work in thy vineyard.'
>
> The Lord said, 'When,' and I answered, 'When I get prepared for the work.'
>
> I told Him I wanted to study the Bible; that I did not understand it well enough. Then there appeared on the wall a large open Bible, and the verses stood out in raised letters. The glory of God shone around and upon the book. I looked, and I could understand it all.[41]

Having received a gift for supernaturally understanding the Bible, Woodworth-Etter set out to find a biblical mentor. "I would go to my Bible and search for teaching and examples," she wrote. "When the Lord put his erring people in remembrance of his great blessing to Israel he said, 'Did I not send thee Moses and Aaron and Miriam to be your leader'?"[42] Although Woodworth-Etter found encouragement in the story of Miriam, the figure that she took as her exemplar was Deborah, the Mother in Israel. "And when there was trouble on hand," she wrote, "Barak dare not meet the enemy unless Deborah led the van. And the noble woman, always ready to work for God and his cause, said, 'I will surely go. God's people must not be prey to the enemy.' Oh no; call out the men of Israel; Sisera's mighty hosts are gathering."[43]

Woodworth-Etter retold the story of Deborah many times in her sermons and autobiographies.[44] She was careful to emphasize the

Mother in Israel's leadership, her responsibility to the children of Israel, and her status as a military leader.

> Deborah, a prophetess, the wife of Lapidoth she judged Israel at that time. See the responsible position God gave her, to sit and judge the hosts of the children of Israel. The children of Israel had sinned and God would not fight their battles, and for twenty years the nations arose against them and defied them to come out to battle. Barak dared not meet the enemy unless Deborah led the van. This brave woman, ever ready to defend the cause of God, said, 'I will surely go.' God's people must not be taken by the enemies. Oh, no; call out the armies of the Lord. Sisera's mighty host is gathering. Every soldier at his post.[45]

Woodworth-Etter referred to herself as a "Mother in Israel; a Deborah,"[46] and her congregation as her "own children."[47] Like Deborah, she spoke of her mission on earth to "lead the van"[48] to protect God's children.

Choosing to model herself on Deborah the Mother in Israel served Woodworth-Etter well. First, the Mother in Israel benefited Woodworth-Etter because Deborah was a biblical figure to whom she could relate as a mother. Unlike Rebecca, Rachel, or Leah who were known for their relationship to their offspring, Deborah mothered people who were not her biological children. By claiming to mother like her, Woodworth-Etter was able to find a way to use her mothering skills even though only one of her children survived into adulthood.

Second, Deborah's title, the Mother in Israel tapped into the ideal educated motherhood of the 1890s–1910s.[49] The Mother in Israel was deployed in a number of positive ways in the turn-of-the-century American Protestantism.[50] For some, Deborah symbolized ideal female American citizenship. "This Mother in Israel does not mean mother of children," wrote commentator Emily Oliver Gibbes, "but is the same as we say that Washington was the father of his country. A Mother in Israel is a mother of her country."[51] The *Baltimore Sun* defined a "true Mother in Israel" in the following manner: "Her life was one of service to her country. She had determination and energy without loss of gentleness. She was a good citizen."[52] Therefore, by calling herself a Mother in Israel, Woodworth-Etter evoked a sense of dutiful American citizenship.

Progressives used Deborah as a biblical precedent for women in public leadership. Deborah was *the first public woman of the Bible, if not of history.*"[53] The Mother in Israel, for women anxious to join their male counterparts in the professions, was an example of "a 'new woman' in an age that is very old."[54] She was called the "first suffragette, the Mother in Israel," a woman who, like her turn-of-the-century descendents, "introduced all the beautiful reforms," although the author did not specify which reforms Deborah was supposed to have introduced.[55] Deborah was a "female head of the people,"[56] and a woman with "much authority, and knew how to use it."[57] Pioneering female lawyer Phoebe Couzins used the Mother in Israel as a prototype for modern female professionals. "Deborah, who judged in Israel," she wrote, "said: 'The highways were occupied, and travelers walked through the byways, until I, Deborah, arose a Mother in Israel.' She took command of the army, routed the enemy, and for forty years there was peace in the land. I tell you, ladies, that is the way we women fight."[58] For progressives, Woodworth-Etter's identification with the Mother in Israel was an apology for her status as a public figure of authority.

For conservatives, Deborah was not a radical reformer but a model of educated motherhood. The Mother in Israel was celebrated as a beacon of ideal womanliness who "stood for home, for domestic purity, and social order."[59] "For the most part," wrote popular commentator J. B. Lightfoot, "the Israel of which she is mother will be her own home, her own social circle, her own parish and neighborhood. By her stronger affections and her finer sensibilities, by her greater sympathy and her truer tact, by her comparative physical weakness, by the direct demands made upon her as a wife and mother, she will commonly be guided to a less conspicuous, but not less useful, sphere of action."[60] From this perspective Deborah was not an example of authority, but of "meekness and humility," and "simplicity and lowliness."[61] Rather than fighting social ills as a suffragette, the conservative Mother in Israel used the weapons of "patience and tact" to improve her domicile.[62] Unlike the progressives who used Deborah as a precedent for female public authority, conservatives praised her "personally humble station, evidently without any ambitious wish, or attempt to elevate her rank or prospects."[63] And, like any educated mother, the ideal Mother in Israel's ultimate calling was to raise "manly boys" and fill her days with "mothering service."[64] Thus, for conservatives, Woodworth-Etter's allusion to Deborah signaled a comforting preservation of the models of womanhood progressives sought to dismantle.

Woodworth-Etter deployed the term "Mother in Israel" in a variety of ways. The narrative that she created for her ministry highlighted aspects that repeated "mothering service." For example, she described pastoring her followers in terms of a mother nurturing her children. She called her congregation her "dear children" or "children of the Lord,"[65] "a son or a daughter of the most high God"[66] (I John 3:2), or as "children of the light"[67] (I Thessalonians 5:5). When she spoke of pastoring other pastors, the role that could have been termed "bishop" became a maternal one. "They look to me," she wrote about the young ministers who came to her, and "as a mother for advice. I feel a care and love for them, as a mother does for her own children."[68] She believed her mothering would lead her children to the eschatological feast Jesus referred to in Luke 13:29 and Matthew 8:11, and keep them from suffering the "weeping and gnashing of teeth," that awaited those outside the feast. "I thought," she wrote of her congregants after a revival meeting, "when I shall sit down with the dear children God has given me, who shall come from the east, west, north and south [Luke 13:29]."[69]

Part of caring for her children meant that she instructed them. She noted with satisfaction that, "multitudes from all parts have received instruction and teaching concerning the things of God."[70] She saw herself as a teacher whom "He [God] could use to enlighten His children and bring sinners to Christ."[71] She warned her followers, "False teachers will rise up having the form of godliness, but denying the power thereof... '*from such turn away*.'[72] Rather, they were to consider her teachings and "exhortations." "You need this knowledge," she told her follower of her teachings, "Do not fail to get this literature. Read them and get faith."[73] "We teach them, and pray with them," she wrote of her followers, "helping them as best we can to trust Jesus for both soul and body."[74] She predicted that upon reading her words, "the children of God will be stirred to more earnestness and diligence."[75]

By portraying herself as a Mother in Israel who loved, nurtured, and instructed her children, Woodworth-Etter constructed a narrative that gave her the same sort of authority claimed by many mother activists. Casting her ministerial acts as motherly meant that she occupied a familiar, socially acceptable position. By infantilizing her congregation, she made herself an acceptable figure of authority. Not everyone had a female minister, but everyone had a mother, and Woodworth-Etter was her congregation's mother. She wrote that her children gave her a "highly honored" place in their congregation.[76]

Woodworth-Etter complemented her invocation of Deborah as nurturing mother and domestic authority by drawing upon images of the manly ministry revivalists desired. Her Mother in Israel story was the tale of a female military commander as well as educated mother.

Woodworth-Etter adjusted the biblical narrative to emphasize the military power of her Mother in Israel. Judges 4:9–15 mentions that Deborah traveled with the army of Israel and commissioned Barak to lead it, but the text does not place her on the battlefield. In Woodworth-Etter's account, Deborah joined the army and fought for her people. "See the brave woman riding with Barak, the commander," she wrote, "at the head of the army cheering on the hosts to victory, shouting victory as she led on the armies, sweeping through the enemies' ranks carrying death and destruction."[77] Woodworth-Etter's Mother in Israel not only nurtured her children but also participated in the manly act of war on their behalf.

Just as Sisera's army had amassed to battle Israel so, "gross spiritual darkness is fast settling low over the people," wrote Woodworth-Etter.[78] While Deborah oversaw a battle between the Israelites and Canaanites, Woodworth-Etter's battlefield was significantly larger. "The whole world will be taken in a snare at the winding up of the awful time with the great battle of God Almighty with the armies of the earth," she wrote.[79] Her role was to lead an army of God to fight the enemy. "God was preparing me," she wrote of her early days in the ministry, "and opening the way for the great battle against the enemy of souls."[80] She wrote that she and "the armies of the Lord and the soldiers of Jesus have left the various battlefields and have come together."[81]

Woodworth-Etter claimed that her part in the battle was to act as God's agent. "I was to be God's mouth-piece," she wrote. "I must trust God to speak through me to the people the words of eternal life."[82] As God's mouthpiece, she, like Deborah, led her congregants into battle. She wrote the following account of a particularly discouraging season:

> As we look over the last year with all its bitter trials and persecutions, the weariness of body, the many hard battles we were engaged in with the powers of darkness arrayed against us, cold professors, and false shepherds to oppose the work when we had to stand alone, leaning on the arm of the Great Shepherd.
>
> Then he [God] would whisper, "I am with you, be not afraid. I will fight your battles."
>
> Then I would shout, "Victory through faith in the blood," and souls would come flocking to Christ.[83]

Woodworth-Etter's commander-in-chief was Jesus. "Our captain," she said, "will soon call us poor weary, battle-scarred soldiers from the field to shout victory together in a grand reunion that will last forever."[84] This captain was a "man of war"[85] who was ruthless in battle. His mission as a warrior was to exact God's will upon the unrighteous. "Jesus comes now as the stern Judge," she claimed in a sermon on Revelation 20:5–6, "not the despised Nazarene; not the bridegroom in all his glory for his bride. He comes in flaming fire, taking vengeance on the wicked."[86] She also identified God the Father as a warrior, "He will send out His arrows," she wrote, "*His* Word dipped in the blood of Jesus, shot out with the lightning of His power, and they shall wound the king's enemies in the head. They shall fall at His feet when God has His way the tent ground looks like a battlefield; men, women, and children lying in all parts, like dead men."[87]

While she depicted herself as an exemplary mother to her congregation and a commander like Deborah in the army of God, Woodworth-Etter also obscured certain aspects of her identity that did not conform to notions of educated motherhood: her status as a divorcee and her unconventional second marriage. As a mother first and foremost, the story that she constructed for herself did not include that of wife.[88] She rarely mentioned her two husbands. The first, Philo Woodworth, whom she divorced for infidelity,[89] appears only as a brief bump in her career. "My husband was not willing for me to go, or to engage in the work in any place,"[90] she wrote, although he eventually agreed to sell concessions at her meetings.[91] She did not give an account for their divorce; instead, she spoke of their separation after his death, which implied that she was widowed.[92]

Although her marriage to Samuel Etter was more successful, she mentioned him rarely as well.[93] The longest description she did provide was not a picture of traditional marriage roles. "He takes the best care of me, in and out of the meetings," she wrote.[94] Taking care of a spouse was part of what traditional husbands were supposed to do, but the ways in which Etter took care were atypical. In essence, Etter served as her assistant. "It makes no difference what I call on him to do," she wrote.[95] "He will pray, and preach, and sing, and is very good around the altar. He does about all of my writing,[96] and he also helps in getting out my books, and looks after the meeting, in and outside. The Lord knew what I needed, and it was all brought about by the Lord, through his love and care for me and the work."[97] By her description, Samuel Etter's primary role in their marriage was as her subordinate.

Nothing, not even her happy marriage, superseded Woodworth-Etter's work as her congregation's mother. Marriage was something she accomplished, literally, on the way to another church meeting.

"On the first day of January, 1902, I married Mr. S. P. Etter of Hot Springs, Ark. Then we went back to Iowa where I had labored several years before," she wrote unsentimentally. "We held meetings for seven weeks."[98]

In addition to obscuring her marital history, Woodworth-Etter found in her warring mother persona a way to frame her run-ins with authorities as spiritual battles rather than causes for disgrace. She had a long history of trouble with the law including riot police called to meetings in 1890, a trial for fraud in 1913, a clash with police in 1915, and an arrest for practicing medicine without a license in 1920.[99] Any of these scandals had the potential to discredit her. While she could avoid the story of P. H. Woodworth's adultery and their divorce because of his timely death, she had no choice but to address her public arrests.

She wrote about these potentially embarrassing events as epic battles that God helped her win. "So the devil brings all his forces into the battle against Jesus and his saints; but He that is in us, is greater than all that are against us; and the Lord will fight our battles, if he has to bring down all the Armies of Heaven," she wrote of her clash with police in 1890.[100] She credited the devil with her 1913 arrest. "Satan, the enemy of Jesus Christ, and His power, surely over reached himself when he caused the chief of police of South Framingham, Mass. to issue warrants," she wrote. "This arrest," she claimed, "gave a glorious opportunity to put upon the witness stand," many who "all told of the wonderful power of God."[101]

Her masculine God and warring language helped reframe her trials and also gave her ministry manly credibility by superseding the aggressive rhetoric of many of her male revivalist counterparts. Manly ministers like A. B. Simpson taught that, the essence of the scripture was an "exchange of strength" between a human and the "perfect manhood" of Jesus.[102] "Scriptural faith," according to Simpson, produced "good soldiers of Jesus,"[103] but Woodworth-Etter supplemented this masculine portrait of the gospel with graphic details of the ruthlessness of God and her part as one of his commanders.

Woodworth-Etter's warring mother gave her credibility by tapping into the avid interest that holiness and Pentecostal revivalists of the era had in all things end times.[104] She took a figure of relatively no eschatological value in the Bible, and put her at the fore of the epic battle for the fate of the world. Thus, Woodworth-Etter's Mother in Israel brought the seemingly disparate aspects of her identity, her status as a mother, a divorcee, and a minister, together into the story of a woman without a husband who upheld the ideals of educated motherhood and also did some very unwomanly things such as go to war, lead men, and hold a public position of power.

THE BRIDE OF CHRIST

Woodworth-Etter's biblical narrative appealed to 1890s–1910s sensibilities, but the story was less attractive by 1920s standards. The Mother in Israel was a lot of things, but she was not a figure of sexual intimacy and marital friendship. In other words, she was no companionate wife. Woodworth-Etter's successor Aimee Semple McPherson found a way to tell the story of female ministry that combined the companionate model of American womanhood with biblical authority.

McPherson was many things: a minister, a denomination founder, a radio star, an entrepreneur, a mother, a divorcee, and a defendant. Unlike Woodworth-Etter's story of a Mother in Israel, the central plot which brought all of these aspects together into one identity, as McPherson told it in her autobiography, sermons, speeches, and tracts, was that of a biblical bride of Christ. When she shared the story of her life and ministry (which she did often), she always began with the story of her earthly bridegroom, Robert Semple, who was her first love and the man she married as a teenager. "He stood some six feet and two inches in stature had a shock of chestnut-brown curly hair," she wrote admiringly, "one lock of which he was continually brushing back from his Irish blue eyes."[105] Semple's preaching had a profound physical and emotional effect on McPherson. "Cold shivers ran up and down my back," she wrote about hearing him preach, "No one had ever spoken to me [from the pulpit or to her personally] like this before."[106] While she admired him as a preacher, she reveled in their relationship as man and wife. "Tall, dark and smiling," she wrote, "He was like a knight in shining armor."[107] McPherson considered Semple to be the ideal companionate husband. He satisfied her intellectually as her "theological seminary," spiritually as her "spiritual mentor," and intimately as her "unfailing lover."[108]

When Semple died, McPherson wrote that her loneliness was overpowering and that she missed the intimacy of her companionate marriage. In her autobiography she recalled her life as a widow:

> I felt increasingly sad and sentimental. Whenever some tall, smiling man would take his lady's arm and help her across the street, I would hastily lower my black chiffon veil. I was as a chip tossed aimlessly in a maelstrom of a definite, classified, well-ordered life. 'Where shall I go? What shall I do?' I whispered to the pillow at night as I lay wide-eyed

staring through the murky darkness at the grimy street lamp that shone in my window or as I turned in utter desolation to kiss my own shoulder a lonely good night.[109]

Although she remarried twice afterward, McPherson never recaptured the ardor of her first marriage. Harold McPherson, her second husband, provided her with companionship and support for her children, but he did not share his wife's love of the ministry. David Hutton, the third, swept McPherson off her feet, but his career as a Vaudeville singer and his relationships with other women dampened their emotional connection.

Lacking that original passion after her first husband's death, McPherson found meaning in the pages of the Bible. For McPherson, reading the Bible was an act of intimacy with Jesus. To illustrate this, she compared the Bible to a temple. "Picture the Word of God," she wrote, "the Bible represented as a building, a temple with turrets and minarets and towers. A temple with a large number of pillars and with blocks-thirty-nine granite blocks, twenty-seven granite and alabaster pillars; a temple with its beautiful, mighty dome, and its doorway."[110] There were many rooms in the Temple of the Bible, and McPherson gave different writings their own room names. The Psalms were the "Music Room," the Pentateuch was the "Art Gallery," and the Song of Solomon was the "Conservatory."[111]

The most important room in the temple was the room that held the four gospels otherwise known as the "Audience Chamber," where Jesus resided.[112] McPherson modeled her experiences in the Audience Chamber after interactions between Queen Esther and Ahasuerus in his audience chamber in Esther 5:1–8. Esther approached her husband in his chamber (Esther 5:1) and touched her husband's scepter (Esther 5:2), and in the Audience Chamber of the Gospels, McPherson experienced the companionate marriage that she could not recapture in her earthly relationships:

Oh! I am so glad I ever got into the Audience Chamber of the King! And there I saw Him whom to see is to adore. I saw His nail pierced hands, His wounded feet, and I said:

"O Lord, may I draw near?"

Then I turned to my Guide. "Would He mind if I went a little closer, think you?"

My Guide answered, "No."

Gently I heard the Master say, "Come unto me! Draw near unto me and I will draw near unto you."

And so, timidly, I went, and as I approached Him He reached out the scepter of His love to me and I touched it. Oh! I will never forget how I knelt at His wonderful feet in the Audience Chamber of the King, how I kissed His nail pierced hands and how they were placed in blessing on my head and how I fell at His dear wounded feet: and bathed them with my tears.[113]

McPherson's ecstasy when she touched the "scepter of his love" and felt the thrill of being in his presence had undeniable sexual overtones. Indeed, McPherson's meetings with Jesus had all the markings of infatuation: she swooned, she longed, she cried, and she begged for him. "Now I had found the one to cling to and fasten my hold upon," she wrote, "One who would never die or leave me. Oh, it was Jesus! Jesus!!"[114]

In addition to consuming passion, the two also enjoyed the sympathy and friendship of an ideal marriage. Jesus was her confidant and companion. She referred to him with the familiarity of a spouse and frequently called him, "Jesus dear."[115] In a sermon entitled "They Have Taken My Lord Away," based on John 20:13, McPherson demonstrated her dependence upon Jesus as her close companion as well as lover. She began the sermon with John's description of Mary responding to two angels at the tomb, "They have taken my Lord away, and I do not know where they have laid him."[116] Then, she imagined Mary's more elaborate inner monologue, "Oh, Jesus—where are you? Oh, Jesus, I want you! All the world is dark and drear, and my heart is gripped with loneliness without you. Jesus, Jesus of Nazareth, Jesus of the Tender Heart—where are you? Oh! He will not answer me! The tomb is empty! They have taken away, they—have—taken—away—my—Lord!" McPherson continued with a personal request, "Oh, miracle-working, prayer-answering Jesus, where are you? I need you—want you so!"[117] She asked Jesus, "Oh, don't you know—can't you see—we of today need you—need you just as much as those who lived nineteen hundred years ago."[118]

McPherson also wrote that Jesus responded to her emotional needs. "Brokenly I began to sob, 'Oh Jesus, forgive me! For—'" McPherson wrote, "Before I could finish the words, it seemed as though the Lord had placed his hand over my trembling lips, saying, 'There, there, my child. Say no more about it'."[119] "My heart is so full," she wrote of her friendship with Jesus, "Oh precious friends, the Lord has been so real to me in these past days. He has been so close to my side, and how I rejoice I ever stepped out on His promises and put my all upon the altar."[120]

McPherson wrote that it was her friend and lover Jesus who called her to pastor. After a moment in the presence of Jesus while reading the Gospel of John, McPherson reported receiving her call. Her story paralleled Simon Peter's three-part commission in John 21:15–17:

> So when they had dined, Jesus saith to Simon Peter, "Simon, son of Jonas, lovest thou me more than these?"
>
> He saith unto him, "Yea, Lord; thou knowest that I love thee."
>
> He saith unto him, "Feed my lambs."
>
> He saith to him again the second time, "Simon, son of Jonas, lovest thou me?" He saith unto him, "Yea, Lord; thou knowest that I love thee."
>
> He saith unto him, "Feed my sheep."
>
> He saith unto him the third time, "Simon, son of Jonas, lovest thou me?"
>
> Peter was grieved because he said unto him the third time, "Lovest thou me?" And he said unto him, "Lord, thou knowest all things; thou knowest that I love thee."
>
> Jesus saith unto him, "Feed my sheep."

Like Woodworth-Etter's treatment of Deborah, McPherson adjusted the original narrative. In her version of the scene, she employed many biblical tropes. She alluded to the John 13 account of the Last Supper and identified with the beloved disciple who enjoyed a physical connection with Jesus.

> Then I drew closer yet. He said I might lay my head upon His bosom and I might rest awhile. It is when we draw close to Him there that our own hearts catch the throbbing of His heart and we say, "Lord, I will never leave you. I am going to stay right here with you."
>
> He then asked, "Do you love me?"
>
> "Yes, Lord, you know I love you."
>
> "Then feed my sheep. Feed my lambs."[121]

As John's disciple "whom Jesus loved," McPherson heightened the sense that she enjoyed a privileged position in Jesus' inner circle. Then, McPherson supplemented the call to Peter with a reference to Jesus' call to evangelism in John 4:35, Luke 10:2, and Matthew 9:38:

> "Go out into the harvest fields of life and gather in the grain for the fields are white unto the Harvest."[122]

Like Mary Magdalene who clung to the resurrected Jesus in John 20:17, McPherson wrote that she was reluctant to leave his chamber and go into the world:

> "Oh no, no, Lord! I don't want to leave you. I never want to leave Thy presence."[123]

Then, she wrote that Jesus gave her a promise of continued intimacy in a vow that echoed the Great Commission in Matthew 28:20 as well as the covenant made between Ruth and Naomi in Ruth 1:16–17:

> And then, with a sweet and wonderful smile, He bends a little closer and whispers, "Lo, I am with you always. Wherever you go, I will go with you, if it is out to the Mission Field, if it is out to the harvest lands. Where thou goest, I will go, and I will hold your hand in mine."
>
> "Oh! that is all right, Lord. If you will go with me, I will go anywhere!"[124]

By putting Ruth's promise to her mother-in-law in Jesus' call, McPherson eased some of the sexual language between the minister and her savior, but overall her additions to Jesus' call in John 15—the description of their physical closeness, his "sweet and wonderful smile," and their whispered conversations—foregrounded the romantic relationship she enjoyed with her savior. In addition, in her vision of her commission, she illustrated her heightened responsiveness to the call. Jesus did not ask McPherson three times—once was enough.

McPherson's romance with Jesus shared little in common with Woodworth-Etter's status as an educated mother and military captain. Rather, it resembled many popular stories of companionate marriage in early-twentieth-century literature and film.[125] The typical plotline of Roaring Twenties romance novels, films, and magazines featured a young white woman overcoming big-city loneliness, poverty, and hardship and finding love, marriage, and a family.[126] McPherson's ministry, located in the heart of the burgeoning film industry, appropriated cinematic plots. Thus, her self-presentation of an adventurous young woman who survived the tragic death of her true love, endured poverty and loneliness, and went on to find happiness in an eternal, divine romance told a familiar story. While viewers watched the "grand romance" of Mary Pickford and Douglas Fairbanks on the silver screen,[127] they read about Jesus and his companionate wife in the pages of *The Bridal Call*.

McPherson found within the Bible a relationship that both captured the romantic intimacy between herself and her savior and authorized her to lead a congregation: she was the bride of Christ and he was her bridegroom. She used the metaphor of Jesus the bridegroom and the church his bride as the central theme of her writings, as her publication's name, *The Bridal Call*, suggests. She often preached and wrote on passages that explicitly used bride/bridegroom language (e.g., Revelation 21:2; 21:9; 22:17, Matthew 25:1–13, Mark 2:18–22).[128] For example, she quoted Matthew 25:6 in a popular sermon series entitled "When Is He Coming" and advised "the bridegroom cometh," and that the church's calling was to "go ye out to meet him!"[129] "The Bridegroom is near!" she wrote, "He is even at the door."[130] She encouraged her congregation to ready themselves for his return by adorning themselves in anticipation of worshiping him alongside the 24 elders of Revelation 4:10.[131]

For McPherson, no text was safe from being subsumed under the divine love story. She turned the story of Ruth and Boaz into the "wedding in the morn" between Jesus and his bride.[132] The marriage of Isaac and Rebecca was a prefigurement of the eschatological bride and bridegroom.[133] Even the eagle face of the four-faced cherubim in Ezekiel 10:14 was the bridegroom, the "Coming King, whose pinions soon would cleave the shining heavens, whose silvery voice would set the milky way echoing as He came to catch His waiting bride away."[134]

McPherson was not alone in her appreciation for "bride of Christ" imagery.[135] Revivalists in the early twentieth century were particularly fond of it. "The Church is the Bride of Christ," wrote Moody Bible Institute Dean and minister Harold Lundquist.[136] "The Bible plainly teaches that those who are truly born again and regenerated in their hearts by the Holy Spirit make up the bride of Christ," said revivalist "Evangelist Smith," referring to Ephesians 5:29–30 in a sermon on Matthew 24:44.[137]

The bride of Christ was immensely popular in the Pentecostal movement and it was one of the most common images used to describe the relationship between Jesus and the church.[138] Pentecostals regularly spoke about themselves as the bride of Revelation 21:2, 21:9, and 22:17 that waits for a heavenly bridegroom, and about Jesus as the Lamb, the heavenly bridegroom. "The members of His Bride everywhere, one after another are longing with unutterable longing for Himself, His Glorious Presence," wrote one early Pentecostal.[139] Popular preaching passages included the parable of the ten virgins in Matthew 25:1–13 and Jesus' discussion of fasting while the bridegroom was present in Mark 2:18–22.[140] References to the bride and bridegroom peppered early Pentecostal preaching and literature. "Every man and woman that receives the baptism with the Holy Ghost is the bride of Christ," wrote Azusa Street Revival founder William Seymour.[141] Bridal language made its way into early Pentecostal publications such as Gaston B. Cashwell's 1907 journal *The Bridegroom's Messenger* and books such as G. F. Taylor's *The Spirit and the Bride*.[142] It also seeped into Pentecostal hymnody; for example, G. T. Haywood's "Baptized into the Body" included the stanza, "Are you in the Church triumphant? Are you in the Savior's Bride?"[143] Unlike muscular Christians' call for manly, aggressive Christians who took charge of their lives, brides of Christ were required to submit to their husband, Jesus. "Christ's bride has but one husband (2 Cor., 11:2)," wrote William Seymour, "She is subject to him (Eph. 5:25)."[144]

McPherson's use of the term "bride of Christ" was distinct from revivalist depictions in two ways. First, her treatment compounded the bride of Christ's inherent femininity. She exploited every detail about the bride's womanly qualities in describing the church as Jesus' betrothed. For example, in a sermon on the Second Coming, she gave special attention to the church as a woman who receives a beautiful dress from her lover. "He gives to us a beautiful white dress. You may have worn beautiful dresses in your life, but you have never had a dress as beautiful as this which the Lord will give you. It is not an outward dress. It is a dress inside the heart – although you wear it without, too. My dear brothers and sisters, the Lord is adorning His bride, His church, His company today."[145]

In a sermon on Song of Songs 2:8–10, McPherson compared the book's sensual lover/beloved relationship to Jesus and his bride.[146] "Ever thus has come the message unto the expectant church, whose yearning, eager soul awaits the literal appearing of her Lord."[147] Like the beloved in Song of Songs, McPherson's bride was "a beautiful woman."[148] Her rhetoric gave concrete features to the figurative bride. "Her eyes," she wrote, "beheld no guile, but they were tender as a dove's eyes. Her lips were pure, and dropped as the honey-comb. Her ears were kept for His alone, her Lover, her Bridegroom, her King."[149] She had grace, tenderness, a sweet voice, and a beautiful fragrance, "as the rose of Sharon."[150] "With the eyes of the soul she hath beheld Him," she wrote, "but within her breast is the burning desire to behold face to face Him whom having not seen she loves."[151]

Second, McPherson used bride and bridegroom language specifically to describe her personal relationship with Jesus. Jesus was the bridegroom and figure of romantic masculinity, and McPherson depicted herself as the bride, Christ's female counterpart. In one *Bridal Call* article, McPherson wrote that she had a vision of a bride of Christ and the bride. "Slowly my eyes traversed the distance from his nail pierced hands to his glowing eyes," and she shivered after hearing a "glorious, soul thrilling voice."[152] The bride had a face, and that face was hers. "As she [the bride] drew nigh," she wrote, "I gazed with amazement into her face, and saw that it was myself. I heard the voice of the Master speaking unto me, saying: 'This is My beloved'."[153] When McPherson's readers read of the bride of Christ in her writings or in the Bible, they were reading the story of both the church and their leader.

McPherson capitalized on the blurred line between the church as the bride and herself as the bride. She relayed a (perhaps hypothetical) conversation with a congregant on the subject. "Sister McPherson," asked one devotee, "are you the bride of Christ?"[154] McPherson responded, "I am only a little part of that company. If I can be a little part of the little toe, I will be happy! Thank God we can all be a little part."[155]

For all of its usefulness in presenting an idealized version of womanhood, and a recognizable Pentecostal biblical figure, McPherson's narrative had distinct drawbacks when it came to establishing her ministerial authority. The bride of Christ was not a soldier who went to war like Woodworth-Etter and her congregation. She did not initiate battle. She received the love of the bridegroom. The question then for McPherson was how to make such a thoroughly feminine story authoritative. Personalizing the biblical image authorized her ministry: as Jesus' bride, she had a special position as his lover and confidant, which gave her power to act on his behalf. Yet sharing the bride's role with the church enabled her to be in partnership with her congregation: they all held the same role, and the same call, and so they worked for the same purpose. For example, when McPherson took on the monumental task of creating her own denomination, the International Church of the Foursquare Gospel (Foursquare), she claimed that it was not her idea, but rather something she received from Jesus while reading the book of Ezekiel:

> In my soul was born a melody that seemed to strike and be sustained upon four full quivering strings as I thought upon the vision of the prophet Ezekiel. I stood still for a moment and listened, gripping the pulpit, almost shaking with wonder and joy. Then there burst from the white heat of my heart the words, "Why—why it's the Foursquare Gospel. The Foursquare Gospel!" Since that day when the Lord gave me that illumination, the term Foursquare Gospel has been carried around the world.[156]

In her narrative the decisions that she made were not her decisions, but those of her future husband. She frequently noted that her sermons and tracts were "writings straight from God, by the power of the Holy Ghost, on the fourfold message of the hour which He has given and sent her out to preach."[157]

McPherson acknowledged and even emphasized her apparent limitations as a woman but she couched them in terms of her dependence on God and relationship to Jesus. "If I were a man," she wrote, "I could do a lot more. But I'm only a woman who yielded herself for God to use."[158] She also foregrounded additional disqualifications, but turned them into assets. "Never have I attended any earthly Bible school. I clung to the promise that I was to take no thought for what I should say, but that he would teach me in the needed hour, also that out of my innermost being should flow rivers of living water."[159]

In McPherson's narrative, these weaknesses worked to give her a kind of apostolic authority. She compared her situation to the Apostle Paul who in II Corinthians 12:10 claimed, "Therefore I take pleasure in infirmities, in reproaches, in necessities, in persecutions, in distresses for Christ's sake: for when I am weak, then I am strong." McPherson wrote, "I found myself preaching the Gospel, weak in myself but strong in Him."[160] "God uses the weak things, and the small to confound the wise," she wrote of her ministry.[161]

Like Woodworth-Etter, McPherson categorized her most scandalous moments as attacks from Satan. "Before those days in 1926," she wrote of her trial that year, "I used to say often as I watched hundreds of people come to Jesus at Angelus Temple, 'Why doesn't the devil fight this work more?' I said jokingly at the time but I guess maybe he took the hint! I would never again give him any more suggestions!"[162] Unlike her predecessor, however, McPherson did not frame her trial as a battle in which she fought, but rather an attack from which she, as a damsel in distress, needed to be rescued. "Weak and trembling," she recalled, "I struggled to my feet, praying for God to give me help."[163] McPherson wrote about her trial not as a triumph of her morals, and her legal team, but another instance of her companionate husband coming to her rescue. "To God we can give all the glory," she wrote about herself and her staff, "for we stood helpless except for divine intervention. But God helped."[164] By making herself the victim and Jesus her rescuer, the story of her trial fit nicely within the frame of the bride–bridegroom narrative.

Other aspects of her biography—her children and her divorces—that did not fit the bride–bridegroom narrative held much less prominent positions in her story. McPherson compared the dissolution of her marriage to Harold McPherson to the story of Rebecca and Isaac.[165] Just as Rebecca left everything to become Isaac's bride, so McPherson left behind her husband and domestic life to become the bride of Christ. In her brief account, McPherson wrote that she felt intense guilt over leaving her husband, but eventually that feeling passed when she realized that she was leaving him to enter into a life of intimacy with Jesus.[166] "Never mind," she wrote, "Rebecca's on her way to the well—to the fountain-head—to the sure source of supply—to the banqueting table of the King, and we'll soon be filled up now."[167] She rarely made mention of Harold McPherson afterward. She was similarly reticent about her divorce from David Hutton. She quickly shifted attention from her failed relationship to her enduring heavenly one. "My romance and sorrows with Mr. Hutton would have been crushing indeed were it not for that ever-present overwhelming divine love that is ours for the taking."[168]

Her two children, Roberta and Rolf, like her husbands, were not major figures in her narrative even though both were actively involved in her ministry. Roberta was a preacher, children's church supervisor, vice president of the Echo Park Evangelistic Association, and McPherson's heir apparent until she left the ministry in 1936.[169] Rolf also served as vice president, was his mother's closest companion as a young adult, and ultimately succeeded his mother as president of her denomination and pastor of her church in 1944.[170] Calling attention to them might have given McPherson credibility as a mother, but it also would have reminded her audience that she was not only the perpetual bride of her romantic narrative, but also a normal mother with very earth-bound concerns. Thus, McPherson spoke of her children, especially if they had been present during a service,[171] but she rarely utilized her status as their mother to bolster her ministerial authority.[172] Mention of Roberta, named after her late father and once groomed to succeed her mother, was usually coupled with a lengthy description of Robert Semple's death, McPherson's grief, and her eventual triumph.[173] McPherson's falling-out with Roberta, also redacted from her story, might explain some of her daughter's absence in her writings, but her son Rolf McPherson, arguably her most trusted confidant as an adult and eventual successor, also received sparse treatment. The central plot was not that of a mother's love for her children, but of a wife's love for her husband.

CONCLUSION

Woodworth-Etter and McPherson harnessed the significant authority of the Bible in a manner distinct from many of their female minister counterparts. Rather than be drawn into an unending argument over whether or not the scriptures prohibited or endorsed a female ministry, they avoided the conversation. The women put their considerable scriptural knowledge to work creating a story of their lives and ministries that engaged popular notions of 1890s and 1920s womanliness as well as the timeless biblical figures of Mother in Israel and bride of Christ. These narratives allowed the women to emphasize aspects of their lives that harmonized with ideal womanliness and ministry, and obscure those aspects that had potential to detract from their status as female ministers. Therefore, in their sermons, autobiographies, and other writings, Woodworth-Etter and McPherson were not divorced single mothers with scandalous histories. Woodworth-Etter was the Mother in Israel who would lead God's people to a final eschatological victory, and McPherson was the lover, confidant, and bride of the coming bridegroom, Jesus.

3

"Pants Don't Make Preachers": The Image of a Female Pentecostal Minister

The goal of this chapter is to show how Woodworth-Etter and McPherson constructed visual representations of themselves as ministers. It begins by discussing how male ministers projected power through dress, and then examines how female ministers negotiated their outward appearance in response to male attire. Then, this chapter demonstrates how Woodworth-Etter and McPherson aimed not to give a female version of male attire, but to give a visual representation of the biblical women that they claimed to be.

"We humans," wrote William LaFleur, "cannot exist without representation."[1] Indeed, images have power to create meaning for church practitioners, provide interpretation of one's life and existence, and connect viewer(s) to a larger worshipping community.[2] Visual sites for meaning making, interpretation, and connection include not only illustrations, paintings, shrines, and monuments,[3] but also the body. The physical form is an enduring instrument of representation as well as a "readily accessible altar or temple" in which devotees claim to house and display the divine.[4] There is more than one way to play this instrument. Some consider the body to be divinely "given" or "natural" and thus not to be altered for any reason.[5] From this perspective, to alter the body is to defile it and deprive it of its spiritual significance.[6] Others see the body as malleable and available for modification.[7] From this perspective, the body is a "ready made canvas" upon which practitioners illustrate their message.[8]

Through the mass distribution of images in print and film, during the late nineteenth and early twentieth centuries, the body in its given or modified state[9] had unprecedented potential as a medium for revivalist messages. Advertising executive Fred R. Barnard's now famous observation, "One picture is worth a thousand words,"[10] speaks to the communicative power of images, and it is no coincidence that the phrase was coined in the 1920s. Between 1890 and 1930, Americans were bombarded as never before with images.[11] These portraits created a heightened celebrity culture[12] and communicated much about what it meant to be an ideal American. Through advancements in print technology, photography, and eventually film, advertisers, publishers, and filmmakers provided the American public with countless portraits of American life.[13] Through fan magazines and newspaper articles, filmmakers and radio promoters gave celebrities unprecedented ways to be seen embodying these ideals. As public figures, ministers were not immune to the power of mass media. Indeed, celebrity ministers used their personal appearance to signal the propriety and authority of their office, as well as their own ministerial message.

McPherson once summed up her views on women in the ministry by arguing that "sex has nothing to do with the pulpit and pants don't make preachers."[14] The sentiment was witty, but inaccurate. Traditionally, pants *did* make preachers. American Protestant ministers represented the authority of their male office by their clothing.[15] In the early Victorian era, professionals wore multicolored suits and accessories. The minister's black (or dark colored) suit, free from ornamentation, expensive fabric, and flamboyant color, as well as the conservatively groomed body in it, was intended both to distance Protestant ministers from their Roman Catholic counterparts and to signal the sobriety, unostentatiousness, and propriety of the office.[16] Although the cut and location of buttons changed over time, American Protestant pastors typically wore black suits with white shirts (with the possible addition of pulpit robes or a white clerical collar in high church settings such as Episcopalian or Lutheran congregations).[17]

By the mid-nineteenth century, the meaning of the black, conservatively cut suit had changed. Magazines and advertisements published portraits of ideal men as rugged outdoorsmen or as white business professionals working in middleclass fields such as medicine, the law, and engineering.[18] In these portraits, professional men of all types eschewed the colorful ensembles of the Victorian era and wore dark-colored, simply designed suits.[19] Ministers were no longer distinguished from their professional counterparts because the black suit signaled the expert, up-to-date authority associated with other modern professions.[20]

Turn-of-the-century male ministers appeared aware of the increasing power of image in American public life and keen to use their personal appearance to lend propriety, respectability, and professionalism to the office. "The pastor's appearance," according to *The Pastor's Guide*, "both as to his person and dress, should be clean and always command respect and esteem."[21] "People expect their pastor to look his part, to dress in keeping with his high calling,"[22] argued one layman, while another cautioned ministers to "magnify your office," with appropriate personal appearance.[23] Male ministers advised one another to provide congregants with a representation of middleclass manliness by being clean (brush their coats, shine their shoes, button their buttons), avoiding "eccentric" dress, keeping their hair neatly (but not too meticulously) arranged, and wearing black, white, or gray.[24]

Many revivalist celebrity ministers augmented the black suit to communicate their version of the muscular Christian message. For example, A. B. Simpson presented hale, dark-suited images of himself in rural settings as evidence of that message. His biographers claimed that his appearance had a number of muscular traits: it was of "sturdy" and "rugged" stock.[25] "One could not fail to see in him," wrote one admirer, "the marks of highest manhood."[26] 1920s revivalist and former professional athlete Billy Sunday traveled with several suits and accessories that complemented his muscular gospel. He tailored his suits to display his physique and allow him maximum movement onstage.[27] Sunday knew that his image was a draw for revivalist audiences, and he regularly took photos in various athletic poses, and helpfully supplied newspapers with his manly image. Similarly, fundamentalist revivalist J. Frank Norris preached frequently about the need to oppose the feminizing forces of modernism through fisticuffs, if necessary.[28] Norris, a Texan, accessorized his suits by wearing cowboy hats and fedoras (a visual signal of cinematic "tough guys"),[29] and carrying a gun to drive the point home.

Revivalist ministers widely distributed images of their manly ministries. Simpson and Sunday had biographers who published their images as well as their life stories. Norris and Sunday's photos often appeared in newspapers. Posters advertising their revivalist meetings often carried images of the ministers in their manly attire.

For female ministers, no traditional attire signaled womanly propriety as well as professional ministerial authority. While women ministers lacked guidance for how to signal their female ministerial identities, for women in general, there were countless portraits of ideal womanhood. *Scribners, Harpers, Good Housekeeping,* and *Life Magazine* published photographs and illustrations of the "American Woman."[30] In print and on film, she was white, middleclass, educated, and wore the latest in hairstyle, cosmetic, and dress fashions. She was pictured going to college and engaging in a variety of domestic activities such as cooking for her husband, teaching their children, or shopping.[31] Mainstream media images did not include women clothed or working as doctors, engineers, ministers, or any other profession. Unlike male professionals who signaled their professional status by wearing dark-colored suits, there was no generally accepted uniform for female professionals.

A few women of previous generations had attempted to create professional images by imitating men. They developed a version of the suit for professional women, but, while a feminine version of a suit emerged as acceptable womanly wear (for going on walks, going shopping, attending church, etc.),[32] their efforts at portraying themselves as respectable members of the business class were largely unsuccessful.[33] Until the mid-twentieth century, women who wore menswear risked their reputation by having their sexuality being called into question or by being dismissed as an oddity rather than accepted as a professional.[34]

Thus, Woodworth-Etter and McPherson had to find a way of "showing forth the mighty power of God"[35] as pastors without the benefit of a male body or a suit. Rather than try to appropriate professional menswear, both presented images that corresponded to their narrative identities.

THE "PLAINLY ATTIRED"[36] PASTOR

Woodworth-Etter represented her warring mother identity with "plainly attired,"[37] old-fashioned, matronly personal appearance. During the 1890s, women discarded the supposedly "unhygienic" Victorian corsets, hoop skirts, and handmade, elaborate clothing, for simpler, mass-produced fashions.[38] Upper-class women often traded the hoop skirts of the Victorian era for bustles and puffed sleeves.[39] They wore their hair long and piled high upon their heads, often augmented with an elaborately decorated hat. Fashionable women demonstrated femininity and sex appeal with corsets, which cinched in their waists and enhanced their busts. Images of graceful, small-waisted, big-busted, college-educated white women like the famed Gibson Girl populated American advertising space.[40]

Maria Woodworth-Etter's typical dress was a simplified, de-sexualized version of turn-of-the-century styles. In contrast with the black suit of the professional male, Woodworth-Etter usually wore crisp, simply cut white dresses. Her unofficial uniform was a plain white dress and a modest, full-length (usually black) coat. While her more fashionable counterparts wore corsets to display their womanly form, her loose-fitting dresses deemphasized her waist and bust; the sleeves were minimally puffed. Her most flamboyant accessories were a chaste black bonnet and thin white gloves. Woodworth-Etter wore this plain ensemble in and out of fashion and in and out of the pulpit.

During her decades long career, her clothing rarely changed (Figure 3.1). Even though magazine and film images showed hemlines becoming shorter as the nineteenth century turned to the twentieth, she insisted on wearing floor-length dresses.[41] She was loath to accessorize and wore little to none of the lace, ruffles, brooches, "frills and flounces," rings, and other jewelry popular during the era.[42] Woodworth-Etter was equally conservative about her hair. She wore it tightly wound at the top of her head with no elaborate hats, or any other decorative accessories.

Although committed to modesty and averse to flamboyant clothing, Woodworth-Etter was not reluctant to display her image publicly. On the contrary, in every autobiography (some of which were self-published), she provided followers with self-portraits that conveyed aspects of her profession and message. Her conservative, matronly wardrobe signaled white, middleclass respectability in a way that her background and her church services did not. Even though they mocked her "unrefined" language[43] and compared her ecstatic preaching to an exotic "voodoo priestess,"[44] members of the press were repeatedly surprised by her bourgeois look. One such reporter observed that Woodworth-Etter "dressed in no unusual fashion," with "hair worn in a high knot above her head, gray eyes, fairly good-looking. She does not," wrote the reporter, "look like a fanatic."[45]

Modest clothing had deep doctrinal meaning in Woodworth-Etter's teachings. Woodworth-Etter, like other revivalist women, believed that modest clothing had a sacramental function: outward appearance displayed inward godliness and power.[46] Disturbed by what they thought of as sinful modern fashions around them, many revivalists, particularly those of the holiness or Pentecostal persuasion, embraced strict codes of modesty. "The society women," wrote one exasperated holiness writer of early-twentieth-century fashions, "nearly all dress like the women of the Red Light.... Of course, women who are virtuous will be looked at, and spoken to, by sporting men, as if she was a fallen woman, if she dresses like the scarlet woman."[47] These codes of modesty were meant to allow women to display their bodies in their most natural, "God-given,"[48] state and thereby sanctify practitioners around them.[49] "When women get saved and a clean heart," wrote

Figure 3.1 (a) Maria Woodworth-Etter, circa 1916. Credit: Flower Pentecostal Heritage Center. (b) Woodworth-Etter, circa 1922. Credit: Flower Pentecostal Heritage Center.

one holiness writer, "it takes the sporty dress, lodge pins, frills and flounces out of their wardrobe. Amen."[50] One early holiness pastor and historian wrote that in obedience to I Timothy 2:9's advice to women, "People who got this great grace of sanctification pulled off their gaudy dress, and stripped off their jewelry."[51] Plain dress thus showed holiness people that Woodworth-Etter was unencumbered by earthly concerns for fashion or beauty and that her heart and mind were set toward heaven.[52] This freedom from the world imbued her ministry with spiritual power only available through modest, clean living.[53]

Woodworth-Etter's commitment to plain clothing made its way into her teachings wherein she equated saved people with those who dressed appropriately. Even the ability to speak with God was interwoven with proper clothing. "To pray," wrote one of Woodworth-Etter's favorite commentators on I Timothy 2:9, "is supposed to be in verse 9 and to be connected with 'in modest apparel'."[54] She warned against elaborate accessories or hairstyles and condemned "bangs and frizzes" as "the devil's implements of war."[55] Extravagant clothing was not only a waste of money; it was also a tool of Satan to distract believers from what was truly important. "People washed their clothing," she wrote of the biblical meaning of modest, clean clothing, "This [appropriate, unblemished apparel] was the emblem of purity. This was the sign of the inward cleansing. The people were in a condition to meet God—clean bodies, clean garments. God help us to get the cleansing power."[56] She discouraged her congregants from following the latest fashions and instead encouraged them to follow Jesus and be "clothed with immortality," and "clothed with the glory of heaven," as Paul instructed the Corinthian church in I Corinthians 15:53, and II Corinthians 5:2.[57] She described Jesus and his followers as "clothed in white linen," like those in Revelation 19:8 and 14, and the coming Christ as a man "clothed in power," which was a possible allusion to Jesus' post-resurrection instructions to the church in Luke 24:49.[58]

Clean clothing signaled class distinction as well as spiritual power. Cleanliness was associated with wholesome middleclass values in the late nineteenth and early twentieth centuries, whereas filth was a signal of lower-class "social pathology, filth, and needless disease."[59] Stories of poorly dressed sinners coming to the altar, finding Jesus, and going away well and modestly clothed were typical narratives of Woodworth-Etter meetings. One convert wrote that before she attended a meeting, she dressed her baby in a "'greased cloth', but afterward, I made him clothes like other children."[60] When speaking of the success of one revival meeting, Woodworth-Etter wrote with satisfaction, "The women and children began to wear cleaner clothes, and came with their bonnets on, and left their dirty aprons at home."[61] These stories indicated that Woodworth-Etter's meetings had power to reform attendees. They may have entered in as members of the lower classes, but they left as respectable, clean, middleclass people.

Holy apparel also served as a buffer between women and the sexual desires of men—a buffer lowered significantly by the introduction into mainstream fashion of skirts that revealed female ankles. Whereas American revivalists were free to admire the "well developed chest," and "broad shoulders,"[62] of her male counterparts, Woodworth-Etter refrained from clothing and undergarments like the corset that gave her audience an opportunity to evaluate the attractiveness of her physique.

Although she adopted a matronly, female look, Woodworth-Etter did not portray herself in photographs as a motherly figure. For example, she did not pose surrounded by children or cooking in a kitchen. Rather, she chose poses that represented her critical mission to fight on behalf of her spiritual children. She positioned herself with one arm pointed up toward heaven and the other holding a Bible. Other times, she posed with one hand pointing upward and another pointing down. Posing with the Bible reminded the viewer of her authority to wield it. Her hand positions illustrated her message about the battle between heaven and hell.

Thus, Woodworth-Etter's personal appearance benefited her ministry in several ways. It served as a visual cue of her identity as a biblical Mother in Israel and her teachings on holiness and modesty. It also gave her and her ministry a visual sense of middleclass respectability. Her posed pictures were portraits of Woodworth-Etter's status as a militant leader engaging in the masculine act of spiritual warfare.

THE "WHITE CLAD LOS ANGELES SOUL SAVER"[63]

Like Woodworth-Etter, McPherson eschewed male professional wear and favored white dresses to black suits. Whereas Woodworth-Etter's holiness and early Pentecostal leanings led her to shun beautification, Aimee Semple McPherson treated her body as a pliable instrument for communicating her romantic bride and bridegroom message. Her personal appearance was constantly evolving to create an image that underscored her status as the leading lady of her flock and as their representative bride of Christ. In her early days as an itinerant preacher, her look was similar to the womanly professional attire that nurses wore (Figure 3.2). "She couldn't afford an expensive dress,"

Figure 3.2 Aimee Semple McPherson in uniform, circa 1924. Credit: Foursquare Archives.

recalled McPherson's daughter Roberta Salter, so she wore a blue and white maid's uniform and accessorized it, "with a cape put on like the Red Cross nurses had."[64]

Her ensemble was simple, but she knew how to make the most of it. "When she rolled into town," said Salter, "she had to have a clean uniform for the next church service and she stopped by the roadside, and washed it in the stream, hung it out to dry...and then when it was dry she ironed it using for the ironing board the backseat of the car. And when she arrived in town, she was beautiful and dazzling. You would have thought she had ten thousand maids at home."[65]

McPherson's uniform did much to promote her middleclass respectability. It was clean and modest, and it gave her a visual association with nursing, a quasi-public acceptable profession for women. The association with nursing gave McPherson a maternal-like role as nurturer who was subordinate[66] to the "Great Physician," Jesus. It also had the potential to heighten her sex appeal in the years following World War I. Nurses were well-known objects of soldier desire in the Great War,[67] and her visual association with that guild allowed

McPherson to capitalize on that kind of appeal. Finally, the uniform harkened back to her respectable Salvation Army roots and she made it the official garb for all female ministers in the Foursquare church.

The simple uniform, however, was out of step with the glamorous celebrity culture emerging from 1920s Hollywood. Therefore, as she gained fame, McPherson departed from earlier women preachers who downplayed their femininity by hiding their curves and refusing to use beauty-enhancing products. Instead, like Billy Sunday, she chose figure-flattering ensembles. Whereas Sunday emphasized his athletic prowess and manly virility, McPherson chose fashionable 1920s clothing that enhanced her feminine sex appeal.

In the 1920s, women's fashions differed from the early-twentieth-century corseted profile.[68] A slimmer, less voluptuous figure replaced the ideal curvaceous woman. Women illustrated their femininity and sexuality by displaying their shapely ankles and calves rather than their small waists and big busts. Hemlines and sleeves also became shorter, as did hair.[69]

Images of women in advertising and film also shifted from the portraits of womanliness popular at the turn of the century. In addition to pictures of women caring for their children in their homes, women were depicted enjoying the world outside.[70] Young women were often shown playing sports, going to college, or grocery shopping. Companionate wives (and future companionate wives) were shown holding hands, kissing, dancing, or even drinking with their husbands (and future husbands).[71]

There was much handwringing among Protestants at the arrival of the "tall, thin, cartoonish young woman preoccupied with dancing, drinking, and necking," that dominated magazine print.[72] Liberals like Harry Fosdick and conservatives like Billy Sunday both criticized portraits of 1920s women enjoying activities that those with supposedly loose sexual morals appreciated.[73] Revivalists, particularly those of the holiness and Pentecostal variety, were also troubled by 1920s images of femininity.[74]

McPherson, however, was unafraid.[75] By all accounts, she embraced the changing fashions. Indeed, she viewed the young generation coming of age in the Roaring Twenties as a field ripe unto harvest. "On the question of flappers," reported the *Boston Daily Globe*, "Mrs. McPherson was content to shrug her shoulders and say, 'I see beyond the cosmetics and the clothes'."[76]

In fact, McPherson embraced many of the same cosmetics and clothes feared by her revivalist contemporaries, and her openness to modifying her personal appearance pushed the boundaries too far for revivalists who believed that spiritual purity was signaled through an unaltered physique. Her usual 1920s and early 1930s pulpit clothing consisted of form-fitting (sometimes sequined) white gowns with long, wide sleeves. "She clings to white," observed one sarcastic observer, "and the fabric clings to her."[77] McPherson's image as a bride waiting for her bridegroom was clearly understood by reporters. When she took the platform, she did so, "Wearing the garb and manner of a bride on her honeymoon."[78]

McPherson's white gowns were not the only signature aspect of her look. She was not afraid to experiment with the latest beauty products. She employed her own "beauty specialists," including a hairdresser and makeup artist to make sure she looked "like her old self," from the pulpit.[79] In addition, flowers were a staple of her apparel. She was often photographed wearing a corsage or carrying a large bouquet. She accessorized with a sequined stole that was designed to rest over her breasts, and she wore glittering symbols such as a cross, a bible superimposed over a shield, or a Foursquare emblem across her chest. The result was a clerically inspired evening gown that fit in nicely with the glitz and glamor of early Hollywood culture (Figure 3.3).

Figure 3.3 McPherson gowned, circa 1933. Credit: Foursquare Archives.

Arguably the most symbolic aspect of McPherson's person to change over time was her hair. Early-twentieth-century revivalists were particularly interested in the relationship among hair, godliness, and worldliness.[80] Long, undyed hair symbolized the "natural" femininity of sound revivalist teaching, while bobbed hair was worn only by those "stupefied by some Satanic opiate" of the "fashions of the day."[81] When McPherson began her career, she had "high-piled, unshorn dark hair."[82] Eventually, she began to experiment with her hair color and it attracted national attention. Newspapers reported that she wore it red,[83] strawberry blonde, and platinum.[84]

Changing her hair color was newsworthy, but as long as McPherson maintained her long locks, she remained relatively uncontroversial. By wearing long hair, she communicated to her flock that she had not completely given herself over to "worldly" cultural norms (Figure 3.4). Given her penchant for sartorial trends, it was inevitable that McPherson would cut her hair into a fashionable marcelled bob (Figure 3.5). In 1927, she did just that.[85] The cut was front-page news, and it was cited as the primary cause in a church split.[86] "Mrs. McPherson hurt her followers beyond endurance," said choir leader and church defector Gladwyn Nichols, "when she had her hair bobbed recently."[87]

Figure 3.4 McPherson's long tresses in 1923.

Figure 3.5   McPherson's sleek bob, circa 1933. Credit: Foursquare Archives.

Had McPherson's teachings about personal appearance, worldliness, and the power of the Holy Spirit been similar to Woodworth-Etter's, Nichols' splinter church would have probably been large and their absence would have damaged her church. Because she had been gradually embracing 1920s fashions, however, many of her followers were willing to stay with her after the bob scandal. The fact that her congregation did not crumble shows a marked shift in Pentecostal revivalist thinking about the relationship between the believer and the world. Unlike first-generation Pentecostal revivalists who usually adopted strict modesty codes, McPherson and her growing circle of colleagues and followers were much more comfortable with fashion. Instead of seeing it as a mark of spiritual deficiency, they used fashion as a tool in service to their revivalist messages.

McPherson was not the only one who was changing her theological tune about the relationship between modest attire and spirituality. Other Pentecostals were beginning to become weary of the strict boundaries around personal appearance that holiness preachers erected. "We criticize each other's dress and clothes as if the kingdom of God depended upon these things," complained Pentecostal preacher Charles Price.[88] Price went on to argue that modesty was secondary to other theological truths rather than an essential reflection of God-honoring living. "We get into the habit of paying more attention to the way some woman does her hair than we do to the fact that thousands are dying around us on every hand and side without God and without salvation. Mark you, I believe in modesty in appearance, yet there are some people who seem to appoint themselves as guardians of other people's rights and liberties to such an extent that dissention is stirred up and the work of the Lord is impeded and marred."[89] Thus, with her short hair and fashionable gowns, McPherson's power and congregation continued to grow.

At the height of her fame and influence in the 1920s, McPherson combined the Hollywood glamor of the emerging film industry with popular, bridal images of womanliness. She took on a number of leading lady roles from the pulpit, and she had costumes that corresponded to each. In some sermon illustrations, she played the part of biblical brides such as Ruth and Rebecca (Figure 3.6).[90] For these parts, she dressed in "authentic Arab garb" that she had

Figure 3.6   McPherson as Rebecca. Credit: Foursquare Archives.

purchased on a trip to the Holy Land.[91] Taking full advantage of her Hollywood surroundings, McPherson frequently called upon film industry costumers to create elaborate costumes with which to illustrate her sermons.[92] Playing the role of a Southern belle in one sermon, she wore a professionally designed antebellum dress (Figure 3.7). On another Sunday, McPherson told a Dutch folktale about a leaky dike. She preached the entire sermon dressed in a Dutch girl costume. When she preached a sermon about staying away from the dangers of sin, she had a tailor-made police officer uniform made to reinforce her message, "Stop! You're going the wrong way!" Her famous sermon about her small town Canadian roots came complete with a farm girl costume.

In many cases, McPherson's costumes bore strong resemblance to popular 1920s films. For example, the farm girl costume was similar to Mary Pickford's clothing in *Rebecca of Sunnybrook Farm* (1918).[93] Her biblical costumes were similar to those worn in biblical epics like *Ben-Hur: A Tale of Christ* (1925).[94] Thus, when her

Figure 3.7 McPherson as a Southern Belle in the illustrated sermon, "Slavery days," circa 1926. Credit: Foursquare Archives.

followers looked at their pastor, they saw images taken directly off Hollywood studio lots,[95] and when McPherson preached, she was often compared to romantic film heroines like silent movie star Mary Pickford.[96]

McPherson's image was ubiquitous in the 1920s. Pictures depicting a perfectly coiffed pastor wearing the latest fashions appeared in *Los Angeles Times* and other newspapers as well as her church building's façade. She graced the cover of magazines, postcards, and her own denominational literature and autobiographies. She sat for numerous publicity photographs and even advertised her meetings in film shorts.

McPherson showed her skill at manipulating her personal appearance during her 1926 trial. On Tuesday, May 18 of that year, McPherson disappeared while on a trip to Ocean Park Beach. Her followers believed that she had drowned. McPherson's mother Minnie Kennedy and church leaders held beachside vigils for several days, and when efforts to recover her body failed, they planned an elaborate funeral.[97] Meanwhile, the Los Angeles Police Department poured hours into a search for her body.

The search became something of a national pastime, and McPherson sightings ran rampant. Some speculated that she had run off to Canada, while others thought that she had left for China.[98] *Time Magazine* satirized the obsession with finding the beautiful pastor: "Her description has been so minutely detailed that it is certain she prepared to go in swimming. Her bathing suit had a white edging around the armholes. It was a one-piece suit with the pretense of a short skirt. The trunks came down almost to her knees. Her legs that day were vague."[99]

On June 23, McPherson came back to the public in dramatic fashion. Emerging from the Arizona desert, she claimed to have been kidnapped by a small ransom-seeking gang.[100] Her congregation rejoiced and showered her with affection and flowers,[101] but from the moment of her reappearance, those outside of her flock were suspicious that McPherson was not telling the truth.

Police searched for the shack in Mexico from where McPherson supposedly escaped. They found no evidence of its existence. Many speculated that she had a personal relationship with her former radio engineer Roy Ormiston,[102] and Los Angeles buzzed with rumors that she had left her pulpit to share a romantic "love nest"[103] at Carmel-by-the-Sea, California. Several Carmel-by-the-Sea residents claimed that they had seen a man with an attractive redhead matching McPherson's description in a romantic cottage.[104]

The rumors of McPherson's alleged sexual indiscretion eventually brought her into conflict with the law. Los Angeles District Attorney Asa Keyes believed that she had run off with Ormiston. He charged McPherson with criminal conspiracy and perjury for allegedly hiding her ten-day affair with Ormiston and sending Los Angeles police on an expensive wild goose chase.[105]

Keyes portrayed McPherson as a highly sexed vixen who seduced a man and ran off to a "love nest," in Carmel-by-the-Sea.[106] McPherson visually countered this depiction in several ways. First, on her first day in court, she eschewed her "picturesque temple garb," and wore instead to court a sober "simple black satin coat suit with soft white shirtwaist and a plain black mushroom straw, high crowned and banded in grosgrain ribbon."[107] For the duration of the trial, she usually wore an equally somber ensemble or the simple, modest Foursquare uniform.

Second, she gave the press images of piety that reminded viewers of her divine relationship. During her trial, she often posed in prayer, with her eyes lifted up toward heaven.[108] She had moments of frustration and "hysteria" outside the courtroom, but during her hearing, McPherson looked angelic and serene.[109] On the first day of her testimony, she augmented her heavenly look by arriving flanked by several young women dressed in white and carrying hymnals.[110] The women, fiercely devoted to McPherson, were pictures of purity and innocence even as their leader faced accusations of fornication.

McPherson also published a series of pictures that depicted her supposed kidnapping. These portraits showcased a modestly dressed figure in poses that mirrored those struck by silent movie heroines. Like Christine Daaé, who struggled to break free from the Phantom of the Opera[111] or Nanette Roland who was endangered by the obsessive love of the villainous Buck McDougal,[112] McPherson's photographs told a story of an innocent damsel in distress who narrowly escaped becoming a victim of corrupt mercenaries.[113] She published poses of herself being kidnapped, tied up, cowering in fear, and then ultimately sneaking away, and then helpfully provided them to her followers and to the national media.

Thus, while McPherson did not subscribe to Woodworth-Etter's notion that plain clothing was the key to spiritual power, she did understand its usefulness and actively modified it to suit her needs. Her openness to bodily modification for the purpose of communicating her message was such that she was rumored to have undergone plastic surgery to preserve her youthful, bridal look. "You see," her estranged mother and former church administrator "Ma" Kennedy told reporters about rumors of McPherson's face-lift in 1930, "Sister believes that everyone is an instrument of the Lord that may be used if His purposes are to be accomplished. According to her philosophy, a plastic surgeon, by making her more beautiful, would be helping along the Lord's work with a modern miracle of science."[114] McPherson never publicly admitted undergoing such a procedure, but she was undoubtedly committed to maintaining her image as a "well-gowned, flashing-eyed and well-preserved" leading lady.[115]

CONCLUSION

Woodworth-Etter and McPherson were able to present ministerial images for their congregations without wearing masculine professional attire by providing followers with images that corresponded to their biblical identities as well as popular images of womanliness. For holiness woman Woodworth-Etter, who believed that attempts to change the body were "worldly," that meant presenting herself as a plainly dressed, matronly figure. For McPherson, to whom the body was a blank slate upon which she communicated her revivalist message, she portrayed herself as an increasingly feminine Hollywood bride awaiting her eschatological bridegroom.

4

"A Glorious Symbol": Building a Female Pentecostal Worship Space

Personal appearance was not the only way of representing 1890s–1920s ministry. The space in which ministry occurred was equally important. Therefore, this chapter discusses revivalist ministers and their meeting places. Many aspects of revivalist sacred space communicated the masculinity and power of celebrity ministers, and Woodworth-Etter and McPherson constructed Pentecostal revival worship spaces to create spaces that displayed their power as ministers and their status as womanly women.

1890s–1920s revivalists were keenly aware of the "capacity of architecture to both embody and broadcast ideas and meanings."[1] Since the days of the early republic, many American Protestant churches had been designed to imitate classically inspired British church architecture and to promote the traditional modes of Protestantism the architecture facilitated.[2] Beginning in the mid-nineteenth century (1840s–1880s), however, revivalists created worship spaces that borrowed as much from theatrical and domestic architecture as they did from traditional church design.[3] One result from this shift was that the church building itself became closely associated with the specific looks, personality, and talents of the (presumably male) presiding minister. Revivalist celebrity ministers who had the financial and political resources to build their own churches took an active role in designing their meeting places.

For the most part, revivalist worship spaces bolstered the masculinity of the minister. One aspect of design that ensured this maleness was that many church layouts were modeled after turn-of-the-century homes[4] with rooms that corresponded to domestic spaces. For example, instead of a child's room, they had a Sunday School room.[5] Where homes had a dining room, churches featured a fellowship hall and often had a kitchen.[6] Turning the church into a home did not imply that women, as keepers of the home, were welcome to exercise authority. By domesticating the worship space, revivalists actually reinforced the masculine gender of the minister. While women were welcome to serve in traditionally wife/mother private spaces such as the kitchen, the children's room, or the dining area, the auditorium, the public space wherein nonfamily members assembled, like any other public space, belonged to the men.

The layout of revivalist worship space was not the only design component that conveyed the masculinity of the minister. Male revivalists communicated masculinity by building "very vigorous and masculine"[7] worship spaces that conformed to late-nineteenth- and early-twentieth-century notions of architectural manliness.[8] For example, A. B. Simpson's six-story church exterior was praised for being "one of the most imposing churches west of New York City,"[9] and admired for its masculine quality of being, "the most aggressive center of evangelism in New York City."[10]

Another indication of 1890s–1920s decorative manliness was "manly simplicity."[11] Ornate décor was described as "weak or effeminate,"[12] but the "finer and franker the lines, the more reserved and powerful the parts," wrote early-twentieth-century architect and critic Ralph Cram.[13] Revivalist ministers' worship spaces were often sparsely decorated, angular structures that resembled armories more than cathedrals.[14] As the leaders of "spiritual armories,"[15] pastors sheltered those inside from the turbulent modern times and fortified the worship space from the attacks of modernism.

In addition to imbuing worship spaces with signals of late-nineteenth- and early-twentieth-century manliness, revivalists sought to convey a sense of supernatural vigor. In order to signal spiritual power, many revivalists gave their worship spaces a moniker associated with extraordinary biblical dynamism. They named their churches tabernacles, otherwise known as the "architectural icon of revival."[16] A staple of the eighteenth- and nineteenth-century revivalist preaching circuit, tabernacles began primarily as large tents named for their resemblance to biblical tents (mentioned in passages such as Exodus 25:8–9, Exodus 33:7–10, and 2 Samuel 2:6–7) wherein the presence of God was supposed to dwell.[17] Like their biblical counterparts, early revivalist tabernacles were portable, temporary structures that housed itinerant ministers in primarily rural settings.

Revivalist tabernacles showcased their ministers in large part because the preacher was often the only design piece. Tabernacles were simply constructed with a small, usually raised platform in the center. This platform, sometimes accompanied by a music stand and a piano, served as a pulpit.[18] Chairs or benches were arranged around or facing the minister. The audience's attention was thus immediately drawn to the platform and the body performing on it.

In keeping with their biblical models, revivalist tabernacles had altars,[19] although they did not serve as a location for the sacrifice of animals, grain, or incense.[20] They were also distinct from mainline and high church altars that held relics or were the tables from which Eucharist was served.[21] Revivalist altars were located just in front of the pulpit and were places where participants stood to accept the sacrifice of Jesus or receive healing from him.[22] In some cases altars included a small table, or were accompanied by a bench or two, but they were often no more than a marked-off space just below the pulpit.[23]

The altar was the place where a revivalist minister proved the power of his or her message by the number of respondents he or she received. Therefore, revivalist altars occupied a public and prominent place in the tabernacle.[24] Next to the minister himself or herself, they were the most talked-about aspect of revival services. "First Church, New Philadelphia, Ohio has been visited with a glorious revival of religion," wrote one Methodist Episcopal publication of the Reverend J. V. Orin's efforts. "In every service held we saw many seekers of Christ at the altar of prayer."[25]

By the end of the nineteenth century, fewer tabernacles were actual tents,[26] and many were distinct from churches or cathedrals in name only. There were wooden, brick, and stone tabernacles. The name nevertheless retained a biblical sense of power. Adherents believed that within their walls they encountered the primordial presence and power of God. Tabernacle worshipers were transients passing through this word and not meant to stay in or partake of the sinfulness of the world around them. They were to be empowered for holy living through their worship. After experiencing the "secret of his [God's] tabernacle," wrote one observer, attendees emerged "armed with faith and buoyant with expectation."[27]

In addition to the promise of biblical power, for late-nineteenth- and early-twentieth-century revivalists, the word tabernacle also carried connotations of the "old time religion" of earlier tented meetings.[28] For the many revivalists fearful of modernism, the idea of worshipping in the manner that predated the modernist-fundamentalist contro-versy had potential to comfort. Revivalists utilized the old-fashioned sensibility that tabernacles brought to worship services and preserved the rural elements of nineteenth-century tabernacle décor.[29] For example, Billy Sunday insisted that host cities include his trademark sawdust flooring in even the most urban settings.[30] One result of this architectural feature was that it let attendees know that he retained the "old time" power of previous generations.

Although they claimed to retain the holiness and "old time religion" of early-nineteenth-century tented revivals, 1890s–1920s revivalist tabernacles were much larger than earlier tents and they utilized modern theater equipment and architecture. "The Revivalists have to deal with a vast crowd in a huge building," wrote one observer, "but they have adapted themselves with remarkable intuitive skill."[31] They maximized attendance using architectural techniques such as sloping floors and stadium seating.[32] They employed inventions such as microphones to carry the minister's voice and theatrical lighting to highlight the minister's performance. These innovations gave attendees the opportunity to admire the minister's "real manhood"[33] in his body, gestures, and vocal patterns, and revivalists adapted their preaching to reach as many hearers as possible. The result of these innovations was an emphasis upon the masculine aspects of revivalist ministers and an increasing focus upon the personality of male revivalist stars.

Female ministers like Woodworth-Etter and McPherson faced a challenge when it came to constructing their own buildings. Without male bodies and corresponding masculine personae, they did not have the advantage of appearing naturally authoritative in the worship space. Thus, they had to find alternative visual cues to signal authority. Just as they did with their use of scriptural narrative and their personal appearance, the women took much different approaches.

THE HOUSE OF GOD AND THE BATTLEFIELD

As a staunch revivalist, Maria Woodworth-Etter made the tabernacle her space of choice. She was convinced that her worship spaces helped her congregants experience the presence of God. "A celestial golden, light-like mist filled the Tabernacle," she wrote about the opening of her Maria Woodworth-Etter Tabernacle, "a glorious symbol of the outpouring of the latter rain, which melted the audience and created in them a desire to be more like Christ."[34]

Woodworth-Etter's "glorious symbol" was no doubt powerful, but it was hardly innovative. In terms of layout and architecture, very little differentiated Woodworth-Etter's itinerant meeting places from the tabernacles of male revivalist ministers. Her tented tabernacles, which held anywhere from several hundred to several thousand attendees, displayed all of the simplicity and roughness of her masculine counterparts' meeting places, even as they reflected her personal commitment to plainness.[35] Her traveling tabernacles had several rows of benches or wooden chairs arranged to face a small wooden platform designated as the altar. From there, Woodworth-Etter stood and preached.[36] When she was in the country, she set her tent up in campgrounds such as the popular Pentecostal destination Montwait. When she was in the city, she erected her tents in empty lots. The only decorations were posters announcing meeting times or short slogans for her meetings (Figure 4.1).

For over 40 years, Woodworth-Etter held meetings in temporary tabernacles. Eventually, she decided to build a permanent home in Indianapolis. "For years the hearts' cry of the saints over the country has been for us to establish a permanent, central place somewhere, where they can come at all times and receive the help they need for spirit, soul and body," she wrote. "California and other places wanted this established place, but the Lord has shown me to build at Indianapolis, which is very centrally located, where the saints can gather together from all parts in one spirit, and have unity and liberty."[37]

Figure 4.1 The Maria Woodworth-Etter Tabernacle, circa 1900. Credit: Flower Pentecostal Heritage Center.

Figure 4.2   The Maria Woodworth-Etter Tabernacle, circa 1920. Credit: Flower Pentecostal Heritage Center.

The permanent Maria Woodworth-Etter Tabernacle retained the modest and austere qualities that characterized her tented meeting places (Figure 4.2).[38] It was a long, rectangular wooden building with a few windows and a small platform at one end. Décor in the Tabernacle was sparse and mainly consisted of posters with popular Pentecostal exhortations to believe in Jesus, seek the Holy Spirit, or prepare for the Second Coming. The Tabernacle's plain appearance was designed to showcase Woodworth-Etter's preaching and healing performances. There was very little to look at besides the warring mother.

Woodworth-Etter did embrace the revivalist penchant for technological innovation, although any amenities she installed were for functionality rather than form. "It is, fully equipped," Woodworth-Etter wrote proudly of the Tabernacle's ability to facilitate revivalist practices, "with baptistery [sic], electric lights and A-1 seats."[39] Woodworth-Etter did allow herself one luxury item. She was given a "large beautiful chair from the Assembly [of God]"[40] that she displayed prominently on the Tabernacle stage.[41] In her later years, she preached and presided over her services from her custom-made perch.[42]

Like her male counterparts, Woodworth-Etter used her plain surroundings and simple pulpit to direct her audience's attention to the altar. In addition to providing the setting for her charismatic preaching, during crowded services, the minister placed three wooden chairs on the platform in order to draw attention to her faith cures.[43]

"Everybody was interested and wanted to see and hear, or get some blessing," she explained. "We placed chairs on the platform; those who wanted special prayer and laying on of hands sat in the chairs."[44]

Her meeting places resembled typical revivalist tabernacles, but they were also places wherein Woodworth-Etter accomplished two seemingly opposing tasks: her masculine duties as a warrior and her womanly responsibilities as a mother. In her sermonic rhetoric, she used two metaphors for her meeting places. Woodworth-Etter frequently referred her meeting places a "house of God," a "home," or a "house of prayer."[45] Whereas revivalist churches often designated the sanctuary as a public place for the head of the household to govern the church service, Woodworth-Etter viewed the entire "house of God" as a classroom wherein she educated her children. All of her building was reserved for the private activity of domestic nurture. She spoke about her tabernacles as places wherein the minister could "teach divine healing pray for the sick."[46] "God showed me one night that I was to build a tabernacle," she wrote, "so that people from all parts of the country could come in and spend some time in a good spiritual mission, and get established in God."[47] She spoke proudly about her children going from the "school of the prophets," as "flames of fire" for the Pentecostal cause.[48]

Describing the tabernacle as a domestic classroom feminized the worship space, but Woodworth-Etter also spoke of her meeting places as battlefields wherein she and her followers engaged in the very masculine act of war.[49] Other revivalists built spiritual armories to protect believers from the onslaught of modernism, but Woodworth-Etter took it a step further and spoke of her buildings as spaces intended to go on the offensive against the powers of Satan. "As the gospel trumpet blew loud and long, the tramp of feet, of the Lord's army could be heard from all parts of the country," she wrote of one Tabernacle meeting. "They had the Lord's armor and the blood stained banners of Jesus floating in the breeze. On they came, [to the tabernacle] marching to the music of Heaven, shooting victory over all the enemies of Christ. Soon they were on the field of battle, ready to fire into the enemy's ranks."[50] Her Tabernacle was a warzone and Woodworth-Etter described herself as one of the Lord's commanding officers. From the stage she executed her divinely inspired battle plan. "I am still pressing the battle to the gate,"[51] she wrote of her duties as a revivalist minister.

Woodworth-Etter's worship space thus held feminine aspects of her identity in tension with the masculine qualities she displayed. Her meeting places were homes where a mother could educate her children, and battlefields where a general could lead soldiers in the masculine act of war. The tabernacles' simplicity repeated Woodworth-Etter's personal modesty and testified to her holiness teachings. This setting served her well in the heartland city of Indianapolis.

THE TEMPLE OF THE LORD

Aimee Semple McPherson, who built her worship space a mere five years after her mentor's, needed something more than Woodworth-Etter's middle-American revivalist meeting place. Her ever-changing, hyper-feminine persona contrasted too sharply with plain, masculine tabernacle architecture, and her California setting required a worship space built on a much grander, more entertaining scale. McPherson's worship space, like her personal appearance, underwent many changes to fit her evolving bride of Christ identity.

During the first few years of her career, McPherson held services in traditional revivalist tents. Like Woodworth-Etter's, her tabernacles were sparsely decorated. They had wooden benches or chairs that faced a simple platform where McPherson stood to preach her sermons and where a pianist or a small band assembled to play music. The tabernacles' exterior had a large sign stating the minister's name and service times (Figure 4.3).

Figure 4.3 McPherson ministering in holiness fashion, circa 1918. Credit: Foursquare Archives.

Six years after she began preaching, McPherson decided to build a permanent center for her ministry. As a young woman newly separated from her husband, the American West was an appealing place to start over. She moved her ministry to Los Angeles and bought a piece of property in Echo Park, a neighborhood famous for its artistic, movie star residents.[52]

McPherson's original vision for her permanent meetinghouse was a tabernacle similar to that of Billy Sunday.[53] When she first arrived, she believed that what Los Angelinos needed was an old-fashioned camp meeting atmosphere, and she imagined attending to their spiritual needs from sawdust-covered floors. She spoke about her desire to "go forth to seek and bring back the old time power into the Tabernacle of the Most High," in Los Angeles.[54]

McPherson's increasingly glamorous persona and her larger-than-life church services hardly fit a camp meeting setting. The more time she spent in Los Angeles, the more she became convinced that her church needed more than sawdust to compete with the burgeoning entertainment industry.[55] "Certainly the term *tabernacle*," wrote McPherson, "was not adequate to describe the building as restructured to class A specifications."[56] She then decided that what Los Angeles needed was a temple, not a tabernacle. Accordingly, what was known formerly as the Echo Park Revival Tabernacle became Angelus Temple.[57]

The name changed the meaning of the worship space considerably. First, while tabernacles were associated with rural gatherings, a temple was urban. Thus, McPherson's meeting place veered away from the rural revivalist images upon which Woodworth-Etter and Billy Sunday capitalized. Second, a temple carried different biblical allusions than a tabernacle. Whereas a tabernacle was a portable place for itinerant people to worship God in temporary settings, a temple was a fixed place where supplicants could worship permanently. This shift had potential to change the relationship between the building (and those inside) and the outside world. A tabernacle was not meant to have a permanent geographical location, and those inside were not meant to stay and make relationship with those around them. Temples, on the other hand, were meant to be the crown jewel of a city and so to be in some sort of relationship with that city. Third, while tabernacles were simple structures by design, a temple was meant to impress visually. Just as the opulent Temple of Solomon was built in the city of Jerusalem, McPherson built her permanent, extravagant Angelus Temple, or the Temple as it came to be known, in her very own "Promised Land" of Los Angeles.[58]

The Temple's design reflected McPherson's identity as a romantic partner to her heavenly husband. 1910s–1920s architects drew sharp distinctions between the "feminine grace" of certain structures, "as compared with the more masculine vigor," of others.[59] "Feminine characteristics" of architecture were defined as "softness and round-ness of physical form, refinement of mentality, and grace and sweet-ness of spirit."[60] Whereas masculine buildings were known for their angularity and straight lines, feminine edifices were identified by their "graceful curve and enticing form, [which] seems to possess an alluring power."[61]

Style Moderne epitomized this alluring power. *Style Moderne*, or art deco as it was later called, was an architectural trend from France characterized by its proponents having feminine "grace," and "com-plete expressiveness" in contrast to the "muscular English" style that dominated American architecture.[62] The clean, rounded silhouettes and curved lines coupled with elaborate, intricate appliqués and art-work were derided by detractors as an "effeminate manifestation" of modern architecture.[63]

Angelus Temple, designed by McPherson with the well-known Mediterranean art deco architect A. F. Leicht, was built in the *Style Moderne*.[64] Whereas Woodworth-Etter's Tabernacle was boxy and plain, the Temple was all rounded edges and soft lines. It had none of the rough-hewn angularity of revivalist tabernacles like Billy Sunday's. It had gracefully arched windows, a domed ceiling, a rounded audito-rium, and a curved stage (Figure 4.4).

Figure 4.4 Exterior of Angelus Temple in a Los Angeles postcard, 1924. Credit: Foursquare Archives.

Figure 4.5 Angelus Temple interior, circa 1930. Credit: Foursquare Archives.

The interior of the Temple, from entrance to exit, reflected its founder's beauty and femininity (Figure 4.5). In detail that rivaled the account of Solomon's Temple recorded in Chronicles, McPherson published page after page about the pulchritude of Angelus Temple.[65] She told them about the Temple's blood-red carpet, velvet curtains, intricately carved wooden chairs, ornate stained glass windows, and the grand entrance.[66] "It is constructed," she told her followers, "of concrete and steel with multi-colored rays piercing great 30 foot stained glass windows which I designed during the journey from San Francisco to Sydney, Australia. Beautiful Angelus Temple! How I love it!"[67]

The Temple's interior design showcased two figures: Jesus the bridegroom and McPherson his bride. The ceiling was a large dome that McPherson commissioned to be "painted as the azure blue of the sky with white fleecy clouds to remind us that Jesus is coming in the clouds of glory so that I and others might look up at it while preaching and wonder, 'Jesus are you coming during this service? Will I be ready to meet you with souls if you come right now?'"[68]

The cloudy reminder was not the only visual reference to McPherson's leading man. "To me," she wrote, "even all this was not enough. I realized that some might wonder, 'How is Jesus coming?'"[69] Therefore, above the stage, McPherson commissioned a 40-foot wide mural of the triumphant, resurrected Jesus. McPherson's Jesus was every bit the leading man: he was handsome, had large, expressive eyes, and was posed with his arms outstretched to receive his bride. On either side of the mural were four stained-glass windows depicting in great detail the life of Jesus in eight stages: birth, baptism, walking upon the waters, talking with the woman caught in adultery, healing the masses, in Gethsemane, on the cross, and ascending to heaven.

The window depicting the Second Coming contained one anachronistic figure: McPherson. She waited alongside the apostles. This placement had strategic importance when it came to establishing McPherson's pastoral authority. It visually elevated her authority to biblical proportions. She was the only woman depicted in the scene, as well as the only extra-biblical figure. Her presence in the window signaled to her followers that she had the same authority and intimacy with Christ as had the ancient apostles.

McPherson's Temple took the revivalist appreciation for the theatrical to extremes. Its large proscenium arch (reportedly designed by McPherson with Charlie Chaplin's assistance) was built to host pageants, cantatas, and plays.[70] The stage had several entrances for theatrical presentations of the biblical stories and morality plays in which McPherson starred. A staircase on the side provided her with opportunities to make dramatic entrances. The Temple was outfitted with professional lighting (McPherson had her own spotlight), theater seats (for comfortable viewing), and an orchestra pit. In addition, it had electric sound that projected McPherson's voice to every corner of the sanctuary. Six ornately carved wooden chairs and a wooden pulpit were placed onstage. The largest and most intricately carved throne-like chair was saved for McPherson who sat under the mural of Jesus and preached about waiting for her bridegroom's return.

Angelus Temple strikingly resembled Interwar era movie theaters. It had similar architecture and décor to famous movie theaters such as Grauman's Million Dollar Theater (built in Los Angeles in 1918), El Capitan (built in Los Angeles in 1926), and the Fox Theatre (built in Pomona in 1931). The movie theater marquee advertised the latest films starring Mary Pickford, and McPherson's Temple exterior featured a large sculpture of the minister and a billboard advertising her latest sermon. Thus by its very appearance, the Temple prompted attendees to expect a theatrical story complete with a heroine.

In addition to signaling its builder's femininity and leading lady status, the Temple was a monument to McPherson's power. Acquiring the funding for such a massive project was a significant display of her leadership, and the manner in which she received funding spoke to the breadth and depth of her influence. Even with large donations of labor and materials from followers, the Temple's construction cost some 250,000 dollars, which would cost over three million dollars in 2014 currency.[71] In order to raise funds for its construction, she spread the word about her project in *The Bridal Call*, and money poured in.[72] Some of the money came 1,000 dollars at a time, some of it came in 25 dollar increments, and some gave as little as one cent. According to McPherson, it was constructed with an average contribution of one cent per supporter, making it a building built by hundreds of thousands of her followers.[73]

The Temple's theatrical façade and technological accessories were also proof of McPherson's media power. In an era that saw a dramatic increase in the reach and role of the media in American public life,[74] McPherson and her Temple were at the vanguard of every major mass media innovation. She advertised the Temple in her periodicals, and national newspapers covered its construction. Soon after it opened, McPherson purchased one of the first radio stations in Los Angeles and proudly displayed radio towers on either side of the Temple dome in post cards and in *Bridal Call Foursquare*[75] (Figure 4.4). The radio towers told followers that McPherson's ministry was powered by exciting new technology that had a nationwide reach. Later, she installed a lighted, revolving cross at the pinnacle of the Temple dome.[76] The cross became a local landmark and a symbol of McPherson's 24 hours a day, seven days per week ministry.

Another demonstration of McPherson's spiritual authority was the famous "500 Room." She designated this small auditorium located off the main sanctuary as a space dedicated to teach, practice, and receive prayer for healing.[77] The meetings there were intense. "From the day the doors opened," McPherson wrote with satisfaction, "a mighty spiritual revival surged into Angelus Temple with ever-increasing power and fervor."[78] The room, which hosted over 80,000 participants in 1924 alone,[79] was decorated with various medical paraphernalia discarded by those claiming to have been healed.[80] Thus, casts, crutches, eyeglasses, etc., surrounded attendees and testified to the power of McPherson's healing ministry.

The Temple's commissary demonstrated McPherson's significant civic presence as well as her spiritual authority. At the commissary, locals in need were served with groceries, clothing, and medical supplies.[81] McPherson was fond of boasting that the Temple surpassed municipal powers when it came to providing for local immigrant and poor Los Angelinos.[82] Her boast was fair. The Temple provided food and social services throughout the 1920s and was one of the city's primary relief organizations in the early years of the Great Depression.[83] "Aimee Semple McPherson-Hutton and her Angelus Temple are something more to Los Angeles than a source of surprising and entertaining news," reported one *Associated Press* writer. "In the last 11 months the 'commissary' of the temple provided free groceries to 40,110 persons, or 10,769 families."[84] The aid that the Temple provided bolstered McPherson's status as a power player in Los Angeles and gave her a national reputation as a community leader as well as a celebrity revivalist. Thus, in form and function, Angelus Temple represented McPherson the ministerial bride of Christ.

CONCLUSION

Like their male counterparts, Woodworth-Etter and McPherson used their revivalist space to convey their ministerial identities and their messages. Whereas male revivalists used the space to showcase their masculine form and manly sensibilities, Woodworth-Etter and McPherson reframed the space to suit their female ministries. Woodworth-Etter's tabernacles displayed all the power of a male ministry, but in her rhetoric she made it the home for a warring mother rather than a manly minister. Her tabernacles' austere architecture and lack of ornamentation were an ideal venue for spreading her message of modesty and holiness; the Maria B. Woodworth-Etter Tabernacle was unencumbered by the things of the world. It was a place for spiritual nomads passing through to the Promised Land.

McPherson's temple on the other hand showcased the minister's leading lady, bridal persona through its elaborate décor and its theatrical design. It also served as a visual reminder of her clout in Pentecostal revivalist circles, her influence in broadly evangelical revivalism, and her political power in the city of Los Angeles. In this way, it was a large-scale proclamation of the minister and her message.

5

"Thunder" and "Sweetness": Authority and Gender in Pentecostal Performance

This chapter examines the heart of Pentecostal pastoral authority—preaching performance. Woodworth-Etter and McPherson's worship spaces and personal appearances gave skeptics and followers alike impressive signals of womanliness and ministerial authority, but the bodily acts[1] performed within them in the form of revivalist preaching were what made them sacred vessels of the ministers' messages. These "spatial practices—the 'techniques of the body', the formalized 'gestures of approach', and the location and direction of embodied movement—all contribute[d] towards producing the distinctive quality of sacred space," in Woodworth-Etter and McPherson's revivalist meeting places.[2]

Pentecostal revivalist preaching performances were "fundamentally a way of doing things to trigger the perception that these practices are special," and as such were ritualized acts.[3] It was during the ritualized act of revivalist preaching, a performance during which the minister received and the congregation gave power,[4] that Woodworth-Etter's Tabernacle became "a glorious symbol"[5] of her powerful work and McPherson's Temple became host to "a mighty spiritual revival."[6]

Woodworth-Etter and McPherson were not alone in their penchant for revivalist preaching. 1890s–1920s celebrity revivalist ministers were not best known for their public image, their buildings, or their biblical interpretations. They were famous for their performances during revivalist services. Characterized as an effort to spontaneously "awaken, alarm, excite,"[7] by proponents, and as "vulgarities wrongfully labeled religious exhortations,"[8] by opponents, revivalist services were the most noteworthy and notorious aspect of any revivalist minister's career.

Revivalist meetings shared a standard structure. Usually, they included singing and prayer, a sermon, an offertory, and an altar call.[9] The order or elements of the service might change slightly (e.g., many services included extended testimony time or a healing service in addition to an altar call),[10] but for the most part, the components of the revivalist service were fixed.

Ministers did not necessarily perform all aspects of the service, but they were the masters of ceremonies, and the responsibility for creating and promoting the revival experience rested primarily upon their shoulders.[11] Instructional books such as *Revivals: How to Promote Them, One Hundred Revival Sermons and Outlines, The Revival and the Pastor, The Revival,* and *Revivalist Addresses* argued that pastors made or broke revival meetings.[12] "The Christian minister," observed one revivalist, "stands somehow at the center of this [revivalist] task."[13] "Nothing moves without the pastor," wrote another, "and nothing moves ahead of the pastor."[14]

Ministers promoted revival through their pulpit performances.[15] The primary goal of the revivalist sermon was to "arrest their [audience's] attention and tell them that Christ will save them *now*."[16] With emotional appeal and a sense of immediacy, revivalist preaching was expected to mediate an emotional, psychological, and physical experience to attendees.[17] The power of the minister's preaching and ability to facilitate revival were evidenced through the "scandalous practices"[18] exhibited by attendees. Weeping, laughing, shouting, kneeling, fainting, shaking, testifying, speaking in tongues, or speaking prophetically demonstrated the minister's authority and "divine blessing."[19]

Revivalist literature testifies to the role that a minister's performance played in setting apart the special time and space of revivalist services. A minister's preaching, according to revivalist Jonas Oramel Peck, brought the presence of God into the lives of the attendees. He wrote that the pastor would "marshal his forces to bring about times of refreshing from on high."[20] Revivalist William Bell Riley wrote that, "when he [the preacher] appeared in the pulpit on Sundays, the people were overawed with the sense of Christ being in the preacher. It was Christ's face they saw beaming on them in the face of their pastor, and his tones thrilled with the power of the voice which once spoke on earth as 'never man spake'."[21] Riley's ideal revivalist minister sanctified himself and his pulpit by setting both apart from everyday moments.

THE "THRONE OF ELOQUENCE"

As ritualized acts, revivalist preaching performances were the site for the creation and negotiation of power.[22] The preacher entertained, inspired, and invited the congregation to agree with the message that he or she preached. The congregation in turn gave power to the preacher through their attendance and participation in the sermon. Every "Amen!" shouted, every dollar given in the offertory, and every testimony spoken, was a way of giving power to the person in the pulpit.

For male revivalist ministers, each performance was an opportunity for the minister to signify[23] his masculinity and authority for his congregation, and for his congregation to recognize, submit, and further constitute that male power.[24] "The work of soul-saving," wrote Peck, author of *The Revival and the Pastor*, "will develop the most robust qualities of manhood [in the pastor]."[25] The primary method for accomplishing this was to present congregants with a "representative man"[26] who possessed a manly body and manly gestures and vocal patterns. "Effeminate habits of voice, of manner, of thought, of method or language," wrote the William Henry Young in his revivalist instructional manual, *How to Preach with Power*, "should therefore be eschewed."[27]

Revivalists showed their masculinity in their pulpit performance.[28] Billy Sunday gave the quintessential manly performance of the early twentieth century. The minister billed himself as the "most vigorous speaker on the platform today," and his body was an integral part of his manly preaching.[29] "Sunday is a physical sermon," wrote his official biographer; "no posture is too extreme for this restless gymnast."[30] Sunday developed several signature moves that showed off his physical form and his virile energy. The former baseball player was best known for sliding into an imaginary home plate in the pulpit or raising his hands over his congregation and making an overhand throwing motion as if his gospel were a baseball and his sermon was full of pitches.[31] He had several other folksy-named signature moves that included the "bucking broncho [sic]," "a balky mule," and "shelling the woods."[32] His raspy voice and intense, rapid, sing-song cadence was known to deliver "word bullets with his Gatling gun which grew almost white with heat at times."[33] His performances gave audiences a demonstration of ideal manhood: physically fit, tough, fearless, and aggressive.

Ministers displayed their masculine authority most clearly during the distinctively revivalist performance of the altar call. This "invitation," as it was also known, was the grand finale of the revivalist service. After the singing, offertory,[34] and preaching, ministers invited sinners and the sick to the altar to pray. Ministers offered followers the opportunity to come forward to pray for salvation or to rededicate their lives to the revivalist gospel, and those who specialized in "faith cures" like A. B. Simpson, William Seymour, Smith Wigglesworth, and John G. Lake added prayer for healing to their altar call.

Revivalist literature was replete with recommendations for the efficacious execution of the altar call. Revivalist William Edward Biederwolf recommended a series invitations for salvation and healing followed by a series of questions such as: "How many of you are ready now to say that if God should call you tonight you would like to be prepared and to know that God would be pleased with you when you meet Him, will you rise?"[35] The pastor "must simply proceed, with all the power God has given him," wrote revivalist Jonas Oramel Peck, "in a legitimate and sensible method, to warn, entreat, and arouse his hearers to accept the invitation of the Gospel and be saved."[36] The job of the revivalist minister, according to R. A. Torrey, was to perform the manly act of explaining the reasonableness of the revivalist gospel. He argued that the pastor was responsible for convincing the attendee of "how utterly irrational and absurd are all the excuses that men make for not coming to Christ," when prompted by the altar call.[37]

During the altar call, the preacher, the masculine initiator, invited men and women to come forward and receive the salvation or healing they offered on behalf of Christ. When women and men came forward to the altar, the act of response was characterized in virtually every revivalist publication as the feminine act of surrender or yielding.[38] "I will guarantee one thing," wrote R. A. Torrey, "that if you will accept Jesus Christ with all your heart and surrender your whole life to Him, and His control, and publicly confess Him before the world, God will send you His Holy Spirit into your heart, filling it with a joy you never knew before."[39] "'Yield yourselves to him'. He leads the yielded one," advised William Bell Riley.[40] Yielding and surrender were the ultimate goal of any invitation. "I do not much care whether you hold a protracted meeting or do not hold one; whether you invite people to the altar or to an inquiry-room, or do not invite them to either; whether you invite people to rise for prayers or sign a 'Decision Card;' whether you draw the line sharply, or do not draw it at all; whether you hold special services, or make services special," wrote revivalist J. H. MacDonald, "so long as in some way—and that your own way—you get men and women, boys and girls, to surrender to Jesus Christ."[41]

These acts of surrender were often accompanied by nonmasculine acts of weeping, kneeling, or embracing fellow worshipers.[42] "When the sermon was over," wrote one revivalist pastor, "the governor as he passed out took my hand, but could not speak. He was trembling with emotion and his eyes overflowed with tears."[43]

The masculine minister and yielding congregation placed the congregants (both male and female) in the role of the feminine. Given that muscular Christians were anxious to avoid labeling their male followers as feminine in any way, many revivalists tried to frame the invitation and subsequent response as a manly task. For example, A. B. Simpson countered the notion that faith cures were expressions of femininity. He spoke of divine healing not a passive, receptive, and feminine practice, but a "practical principle"[44] in keeping with the manly, "strenuous life."[45] "It is a manly, robust thing to follow Jesus Christ,"[46] preached revivalist Gipsy Smith to young men who believed that only women "grip God's altar;" "'Put on thy strength,'" he wrote quoting Isaiah 52:1, "Pull your full weight, man! Play the game! Pluck out everything that saps your manhood and palsies your spiritual achievement."[47] Billy Sunday's altar calls went out to women and men, but he paid special attention to the men in the audience. The altar calls were often accompanied by appeals to men in the audience to "show your manhood. In the name of your pure mother, in the name of your manhood, in the name of your wife, and in the name of the pure innocent children that climb up in your lap and put their arms around your neck, in the name of all that is good and noble, fight the curse."[48] One revivalist even tried to show that the emotionality that characterized revivalist meetings was not a womanly response, but an act of masculine bravery. "If you are afraid of emotions," he challenged his readers, "you'd better give the revival a wide berth."[49]

Celebrity revivalists were known for their ability to encourage followers to yield money as well as their person, and large public offerings were opportunities for followers to display their masculine prosperity. For example, late-nineteenth- and early-twentieth-century revivalist A. B. Simpson was famous (and infamous) for his ability to collect money and converts simultaneously. At the end of a typical sermon, Simpson said to his congregation, "I want to ask everyone here who is willing to devote his life to the work of spreading the Gospel in heathen lands to rise."[50] He paused and waited. Several women and men stood. "The first pledge," reported the *New York Times*, "was one of $50. Then there followed several of small amount, and then there came one for $400. The next two were small, but were followed by a pledge of $1,800. The next was for $100 and the next for $3,000. As this last was announced the congregation began to sing, 'Oh How I love Jesus.' Then there came pledges of $1,200, $1,000, $1,600, $2,000, and $4,000."[51]

In spite of efforts to make male respondents seem masculine, the minister-congregant revivalist performance was essentially a masculine-feminine exchange. While large offerings showed the prosperity of the follower, in the 1910s and 1920s, when financial prosperity was closely aligned with masculinity, Simpson and other revivalists' ability to evoke financial submission ultimately underscored the minister's manliness and the congregation's status their feminine respondent. While it may have taken courage to show emotions, stereotypical weeping and wailing of a revivalist meeting departed from rational late-nineteenth- and early-twentieth-century masculinity. The altar call, with its feminine response of yielding and surrender, made the role of the minister seem naturally male and the role of the congregant female. On one side was the aggressive masculine minister and on the other side, the receptive feminine audience.

A female stepping in to the role of altar caller disrupted this neat binary and threatened the sanctity of the masculine pulpit. Many believed that women in this role went against nature. The "Discontented Man's" argument that, "there is in most of us an inwardness of instinct against setting up a female in the prominence of the pulpit to lecture on their sins to a mixed congregation of men and women," gave voice to this popular opinion.[52] 1890s–1920s Protestants worried that female ministers would neuter the pulpit's power with their womanliness. "Everything," wrote revivalist William Henry Young, "that savors more of the woman than the man [in the pulpit] is a virtual abdication of that [pulpit's] 'Throne of eloquence'."[53]

In spite of the danger of abdicating the "throne of eloquence," female revivalist ministers were required, like any other revivalist, to demonstrate power in the pulpit. Woodworth-Etter and McPherson's preaching showed that demonstrating power without manliness was a complex task. On the surface, the women appeared to run business-as-usual revival meetings. Their services included music, sermons, offertories, and altar calls, but their performances could not be the exchange of power between a male minister demonstrating and receiving power and his feminized audience. Thus, the challenge was to perform powerfully enough to induce submission and surrender, yet not to compromise their womanliness.

The Mother and the War at Home

Woodworth-Etter made up for her nonmaleness by emphasizing her status as a receptacle of God during her preaching performances. After beginning her meetings with several minutes of singing, shouting, dancing, and crying, her audience was "held as under a spell," ready to hear from their pastor.[54] Woodworth-Etter came to the platform. Instead of preaching her sermon immediately, as her male counterparts did, she stood in front of her congregation and waited to receive power from God.[55] "At the meeting when Sister Etter entered," wrote one observer, "the power of God came upon her and she stood with uplifted hands looking out into the beyond, for a long while."[56] "She rose on her toes a number of times and her eyes assumed a glassy stare, wide open," wrote the *Indianapolis Star*.[57] "She remained in this position half an hour. After a time, all was deathly still. All waited to see what she would do."[58] "Her appearance was so striking," wrote one observer, "so supernatural that it would have impressed anyone."[59]

This moment of silence gave the audience opportunity to observe Woodworth-Etter receive direct, unmediated access to God.[60] Her silence deemphasized her agency by highlighting the role that God played in and through her. Woodworth-Etter always vehemently denied being a medium or spiritualist, but her words and actions tended to undermine her objections. "God has had possession of my body," she said in a typical utterance.[61] "He is giving you a warning. I am not God, but he is here. The gates of heaven will soon be shut. Christ is coming again, while many of you here are living. You will see Him."[62]

Once she had received power, Woodworth-Etter wielded it freely. Rather than adopting gestures that displayed feminine virtues of submission, deference, or domesticity, such as kneeling or bowing, she assumed the role of commanding officer in the coming, "battle against the enemy of souls."[63] From the pulpit, she executed her battle plan by dispensing male and female "praying lieutenants" to pray with attendees.[64] As a spiritual military leader she used large, commanding gestures similar to those of her male counterparts.[65] "I raised my hand in the name of the Lord and commanded them to listen. I said the Lord had sent me there to do them good, and that I would not leave until the Lord told me to—when our work was done. The power of God fell," she wrote of their response to her gesture and message, "and the fear of God came upon the multitude. One Catholic said that I had struck him down, and showed him hell."[66]

Woodworth-Etter used her "strong and clear" voice to transmit her message.[67] When she preached, she had none of the softness, quietness, or "too high pitched" qualities associated with the "feminine voice."[68] The small woman boomed her messages about the end of the world with a raspy, resonance. "God gave me voice and power to hold the people still as if death was in our midst," she wrote after a particularly rousing "battle."[69] Her followers wrote that her voice even had authority to exorcise and resurrect. "In Jesus' name [Woodworth-Etter] commanded the drug demon to come out of him, it threw him on the ground and fought like a snake. Some thought he was dying, and apparently he did die; but when the Resurrection Power struck him he arose from the floor and walked back and forth across the platform, shouting and praising God, very much alive."[70]

With her strong voice, she ordered local pastors, her fellow soldiers in the fight, to the platform for prayer and exhortation.[71] She charged her attendees to support the future work of the church by supporting the "dear boys" (usually men) that were the area's permanent ministers.[72] Referring to the pastors as boys likely reinforced her role as mother and it bolstered her authority because it showed that Woodworth-Etter had power even to command male ministers.

Woodworth-Etter domesticated her performance with acts reminiscent of an educated mother, including childcare, and providing "the benefits of education" to the public sphere of her congregation.[73] For example, she dedicated time to teaching her congregants the proper use and meaning of Pentecostal practices. The *Topeka Daily Capital* reported one such instance:

As two young people danced frenziedly back and forth on the stage Mrs. Woodworth-Etter smiled at them approvingly.

"The Spirit of God," she frequently exclaimed.

As they danced the young woman's hair had become loosened and hung below her waist. She frequently brushed aside the locks that fell over her face. The two danced unceasingly for 22 minutes. As they paused, the young woman stretched out her arms toward the audience and began uttering unintelligible words, mostly made up of sibilant sounds and ending in vowels.

"God speaking through lips and tongues of clay," exclaimed Mrs. Woodworth-Etter.

The young woman continued and spoke rapidly. Occasionally her words could be distinguished. Her eyes were closed as she spoke. Finally she stopped and retired to a nearby seat. The young man who had stood by with his hands covering his face suddenly stepped forward and began talking in the same manner that his companion had, but his words were more inarticulate, though louder. After speaking for several moments, he stopped abruptly and put his hands over his face. He was silent a moment and then began groaning in a wailing tone, not unlike a patient first recovering consciousness after an anesthetic.

"Heed the Spirit's warning," said Mrs. Woodworth-Etter.

"Amen," shouted a dozen others.

Mrs. Woodworth-Etter explained that the two converts had received the gift of tongues. She said that they spoke in different languages and could be understood by a linguist or parts of their speech could be understood by those familiar with the language in which it was spoken.[74]

This account is a typical example of how Woodworth-Etter used the pulpit to teach her children about Pentecostal practices (in this instance, glossolalia) and their proper execution. She permitted and encouraged certain expressions such as dancing and tongues, and gave these practices doctrinal support. According to her teachings, they were not freakish expressions, but the "Spirit's warning" and "words of God."[75]

Like other revivals, Woodworth-Etter meetings ended with an altar call for salvation and for healing. "I prayed for God to display his power," she said of one altar call, "that the sinner might know that God still lives."[76] During crowded meetings, she used her onstage chairs to expedite the process. "We had three chairs on the platform in which the sick sat to be prayed for. I had one of my best workers at each chair; they would talk to the sick—some spiritually, and others physically sick – and teach them the Word of God, and how to receive; then I would pray for them."[77]

Woodworth-Etter could have performed healings with the demeanor of a medical professional. She could have invited people to the stage, diagnosed them, and then prayed for healing. She could have imitated her male contemporaries and taken on the role of masculine healer warring with sickness on behalf of her congregation. Unlike male healing revivalists such as A. B. Simpson, who presented the "faith cure" as an opportunity for followers to display muscular energy,[78] Woodworth-Etter's healing services were an invitation to experience healing from a "mother's hand."

Rather than taking on the role of military coordinator during altar calls, Woodworth-Etter's plump, diminutive frame changed when she prayed for healing. The extended arms and grand gestures that elongated her frame and filled the stage with energy while she preached were replaced by smaller gestures and more personal body language during healing services. She went from being a warrior to a caregiver. As Woodworth-Etter reached down from her podium to pray for sick attendees, she struck a nurturing, motherly pose. She touched people's faces, arms, backs, and stomachs and prayed for healing.[79]

She spoke quietly with the sick, nodding with understanding as men and women told her about their illnesses. She made a point to pray individually with as many sick or injured people as she could during her services. She made house calls.[80]

The *Chicago Herald* recorded one such healing moment. "Stooping over, the evangelist began removing the bandages, speaking words of hope all the while. Other assistants were around the woman singing and calling on the Lord for help. Finally Mr. [sic] Sea arose with a look of happiness and relief. She moved her arms and joined in the demonstrations made over her recovery."[81] Woodworth-Etter frequently replicated the actions she performed for Mrs. Sea as she bandaged, wiped brows, hugged, and held the hands of her followers. Attendees regularly came forward to ask "Dear Mother Etter"[82] to lay hands on them, pray for them, and heal them.

By all accounts, Woodworth-Etter's followers accepted her role as their educator and nurturing healer. "Mrs. Etter gave us some motherly advice and encouraged us very much," wrote Herbert W. Thomas and Wife, of their time at the Tabernacle.[83] "Mother Etter preached the most wonderful sermon," wrote admirer W. B. Oaks of the "power and victory" of her ministry.[84] Attendees sang songs and recited poetry celebrating her spiritual motherhood. "Many rise up to call you blessed, dear," wrote one poet whose sonnet echoed the ideal woman and mother in Proverbs 31:28.[85] Her pastor disciples gave her motherly authority over their lives and ministries. Her protégés Reverend Birdsall and Reverend F. F. Bosworth acknowledged her role in their lives as that of a "mother in Israel," and that they were her "two dear boys."[86] Pentecostals who came to the movement through her ministers referred to her as their grandparent. "He said he had been converted through a minister who was converted through me. He had heard so much about me," Woodworth-Etter wrote about one young attendee, "he had come fifty miles to see his grandmother."[87]

Woodworth-Etter's mother–child performance was in line with celebrated popular images of womanliness, but Woodworth-Etter's preaching evoked more than a mother–child relationship from her attendees. It also garnered powerful responses from her followers. Their effusive physical and emotional reactions outstripped occasional hand clapping, shouting "amen," or crying. They flailed, shouted, cried, and danced when they heard her preach.

Going beyond the typical altar call response, they performed acts known as falling "under the power."[88] During this "religious fervor," congregants came forward to the altar, fell at Woodworth-Etter's feet, and lay there anywhere from several minutes to over an hour.[89] These acts of submission were not necessarily to the minister herself, but to whom she served as receptacle. "I hadn't been praying for three minutes," wrote one Atlanta revival attendee, "until I began swaying under the power of God. I had just told him everything I had was on the altar, even husband and baby; and I wanted all He had for me. I knew it was the power of God and did not resist, but gave up completely."[90]

Often when under the power, attendees reported having visions of their pastor.[91] These visions elaborated on the warring mother with military authority that Woodworth-Etter created in her biblical script, dress, tabernacles, and pulpit performance. They were often imaginative riffs on her own self-description as a warring mother like Deborah. "I had a wonderful vision, which made a stir in the congregation," wrote one anonymous follower; "I saw the devil and his army, and on the right was the Lord and his army. I saw the army of Heaven and Sister Etter was in front; she was leading the army and the Lord was leading her."[92]

These accounts were flavored with language borrowed from biblical apocalyptic imagery. In the visions, the minister often stood alongside the "Lamb that was slain"[93] in Revelation 5. "While Sister Etter was standing addressing the audience," wrote Elder H. C. Mears, "I saw a great concourse of angels, and a Large Golden Two-edged Sword was in her hand."[94] This imagery put Woodworth-Etter in the company of the angels in Revelation 1–2, one of which received a message from "one like a son of Man" with "sharp, double edged sword" (Revelation 2:12). For Mears, the two-edged sword likely meant the word of God as described in Hebrews 4:12, "For the word of God is quick, and powerful, and sharper than any two-edged sword, piercing even to the dividing asunder of soul and spirit, and of the joints and marrow, and is a discerner of the thoughts and intents of the heart." Thus, in this vision, Woodworth-Etter stood alongside angels with the powerful word of God in her hand.

These visions of a divine showdown between Satan and Jesus illustrated her followers' understanding that Woodworth-Etter was an important player in cosmic spiritual events and so more than an 1890s–1910s mother. Outsiders saw a frumpy, middle-aged holy roller. Her followers believed that their visions revealed their pastor for the figure that she really was: a commanding officer in God's army.

These reactions to Woodworth-Etter's performances crossed a gendered line. Warm tributes to a mother from her children were to be expected and lauded in mainstream revivalism, and previous generations of preachers like Phoebe Palmer proved that a female preacher could gain mainstream acceptance by evoking this sort of response from her followers. Flailing, visions, and falling under the power, however, were outside the purview of mother–child relations.

Woodworth-Etter's authority was pronounced in holiness and Pentecostal revivalist circles. Smith Wigglesworth, Paul Rader, Roscoe Russell, Thomas and Lyda Paino, and other early revivalist greats traveled to her Tabernacle to hear her teachings and to learn about her revivalist style.[95] Well-known Pentecostal revivalist Carrie Judd Montgomery praised her work regularly in her periodicals. "After hearing Mrs. Woodworth handle the word of God with such Divine unction," wrote Montgomery, "it would seem like sacrilege to speak one word against her or against the work God is now doing through her."[96] Her autobiographies sold thousands of copies and their value was seen by many as tantamount to scripture. "I wish all the saints in the pentecostal movement had a copy of Sister Etter's book," wrote revivalist radio celebrity F. F. Bosworth; "it is such a help to faith! There has been no such record written since the 'Acts of the Apostles' recording such victories by the Lord in our day over sin and sickness as this book."[97]

Despite her skillful, charismatic performance, her sizeable, responsive audiences, and her influence in holiness and Pentecostal revivalism, Woodworth-Etter never achieved the broadly evangelical influence of her revivalist contemporaries J. Wilbur Chapman or A. B. Simpson. One reason for this was that interwoven with issues of gender, Woodworth-Etter's ministry faced hurdles of race and class. That is to say, her meetings, in contrast to her male colleagues, seemed (at least to reporters) to include more working class, African-American attendees.[98] In contrast, A. B. Simpson and Billy Sunday's meetings were reported as being "conspicuously middleclass."[99] Reporters noted that Simpson's meetings were made up of people with money enough to finance extensive missionary ventures.[100] "The crowd," wrote an official Sunday biographer, "is quite respectable. It is comfortably dressed, well behaved."[101] Outside observers did not typically note people of color in attendance at Simpson meetings.[102] Although deeply interested in "converting the heathen" of all creeds and colors abroad, his revivals were overwhelmingly made up of European Americans.[103] Likewise, besides describing a few "swarthy human curiosities" or the occasional "old, white-wooled negro," that attended Sunday's meetings, reporters wrote that his services attracted prominent community leaders, businessmen, "society folk," and other examples white middleclass life.[104]

Woodworth-Etter's ecstatic meetings, on the other hand, were often associated with working-class audiences.[105] These audiences occasionally benefited her public image, such as when Salem, Oregon reporters politely noted that she extended "cordial invitations to the poor."[106] More often than not, she was criticized for the class of attendee she attracted. The *Atlanta Journal* described with horror the men who arrived at a meeting as "rough fellows in working clothes!"[107] One newspaper reporter in Warsaw, Indiana ridiculed the poorer, less-educated people enamored with her work. "The educated class of the community," he wrote, "take no stock in the affair."[108]

In addition to her working-class audiences, Woodworth-Etter actively sought to preach to African-American and white crowds.[109] Indeed, she wrote proudly of the clashes surrounding her efforts to incorporate black congregants into her services. For example, Woodworth-Etter wrote the following account of a meeting in Louisville, Kentucky:

> The white people said that if the colored were permitted to come, they would stay home. Then we gave the colored people one corner of the tent and had them sit by themselves. Some of the wealthy citizens said that they like the meetings, would support them, but they would not do anything if we let the negroes come. Ministers and professing Christians said the same. They said that all evangelists who had been in the city could do no good until they drove the negroes away. I told them God made the whole human family of one blood.[110]

In spite of Woodworth-Etter's apparent satisfaction with interracial or at least semi-desegregated worship, white commentators compared her meetings with black revivalist expression, which they denigrated. "No one who has respect for Holy things or reverence," wrote one editorial, "can give bold utterances to such as 'a cyclone of the Holy Ghost', . . . I have not witnessed the like since I attended the meetings of the poor black slaves in Kentucky, thirty years ago."[111]

The actions and the reactions she induced from her followers also contrasted with the relatively subdued "amens" and hand clapping in Chapman or Simpson's white middleclass meetings.[112] "These physical manifestations," wrote Unitarian pastor Charles Wendite of Woodworth-Etter meetings, "are of the same low order which characterizes the African Voodoo, the frenzied leaps and gushings of the Mohammedian Dervishes, and the delirium of the Indian Medicine man."[113] That the uncivilized "wailing, hollering, and screeching," done by the "voodoo priestess" and her "holy rollers," was performed on primitive, straw covered grounds further served to restrict Woodworth-Etter's influence in large part because it rendered the minister and her people, non-Christian and non-European.[114]

Woodworth-Etter's meetings were also known to attract a rowdy sort. Riot police were called to a meeting in Oakland, California when local health officials, annoyed neighbors, and enthusiastic attendees clashed and had to be subdued with clubs.[115] During meetings near Framingham, Massachusetts, unruly boys threw rocks and eggs and tried to set fires, while people were carried away in "trances."[116] Woodworth-Etter's critics were quick to point out that none of the lowbrow mayhem from the "weaker minded" that characterized Woodworth-Etter meetings was present in Chapman's meetings.[117]

Woodworth-Etter did little to change her reputation for holding rabble-rousing meetings. On the contrary, her response was often defiant. "Some of the drunken police got mad at some of the workers, and they hated us all," she wrote of her clash with law enforcement officers in Oakland, California. "It was dark and rainy, and they gathered up a mob, and were going to tear down the tent, and mob us all."[118] Woodworth-Etter wrote that rather than speaking to the police about the meeting, she treated them to a demonstration of what she believed to be an impressive display of spiritual power:

> The Spirit of the Lord came on me. I stepped up on the altar, and stood looking at them, then began talking as the Spirit gave utterance. I began to walk down the long altar that led down amongst them, talking as the Spirit gave utterance, with power. The Holy Ghost had control of my whole body, arms, hands, and feet. I felt as though I had turned to be a giant, and believed that if they had moved towards us, that God would have smitten them dead.[119]

Woodworth-Etter's followers were moved, but neither the police nor most other nonholiness or Pentecostal revivalists were impressed with her ecstatic display.[120]

Thus, to her followers, Woodworth-Etter's performance in the pulpit knew no equal. By enacting the role of mother and warrior in the pulpit, she gave her followers a figure of authority and womanliness. Her meetings, while exceedingly efficacious for her followers in holiness and Pentecostal circles, had limited authority outside the fold. Her inability or refusal to translate the ecstatic revivalist experiences to outsiders or make it palatable to white middleclass audiences meant that many simply stayed away.

The Bride and Her Bridegroom

In addition to performing her role as a woman and a minister, Aimee Semple McPherson succeeded where her predecessor did not. She created a revival experience that was considered to be authoritative, female, white, and middleclass. Unlike Woodworth-Etter, whose revival services were set in a symbolic battlefield and incorporated both the womanly acts of nurture and instruction, and the masculine act of war, McPherson presided over services that were a complete departure from the manly ministry. Like the decor of Angelus Temple, McPherson's performance was all things feminine. She transformed her revival services from an opportunity to display masculine authority into a romantic epic.

McPherson put her "good-looking, red-haired, and white-robed,"[121] physical form to its best use during events that she called "illustrated sermons," a combination of sermon, musical revue, and scripted play. Journalist Sarah Comstock described them in 1927 as, "a complete vaudeville program, entirely new each week, brimful of surprises for the eager who are willing to battle in the throng for entrance."[122] Each week, McPherson chose a passage for a sermon— the Second Coming, the need for evangelism, and the love of Jesus were all popular topics – and came up with a story that illustrated it.

Then, McPherson directed songs (many of which she composed) sung by vaudevillian singers, hundreds of choir singers, and backed by a professional orchestra, as well as dances, and skits, and various other forms of stage performance. These entertainments, highly anticipated by Temple attendees, were merely the warm up for the most important performance of the service—McPherson's sermon dedicated to her chosen theme. Although there are no available scripts of McPherson's illustrated sermons, first-hand accounts of McPherson's sermons, and photographic evidence, provide insight into the form and function of these events.

In every illustrated sermon, no matter what the theme, McPherson had the starring role. Her most popular sermons reinforced her bridal status as well as her role as a leading lady. For one illustrated sermon on the subject of the Second Coming, McPherson chose to illustrate the parable of the wise and foolish virgins in Matthew 25:1–13. In this passage, Jesus compared the kingdom of heaven to ten virgins who go to meet their bridegroom. Five were wise and had plenty of oil to keep their lamps lit while they waited for him. Five were foolish and did not take oil with them. When the foolish virgins realized they had run out of oil, they asked their wise counterparts for more.

The wise virgins refused, the foolish virgins had to go and buy their own, and then missed their opportunity to go to the marriage. When they returned the bridegroom told the virgins, "verily I say unto you, I know you not," [Matthew 25:12]. Jesus ended the story with an admonition: "Watch therefore, for ye know neither the day nor the hour wherein the Son of Man cometh," [Matthew 25:13].

In McPherson's interpretation, the Bridegroom was Jesus, the wise virgins were those in a prepared church, and the foolish virgins were those unprepared for his coming.[123] The service centered upon the story of virgins getting ready for their wedding day. "The blessed Bridegroom of the Church, [will] return to take His Bride away," she told her congregation.[124]

To illustrate this passage, McPherson assembled on the Temple stage attractive young women dressed in simple white gowns. The biblical passage had only ten virgins, but twelve young women filled the stage more impressively and McPherson bolstered the number with two additional women in wedding apparel. The women symbolized bridal purity as well as sensual anticipation of the wedding night. Then, descending from the stage staircase, McPherson appeared, dressed in a more elaborate satin white gown, as the most beautiful and bridal of the group. With her Bible in hand, she preached about the need to be prepared to be Christ's bride (Figure 5.1).

Figure 5.1   McPherson and the Twelve Virgins (two more than in Matthew 25:1–13), 1933. Credit: Foursquare Archives.

In another sermon entitled, "The Rose of Sharon," McPherson claimed that Jesus was the lover in Song of Songs 2:1 who said, "I am the rose of Sharon, and the lily of the valleys."[125] To illustrate that point, McPherson stood in front of a giant rose that bloomed in a staged garden (Figure 5.3). As its most ardent gardener, she preached about the rose's beauty, lovely scent, and sweetness.

Unlike Woodworth-Etter, who took the role of military commander in the pulpit, McPherson portrayed herself as the perpetual bride to her eternal groom. During her illustrated sermons, she usually upstaged her heavenly leading man. "In this unique house of worship called Angelus Temple in the city of Los Angeles," wrote Comstock, "the Almighty occupies a secondary position. He plays an important part in the drama, to be sure; but center stage is taken and held by Mrs. McPherson."[126] When she preached, she was not simply assuming the ordinary role of companionate wife to an earthly husband. She was an exemplar for her followers. She was the ultimate of what they all aspired to be and that status gave her power over her fellow brides of Christ.

McPherson's body, like her Temple, was curvaceous, soft edged, well decorated,[127] and she used it to provide illustrated sermon attendees with living, breathing displays of a biblical bride of Christ and as well as a leading lady. McPherson did use bold, large gestures associated with masculine pulpit performance. She lifted her arms to toward the Temple dome in prayer to Jesus. She frequently preached with one arm extended confidently over the audience while holding a Bible in the other. She made a fist and shook it passionately when she preached about the dangers of sin. She also used strong gestures to perform typical priestly acts. For example, McPherson extended her arms and blessed her congregation in a typical benediction.

Despite these strong movements, McPherson's surroundings and wardrobe tempered her more powerful gestures. She raised her arm over her congregation, but that arm was clothed in shimmering, draping white material that made the sharpest movement flowing and graceful. She offered a priestly benediction, but that offering was made from a pulpit covered with roses. She moved across the stage with vigor, but as she moved, she showed her attractive curves in motion. Thus, even in her most authoritative moments, she performed the feminine.

As she preached, McPherson repeated many of the same gestures that starlets performed in romantic films, but her repetitions of the gestures contained within them small changes that altered their meaning. She knelt, clasped her hands, and looked up adoringly not at a handsome leading man like Rudolf Valentino, but at the cross, which was a symbol of her heavenly hero (Figure 5.2). McPherson's pose redirected the passion of two film screen lovers to the passion between the minister and her savior. This pose reinforced her status as the most intimate, the most dedicated lover of Jesus.

She also frequently clasped her hands across her chest as film stars like Mary Pickford did in a promotional portrait for her 1929 film *Coquette*. Whereas Pickford was contemplating a human relationship, McPherson clasped the Bible to her chest. She posed in front of a round, lighted circle, which gave her a saintly halo in addition to her feminine gestures. This pose depicted McPherson as a womanly woman, but one with the scriptures close to her heart (literally in this case), and one with sainted, haloed, authority.

Like her film star counterparts, flowers were a part of her performance. For stars like Mary Pickford in *Coquette*, the flowers were related to a romantic relationship. For McPherson, posing with flowers (usually roses) was a way of communicating her special relationship

Figure 5.2 McPherson in *Cavalcade of Christianity* at Angelus Temple, 1931. Credit: Foursquare Archives.

Figure 5.3 McPherson and the Rose of Sharon, circa 1929.

with her spiritual Rose of Sharon (Figure 5.3). She often began services by making a dramatic, unmistakably bridal entrance in a white gown while holding a bouquet. She brought the flowers with her to the pulpit and clasped them with all the anticipation of a Hollywood ingénue. In her sermon *The Rose of Sharon*, McPherson raised the flowers triumphantly over her head and spoke about the value of intimacy with Jesus. In her sermon, *The Year of Jubilee*, she stood with her armful of roses and told her audience that "The Rose of Sharon, "will be so completely entwined with your life, interlaced and interwoven, that you can be taken to the house of the Lord and you will grace His service and shine in His beauty."[128]

In addition to imitating familiar movie poses and accoutrements, McPherson used her voice to signal her femininity. Whereas Billy Sunday's raspy, stilted delivery signaled his masculine roughness, and Woodworth-Etter's voice boomed with power, McPherson's cheerful, casual cadence, and conversational manner bespoke femininity.[129] Her pleasant, alto intonation, similar to the female voices that 1920s audiences were hearing in film and on the radio, was another auditory signal of ideal popular femininity.[130] The result was both powerful and feminine. "Her voice," wrote one journalist, "is the roar of thunder and the sweetness of a woman."[131]

Her altar calls were also demonstrations of ultra-femininity. In contrast to the pleas for a "show of manhood," she invoked passionate confessions of love for Jesus and offered wooing invitations to receive Christ. "Come, brother! Come, sister! There is room at the Fountain for you," she preached. "Come, radio land! Right where you are the Savior is waiting to save you and make you whole. Open your heart to receive Him. The door of mercy swings wide before you – enter while you may."[132]

Admirer and fellow revivalist Charles S. Price wrote the following flattering portrait of McPherson's desire for Jesus and her congregation's response:

> There is a power in her message, a note of victory in her voice, as she tells of the Christ whom she loves and whom she serves.... And then she stops – eyes are closed and heads are bowed; a hush has settled over the building while Sister prays – 'Jesus, won't you give me souls at this opening meeting? I want them, Lord, and you want them, too.'[133]

McPherson's palpable desire for new converts made for an exceedingly effective altar call. "Her prayer was answered as they came streaming down the aisles," wrote Price. "The altar was full to overflowing and soon the sweetest music that was ever heard rolled up beyond the great dome to the city whose streets are of gold and whose walls are of jasper. It was the music of praying people finding Jesus as a personal Saviour."[134]

Actor and former Temple band member Anthony Quinn recalled in his autobiography Temple audiences' responses to McPherson's preaching:

> "Then that rich melodious voice began slowly, 'Glory! Glory! Glory!' I could feel the audience exhale. We shouted, 'Glory!' She smiled and the congregation felt truly blessed. She closed her eyes, leafed through the Bible, and let her finger fall. She read the passage, caressing each word. She began to interweave sudden bursts of emotion, 'Hallelujah! Hallelujah, brothers and sisters!' All the congregation replied, 'Hallelujah!'"[135]

McPherson's healing services were likewise performances of the romantic bride-bridegroom relationship. Simpson presented healing as an opportunity to exercise a manly faith and Woodworth-Etter performed healing as a motherly act, but McPherson's divine healings were an opportunity to have an intense, sensual physical experience with Jesus, the "personal healer."[136] She told her congregants about her own experience with healing: "I suddenly felt as if a shock of electricity had struck my foot. It flowed through my whole body, causing me to shake and tremble under the power of God."[137]

For McPherson, healings were the ultimate feminine act. The petitioner, after a passionate moment of intimacy, received an influx of the presence of an all-powerful bridegroom. She encouraged her congregation to "receive your healing," from a loving Christ rather than to take hold of it.[138] She presented healing as one more moment to have an encounter with God that left the healed, "trembling with excitement and joy."[139] She called followers to come forward in a "soft voice, almost a whisper."[140] She stood or knelt near the supplicants with one or two hands touching them. She closed her eyes and then, "gently implored" the Lord to, "gently touch them with the magic of his love," and heal them.[141] She clasped people's hands; she "clung" to her congregants and prayed and cried.[142]

McPherson's romantic, feminine atmosphere eliminated any need for traditionally masculine gestures. Priestly functions like delivering benedictions and demonstrations of supernatural power like divine healing were all subsumed under the persona of a womanly bride. From beginning to end and head to toe, McPherson was femininity personified.

McPherson's elaborate, sometimes humorous costumes and her feminine poses and gestures served to establish her authority. She was not leading troops to war or men into muscular health. She was going to a wedding and then to the bridal chamber. She was leading fellow adorers to the object of their adoration by being the most devout, submissive, and ardent lover of Jesus. Thus, the more womanly she behaved, the more extravagant her performances, and the more she heightened her intimacy with Jesus, the more qualified she was to lead her fellow brides of Christ.

McPherson was assuring her congregants that she was fulfilling the companionate ideal even as she was undermining it with her public, man-less performances. The companionate wife in McPherson's hands had much more porous boundaries than 1920s literature suggested. Rather than being restricted by popular notions of a middleclass, white wife who saved her sexuality for her husband, she epitomized it and harnessed it for her use.

McPherson's influence over her congregants, male and female, was profound. One Los Angeles housewife was so desperate to experience a McPherson service that she reportedly slit her throat after her husband refused to let her attend Temple services.[143] Most reactions, however, were less extreme. Attendees wept when she cried, laughed at her jokes, raised their hands with her to Jesus, and submitted their bodies to her altar for healing and prayer.[144] Newsman Grover C. Loud wrote that they wept "till sobs blend into hallelujahs and the redeemed, weeping, 'talking in tongues,' shadowboxing with the Spirit, choke the aisles in a rush to gather as near as they can to the hem of her stainless garment."[145] "Old women and men, tear-cheeked flappers on their sweethearts' arms, little bewildered children move toward her," wrote journalist Allene Sumner, "like moths to the candle. Sometimes, hysterical, they cling to her body, wetting her hands, her dress, with their tears. They will not be pulled away."[146]

Outsiders speculated that her power was tied to her sex appeal. "She particularly exhorted the young college boys to come forward," wrote a reporter for the *Berkeley Daily Gazette* after commenting on McPherson's beauty. "Many did."[147] "Can anyone believe," asked Loud, "that this could be accomplished by a pinch-faced, wan, sad-eyed, wapper-jawed, slab-sided, long-skirted holy woman, virtuous because no man ever looked upon her with the eyes of desire? It is more plausible that the achievement is due to the fact that the inspirative message was borne by a warm and beautiful creature enhanced by an aura of intriguing mystery."[148]

It is clear that at least one celebrity minister agreed with Loud. The flamboyant Bishop Frank H. Rice of the Liberal Church, Inc. in Denver, Colorado imagined himself as her bridegroom. He was so taken with McPherson and her ministry that he offered to make her his "38th spiritual wife."[149] He offered "full assistance in faith healing and any miracle the proposed union might produce,"[150] and did not have a problem with McPherson's rumored penchant for plastic surgery to enhance her looks. "I don't quite believe it," he told *The Pittsburg Press* about the rumors in 1930, "But if she wants her face lifted and will come to Denver, I'll see the operation costs her nothing."[151] Even though the marriage offer to McPherson was purely "spiritual," Rice's legal wife apparently did not approve of his proposed alliance with the beautiful McPherson. "I hope she doesn't sue me for divorce,"[152] he said reflecting on her displeasure.

Her followers would have probably refuted Loud's analysis of her "inspirative" presentations, but the way that they praised her showed that McPherson's good looks and winsome stage presence was at least part of the reason why they loved her. In a lengthy 1928 *Bridal Call* editorial entitled, "A Tribute to Aimee Semple McPherson from Her Elders, Workers and Members in Honor of Her Birthday," her followers praised her in sensual language from the Song of Solomon. "Like a 'lily among thorns,' as Solomon describes the victorious Christian," wrote her followers, "our Sister has kept sweet and pure amid the trials, sorrows, and cares that have crowded in upon her."[153] The article went on to use the Song of Solomon to describe the ways in which McPherson's person embodied ideal Christian living:

Her lips have been touched with the scarlet [Song of Solomon 4:3] thread of His blood... Her heart has been close to the fountain head of the Throne of God, and therefore from her lips have flowed [4:11] forth the living water of His Word upon a dry and thirsty ground.

Her teeth are even and symmetrical [4:2] as they partake of the whole Word of God....

Upon her cheeks is the veil of humility [1:10]....

Her eyes are constant and true and fixed unwaveringly upon the Savior whom she loves...

Her neck is strong [7:4] and has never yet bowed beneath the attack of the enemy....

Her hands, strong and lovely, have ministered to hundreds of thousands, patting the tired head of the little mother, clasping the afflicted child to her bosom, shaking the hard, toil worn hand of the laborer, caressing the silver hair of some dear old mother in Israel. Gently, those hands have been laid upon the heads of countless thousands in the name of Jesus....[154]

Unlike Woodworth-Etter whose followers loved her for her motherly care, McPherson's followers credited their leader for her "unwavering" love for Jesus and her strong and lovely body. For McPherson's followers, therefore, at least part of her power was due to her beauty and the way that she used her beauty in relationship with her bridegroom and on behalf of her people.

"Countless thousands love her,"[155] her followers wrote about their beautiful minister, and their claim was based in truth. In contrast with Woodworth-Etter, McPherson and her Temple were enormously powerful in general revivalist circles, and in popular culture. The *Moody Bible Institute Monthly*, a staple of mainstream revivalism, gave McPherson a cautious editorial endorsement in 1921.[156] William Jennings Bryan recommended McPherson's ministry and spoke at the Temple.[157] Billy Sunday came for a visit.[158] McPherson was a member of the Los Angeles elite and rubbed shoulders politicians and entertainers like Upton Sinclair and Charlie Chaplin. After its dedication, Angelus Temple quickly became one of the most visited buildings in

Los Angeles. Hollywood tours included a drive to Grauman's Chinese Theater, the Hollywood sign, and Angelus Temple.[159] Postcards of the Temple were commonplace in Los Angeles, and a replica of the Temple was a prize-winning float in the Pasadena Rose Parade.

Part of McPherson's broad influence can be attributed to her location in America's emerging media capital. She attracted national press and a following simply by virtue of being the biggest celebrity minister in the celebrity capital of the country. Her radio ministry gave her access to a national audience. On any given summer night in Los Angeles, a person could walk for blocks and blocks and listen to uninterrupted Temple sermons broadcast through open windows.[160]

McPherson also presented a decidedly more middleclass, white revivalist experience than did Woodworth-Etter. One way that she did this was through her worship space. Her state of the art sets and extravagant décor attracted members of the upper and middle classes more readily than the sawdust flooring and bare walls of Woodworth-Etter's Tabernacle.

Another way she made her services more mainstream was by moving away from the unplanned feel of traditional revivalism. When McPherson began her itinerant preaching, there was little to distinguish her meetings from the rowdy, seemingly chaotic programming of Woodworth-Etter's revivalist services. By the time she built Angelus Temple, however, she had dramatically changed her meeting style. McPherson's 1920s meetings were polished, seamless, well-orchestrated productions. "As a show-producer with unflagging power to draw she knows no equal," wrote reporter Sarah Comstock. "Many a revivalist of the past has played upon his audience by the old methods of sensational preaching; but Mrs. McPherson has methods of her own."[161] Unlike previous Pentecostal revivalist meetings that might oscillate between prayer, praise, and testimony for several minutes or even hours, McPherson kept audiences engaged at all times through structured plays, musical numbers, and her own preaching. "The director," Comstock wrote of McPherson, "knows the value of rapid movement, of the quick shift that anticipates boredom."[162]

Some of McPherson's Pentecostal critics complained that her services were so programmed that they were moving away from her Pentecostal revivalist roots.[163] The 500 Room, with its healings, prophecies, and other ecstatic expressions, did much to assuage their fears. It also helped to make her ministry mainstream by segregating the more ecstatic audiences from the main auditorium's illustrated sermons and musical numbers. It therefore (indirectly) increased

McPherson's mainstream evangelical power. The layout innovation made the Temple friendly to non-Pentecostal attendees because those who came to hear William Jennings Bryan or Billy Sunday preach were not required to participate in more extreme Pentecostal expressions.

McPherson faced a dilemma when it came to African American, Latin American, and other non-white attendees. On the one hand, she had relatively progressive practices when it came to race. She had many Hispanic members in her Los Angeles congregation and hired interpreters (including a young Mexican-American Anthony Quinn) to translate her sermons to bilingual audiences. She celebrated "Gypsy" church members.[164] She also worked with African American preachers like Emma Cotton and Jennie Seymour. In addition, like Woodworth-Etter, she encouraged black and white revivalists to worship together.

Unlike Woodworth-Etter, McPherson was not often accused of performing "African Voodoo" or "Indian Medicine." One probable reason for this was that she restricted ecstatic practice to the 500 Room. She also subtly distanced herself from black audiences in her services. For example, McPherson preached sermons declaring the evils of slavery to sin. Choosing for her illustrated sermon theme the antebellum South, she dressed not a formerly enslaved heroine like Harriet Tubman, but as a Southern belle. Thus, even while she condemned slavery, she was (at least visually) a representation of the white enslaver.

In addition, McPherson occasionally told "Sambo"[165] stories about African Americans sharing their faith; these stories upheld stereotypes of childish African Americans.[166] For example, she used the following exaggerated dialect when she wrote about exchanges with African American attendees:

Only a poor colored man was he, but: "Oh Lawd! Ah done see again – Ah jes knowed ma Savior could do it!" he affirmed. "Fo' twenty years Ah've lived in de da'k; but now – bless de Lawd – Ah kin see!"

"What am I holding up in front of you?" we asked, expecting him to say, "Your hand." We are startled and the audience convulsed with relieved and happy laughter when he replied with ceremonious exactitude:

"Fo'r fingers – and – one – thumb."

"How many now?" we asked.

"Two."

"How many?"

"Three."

"How many now?"

"You've put yo' hand behind yo' back."

"Correct – can you follow me, brother?"

"Sho' Ah I can –" and in and out, through the line that waits for prayer he follows us, then down the steps where a colored 'mammy,' evidently his wife, is wiping the tears from her eyes.[167]

There is no evidence that McPherson consciously distanced herself from black Pentecostal revivalists. But by using terms like "Sambo," and "mammy," by portraying her encounters with black attendees in exaggerated dialect, and identifying (at least visually) with antebellum enslavers rather than the enslaved, she created a divide between her own ways of talking and worshiping and those of her African American counterparts. These acts reinforced the whiteness as well as the middleclass qualities of her meetings and placed McPherson comfortably in the mainstream of American revivalism.

By all accounts, her followers adored their white, middleclass sweetheart as illustrated in the testimony of one devoted disciple:

What a small bundle our pastor is, but what a precious bundle! In her snowy white gown, with her glorious red gold hair piled high, and her arms outstretched, one does not need a vivid imagination to see an angel of the Lord before him. (She does not like that we should say such things about her, but we cannot help it, for when we see the Christ in her we must admire and love).[168]

CONCLUSION

Woodworth-Etter and McPherson's pulpit performances repeated many standard revivalist practices: they had music, preaching, offerings, and altar calls. Whereas male revivalists used the preaching moment to reinforce the masculinity of their message and person, Woodworth-Etter and McPherson performed their roles as a Mother in Israel and bride of Christ. By putting the emphasis on her status as channel of God, Woodworth-Etter deemphasized her agency from the pulpit. As an instrument of God, she was free to assert her authority in her rhetoric and bodily movements with her strong voice, her bold gestures, and her performance as a spiritual military leader. Woodworth-Etter's role as a healer gave the minister an opportunity to perform nurturing motherly tasks like caring for her sick children. Her followers were mesmerized and readily submitted to her altar calls. Her influence was limited to holiness and Pentecostal circles, however, because of her ecstatic services, her working class followers, and her association with African American attendees.

McPherson used her status as exemplary confidant of Jesus to give her performance power. By striking film star poses and putting on elaborate productions that featured McPherson as the star, she made herself out to be the leading lady of her temple and of her savior. By performing a heavenly romance, McPherson showed her followers that she was Jesus' most devoted follower. Her power came from her ability to be the ultimate female consort to Jesus and so even her most powerful gestures were clothed in femininity. McPherson successfully broadened her mainstream revivalist authority by partitioning ecstatic expressions in the 500 Room, by distancing herself from African Americans through her performances, and by acting as master of ceremonies of a comfortable, orderly, middleclass production. Therefore while neither A. B. Simpson nor John Chapman came to Woodworth-Etter meetings, William Jennings Bryan and Billy Sunday happily visited Angelus Temple.

Woodworth-Etter and McPherson's performances can be interpreted as exceptions that prove the rule. In other words, the women gave such extraordinary performances that their charisma overrode the social constraints of the day as well as the taints of womanhood, scandal, and even divorce. Yet the strategic acts used by each woman show that they are also exceptions that display how the boundaries around the educated mother and companionate wife were not always hard and fast. Indeed, even as Woodworth-Etter and McPherson performed ideal womanhood as a ritualized action, they demonstrated that performing these roles created opportunities for women to subvert ideal womanliness while they ostensibly upheld it. In this way, performing popular models of womanhood was both a vehicle of suppression and opportunity.

6

"A REGULAR JEZEBEL":
FEMALE MINISTRY, PENTECOSTAL
MINISTRY ON TRIAL

Even though Maria Woodworth-Etter and Aimee Semple McPherson's followers accepted the women as female ministers, and they had considerable influence in 1890s–1920s Pentecostal revivalism, some reactions from their contemporaries suggest that the women's work was not entirely successful in transgressing the boundaries surrounding womanhood and the ministry. In fact, many revivalists disapproved of the women's ordination and subsequent work as pastors. In some cases, they actively opposed their work. This chapter examines the efficacy of Wooworth-Etter and McPherson's work through the public response to the women, especially during their criminal trials.

Woodworth-Etter had enthusiastic critics. Her ordination in the Indiana Church of God was revoked after "protest against it from the [male] Indiana Eldership."[1] Flamboyant restorationist and fellow heartland minister John Alexander Dowie denounced the "infernal woman named Woodworth," after the two had clashed personally and theologically, and some of his followers began to attend her meetings.[2] According to Dowie, Woodworth-Etter's teachings on divine healing were ineffective and her trances were "a witness of Satan."[3] "She was," he wrote, "a regular Jezebel, like her of Revelation."[4] "I saw one of my people who had been blessed by God – an ex-doctor of medicine – on his knees howling,"[5] he wrote after visiting one of Woodworth-Etter's meetings and seeing a former congregant now in her company. In addition to her tussle with Dowie, Woodworth-Etter frequently clashed with other celebrity healing revivalists in holiness and Pentecostal circles. For example, her fellow Midwestern healing revivalist John Bunyan Campbell accused her of incompetence and insanity. "She like the rest," he opined, "do not know how to use it [healing power] and may use it too much and thus do much harm."[6]

McPherson also had her share of detractors. A group of Baptist revivalist ministers called her ministry "under serious question" and protested her Baptist ordination in California.[7] Robert "Fighting Bob" Shuler, a fellow Los Angeles revivalist celebrity, made McPherson his particular target. Shuler dedicated several articles of his periodical, *Bob Shuler's Magazine*, to criticizing McPherson (in prose and in limerick form).[8] One poetic offering about McPherson demonstrates a high level of vitriol:

> I am going to name a lady with a record long and shady,
> One who in this world has caused a lot of strife!
> Now I know you're laughing hearty – but I do not mean that party!
> For the one I have in mind is the devil's wife![9]

Observers also skewered Woodworth-Etter and McPherson's scandal-ridden careers. Woodworth-Etter's 1913 trial and McPherson's 1926 courtroom drama provided critics with ample opportunity to punish the women for stepping outside 1890s–1920s models of womanliness and into the public sphere of the masculine ministry. The women's legal battles were not simply about the crimes the women were accused of perpetrating. The aspects of Woodworth-Etter and McPherson's identities that subverted gender norms were also on trial.

THE HYPNOTIST

In August of 1913, Maria Woodworth-Etter pitched her revival tent at Montwait, a campground and popular venue for Pentecostal meetings near South Framingham, Massachusetts. Initially, the meetings went as planned. The *Framingham Daily Tribune* reported with interest the "peculiar traits and manifestations" of Woodworth-Etter meetings.[10] The *Tribune* also published an editorial encouraging local residents to come and see the "signs and wonders" that accompanied the services.[11]

Although some showed interest in seeing Woodworth-Etter's "signs and wonders," not everyone was happy with the meetings. Several young men deemed "hoodlums"[12] by local police threw rocks and eggs at revival attendees, dumped buckets of water on stage, and caused enough general mayhem to warrant intervention from local law enforcement officers.[13] Others chose less physical but ultimately more damaging ways of expressing their displeasure. Local doctors came forward and accused Woodworth-Etter of leading meetings that were detrimental to her congregants' health.[14] Concerned citizens believed

Woodworth-Etter's healings were fraudulent and complained about the loud meetings.[15] Their complaints led South Framingham's prosecuting attorney David C. Ahearn to arrest and charge Woodworth-Etter with obtaining money under false pretenses. Ahearn claimed that she cheated her devotees out of 100 dollars in offerings.[16] According to Ahearn, Woodworth-Etter had agreed to heal attendees in exchange for their offerings, and then failed to cure her subjects.[17]

Woodworth-Etter's trial was more about the "nefarious means" she used to control her adherents than it was about whether she stole from them. In fact, throughout her trial, her fiscal policies got very little attention. Instead, the overarching question was: from where did she get such "superior Pentecostal power" over her followers, particularly the men?[18] On behalf of the people of Framingham, Ahearn argued that she used hypnotism to impose her will on the "credulity of weaker minded people."[19]

Hypnotism figured prominently in several high-profile trials of the era,[20] and it had very specific, usually negative connotations.[21] It was most commonly associated with two unsavory practices: the occult and quackery. Newspapers characterized hypnotism as a cultic practice brought from the mysterious and dangerous "Far East" to America, with power to harm participants as well as practitioners.[22] Reporters chronicled tales of hypnotisms gone wrong and blamed deaths, illness, and injury on the practice.[23]

The underlying presupposition of Woodworth-Etter's trial was that she was doing something menacing and even dangerous, and Ahearn's accusations were nothing new. Opponents of Woodworth-Etter's ministry had long been uncomfortable with her supposed hypnotic influence over male minds.[24] A headline reporting on an 1890 Woodworth-Etter meeting warned that the evangelist "STEALS MEN'S WITS AWAY," through hypnotism.[25] In 1891, she was accused of using hypnosis to procure more substantial offerings.[26] The *New York Times* reported a story of a young man who put himself under Woodworth-Etter's hypnotic influence and shortly after experienced hallucinations and insomnia from which his doctor believed he would never fully recover.[27]

Classifying Woodworth-Etter as a hypnotist allowed Ahearn and other critics to construct an identity other than what she created for herself. She spoke of herself as a minister, but as a pastor she was the epitome of the "Malcontent Woman"[28] bemoaned in 1895. Not only did she publicly associate with men as peers, she ordered many of them around, claimed to have authority over sickness, presented herself as God's mouthpiece, and did it all in the male *métier* of the ministry. In addition, despite her many efforts to position herself as a mother who fulfilled her motherly duties with her congregation, she did not spend her time "mothercrafting" in the home. Ahearn's portrait of Woodworth-Etter as a hypnotist was a rejection of her identity as a powerful revivalist. Detractors therefore did not accept that she was a powerful minister. To them, she was a quack who dabbled dangerously in the occult.

Ahearn's case, although passionately argued, was flimsy, and a few days after her testimony, Woodworth-Etter was cleared of any wrongdoing. Many had lingering doubts, however, about her methods of ministry. The Framingham judge's ruling was hardly an endorsement of the minister. His comments reveal the ways in which nonbelievers thought she transgressed gender lines.[29] "There are sections of the country, perhaps, where these defendants have preached where the laying out in straw on or near a public platform, of a dozen or more persons of both sexes and all ages in an unconscious state might pass as one of the usual and proper incidents of a meeting intended for the worship of God," said Judge Kingsbury. "But it is repugnant to the general public sentiment of this Commonwealth and these defendants will be wise if they recognize the fact as long as they stay with us."[30]

Woodworth-Etter's 1913 trial showed that even though her followers found her performance of the warring Mother in Israel to be compelling, her power over her congregants was unacceptable to those not in the fold. During her trial, her opponents argued that the acts that constituted an eschatological warring mother for insiders were the very acts that discredited her. Woodworth-Etter's acts of motherly healing were seen by doctors as public health concerns. Her act of receiving a word from "under the power" was seen as a symptom or cause of insanity. The revivalist meeting with "both sexes" was seen as a "repugnant" fraud. The strategies that served her so well were also used as evidence that she was not a minister at all but a (possibly insane) hypnotist and probable fraud. In short, according to the prosecution and the Framingham court of public opinion, she was anything but a legitimate female minister.

PSYCHOPATHIA SEXUALIS

As it was with her predecessor, McPherson's career was characterized by a number of legal dramas, but none eclipsed the public scandal surrounding her 1926 disappearance, reappearance, and criminal trial. McPherson's trial was a goldmine for scandal seekers.

It involved an alleged kidnapping, a body double, a missing person, and even a suitcase full of lingerie.[31] Most of all, it involved sex. The sex appeal McPherson had focused toward her heavenly bridegroom was now redirected in the media to the "love tryst" she supposedly shared with an earthly partner.[32] Reporters were only too happy to speculate about McPherson's supposed affair. Much of the trial focused not on whether or not she and her staff had conspired to deceive the police, but rather on her alleged affair with Ormiston.[33]

Like Woodworth-Etter before her, McPherson found that news coverage of the trial was focused upon the power she wielded during her revivalist meetings, not on the charges themselves. Reporters noted that her trial galvanized her congregation. "The temple rafters rang with the applause of thousands of her followers who rose in their seats and, lifting their right hands, pledged their support," wrote one United News observer; "'We are with you!' they shouted as one."[34] They were fascinated by McPherson's authority over her congregants in spite of her legal troubles and rumors of her sexual indiscretions.[35] "While Aimee Semple McPherson is being drawn into a quagmire of public scandal that each day reveals some new sensation," wrote one disbelieving newsperson, "her followers believe her to be a holy Christian martyr."[36]

To explain her followers' attachment to their pastor, reporters used popular (and usually misinterpreted) versions of Freudianism,[37] the rage in the 1920s, to psychoanalyze McPherson's authority. McPherson's critics "talk of psychopathia sexualis. They say that when Aimee on her platform dances and sways from side to side, clapping her hands, chanting, shouting, she is sending forth emotional vibrations that the thousands catch like a contagion to sway and chant and moan and sing with her. They say that the religious orgy is really a sexual orgy."[38] In other words, like Woodworth-Etter who supposedly hypnotized her followers, McPherson could not simply be an authoritative minister. She was a hypersexual being whose "vibrations" infected otherwise sane individuals. She was the sexy leader of a "new cult" with a "career of color."[39]

For all of her supposed sexual indiscretion and legal misconduct, McPherson's case concluded rather anticlimactically.[40] Keyes ultimately decided that he could not produce conclusive evidence of McPherson's guilt, and in 1927 he dropped the charges.[41] McPherson claimed to be satisfied to return to Angelus Temple without a criminal record, but the lack of official vindication was a stain on her reputation.[42]

Reaction to McPherson shows that while sex appeal might have been acceptable for male ministers, it was not for women. Billy Sunday's athletic, virile performances were known to "just border on the questionable and prohibited phases of sex relations," but he was absolved by those who argued that, "these raw, vulgar, nasty suggestions are just what our boys and girls need."[43] McPherson's sensual preaching, however, veered too far from the companionate wifedom she purportedly represented. While Sunday kept his status as a "Reverend," no matter the accusation, McPherson rarely received such an honorific title in the press. In her publications, she referred to herself as the "pastor of Angelus Temple," and her practices there as "pastoral duties."[44] In newspapers, she was categorized instead in exotic terms, such as the "high priestess of the four square gospel," the P.T. Barnum of American Protestantism, the "Prima Donna of Revivalism," "Aimee the Actress," or "the Mary Pickford of revivalism."[45] McPherson was an actress and entertainer, reporters readily admitted, but she was not a minister.

CONCLUSION

In many ways, Woodworth-Etter and McPherson's trials show that the women were celebrity revivalists in every sense of the word. Their scandals were (and are) nothing new in celebrity revivalism. Indeed, many of their male contemporaries were also involved in controversy. A. B. Simpson was accused of misusing congregational funds.[46] Billy Sunday's ministry was riddled with rumors of financial improprieties,[47] and his son's numerous brushes with the law shamed the revivalist.[48] In the same year that McPherson was accused of breaking the law, J. Frank Norris killed an unarmed man in his office and was tried (and was subsequently acquitted) for murder (in addition to arson).[49] None of these scandals dimmed the ministers' popularity or influence. Therefore, in many ways, Woodworth-Etter and McPherson's scandals made them full members of the revivalist celebrity club.

The women's trials show that they did not perform their identities as female ministers so well as to escape punishment for unconventional gender performances. Indeed, the women were penalized much more severely their male colleagues. A. B. Simpson was rumored to have spurious financial practices, but unlike Woodworth-Etter, he was never taken to court. J. Frank Norris' 1926 murder trial had the potential to be more sensational than McPherson's 1926 trial for criminal conspiracy and perjury, but it did not attract a fraction of the media attention McPherson's garnered. Norris, every bit as flamboyant as

McPherson, faced no questions about his credibility as a minister. Nor was his legitimacy as a preacher called into question, despite having taken a man's life.[50]

In addition, the courtroom dramas reveal the double-edged relationship between celebrity and gender performance. As celebrity ministers, Woodworth-Etter and McPherson were able to cross gender lines. For example, men willingly subjected themselves to their ministries in part just to see someone famous in action. Their public scandals proved that celebrity cut both ways. Their status made them famous, but it also made them easier targets and the subjects of great vitriol. The rewards for Woodworth-Etter and McPherson's revivalist ministries were significant: they were adored, followed, and celebrated. Celebrity revivalist ministry was risky too, however, and for female ministers, the punishment for scandal was severe.

CONCLUSION

It has been many years since anyone experienced a Woodworth-Etter or McPherson meeting live. Woodworth-Etter, although just as pivotal in founding the Pentecostal movement as William Seymour or Charles Parham, is virtually unknown outside holiness and Pentecostal historical circles. Although certainly more well known than her predecessor, McPherson's once-luminous star has largely faded into obscurity. In order to conclude a study on their authority, therefore, it is important to evaluate their legacies (or lack thereof) in Pentecostalism.

This project has shown that by employing revivalist methods infused with popular notions of womanhood, and combined with Pentecostal biblical and theological tropes and sensibilities, Woodworth-Etter and McPherson created personas that reconciled the seemingly discordant identities of minister and woman. Woodworth-Etter used the Bible to create a womanly model of leadership that was a celebration of turn-of-the-century motherhood, a reaffirmation of Pentecostal eschatology, and an invitation to lead women and men into the masculine act of war. McPherson created a biblical model of femaleness that allowed her to revel in the romantic aspects of 1920s companionate marriage, put forth a living version of the popular Pentecostal image of a bride of Christ, while at the same time qualified her to minister based on her exemplary intimacy with Jesus. The women manipulated their bodies to create visions of their biblical personas. They utilized revivalist worship spaces to proclaim the message of their womanliness and leadership. Finally, they achieved authority through Pentecostal preaching performance.

Their sizable congregations, enthusiastic followers, and publication circulation testify to the fact that Woodworth-Etter and McPherson evoked love, admiration, respect, devotion, and submission from their followers during their preaching performances. The degree of vitriol leveled at the women compared with their male revivalist counterparts, however, suggests that their efforts to become authoritative ministers were not entirely successful. Therefore, the issue of whether or not they were truly gender transgressive or simply the exceptions that proved a gendered rule remains.

Historians have argued that their legacies show that their gender transgression did not last beyond the women's lives.[1] Many aspects of the events following each woman's death seem to support this position. Woodworth-Etter and McPherson's churches still thrive, but men have led them since their famous founders died.[2] McPherson's L.I.F.E. Bible College (now Life Pacific College) once boasted that three of four ordinations per graduating class were female,[3] but it now ordains about 37 percent women.[4] Few of its female graduates take on senior pastor positions. The Assemblies of God, the largest Pentecostal denomination in America and the one Woodworth-Etter was instrumental in founding, has never had more than 19 percent female ministers.[5]

In addition, although many in Foursquare's institutional leadership sought to uphold McPherson's legacy, it was rumored that some in the denomination she left behind felt her scandals were shortcomings and attributed those shortcomings to all women. Regardless of whether or not the rumor was true, women were absent from upper echelons of leadership in Foursquare until very recently. Tammy Dunahoo, Foursquare's current vice president, is the first woman to hold the office since Roberta Semple Salter left the church in 1937.[6]

Evaluating the women's status as ministers based on their institution's continued ability to empower female leaders, however, would be to hold the women accountable to a standard that they did not seek to uphold. Neither Woodworth-Etter nor McPherson showed significant interest in attaining lasting political power for themselves as women or for women in general. Neither their writings nor their actions suggest that they saw themselves as representatives for their gender or as activists for women. Although Woodworth-Etter's ministry reached its zenith concurrently with the suffrage movement, unlike Congregationalist Antoinette Brown Blackwell or Methodist Anna Howard Shaw,[7] she did not campaign for the right to vote. Unlike Presbyterian Louisa Woosley, who campaigned for female ordination and wrote extensively on the subject,[8] McPherson made no special attempt to promote women's ordination. Gender transgression for all women for all time was Brown Blackwell and Woosley's goal, not McPherson or Woodworth-Etter's.

Yet, at their expressed goals, the women were wildly successful. The women's funerals show that followers embraced them as mother and bride in life and death. At her funeral, Woodworth-Etter's followers remembered her for her authority over her congregation as their mother and as their commander. Her followers had gathered at the Tabernacle and mourned the loss of their spiritual military leader and mother. "A mighty warrior has fallen in the battle," wrote Pastor R. J. Craig. "Would that her mantle [of leadership] might fall on me."[9] "She was called from the battlefield of sin and has got her reward," wrote another of Woodworth-Etter's "praying lieutenants," of her, "Dear Mother Etter."[10] An "anonymous friend" composed a poem commemorating her life and pledging to continue her work: "Oh, Mother, Mother, we'll know you there, for a crown of righteousness you'll wear, And the flowers you planted here below, we will water them and make them grow."[11] "Though her voice is silent," they claimed, "she still speaks."[12]

McPherson's followers mourned her death twice: once in 1926 when they believed she had drowned and again in 1944 when they discovered that she had died from complications most likely related to a "tropical fever" she had contracted in 1943; and her use sedatives, she used as sleep aids. Each time, they mourned the loss of their bride of Christ. She was not their dearly departed mother, but their "Sister," who was a "friend and spiritual partner."[13] Their grief was for their pastor, but also their sibling. Newspapers reported on the "hysterical men and women" who were "wailing and shouting hallelujahs with the energy of fanaticism," while they held vigils for her in 1926.[14]

When she was finally laid to rest in 1944, McPherson's status as a leading lady and bride of Christ was evident in the way her followers mourned. Over 35,000 people came to see her fully made-up, 53-year-old body in state before it was buried with Los Angeles's most famous movie stars in Forest Lawn cemetery. *LIFE* magazine reported that of the over 10,000 people who attended the minister's funeral, 8,000 brought flowers.[15] One devotee made a replica of McPherson's stage chair from orchids and asters.[16] Another made a harp of flowers to accompany the minister in her heavenly musicals.[17] Surrounded by cascades of flowers and dressed in white, McPherson was a bride of Christ to the end. Followers consoled themselves by declaring that McPherson had achieved her goal of union with Jesus. "Then she heard the Master's voice," said one mourner, "'Come up a little higher', and she who had walked in the light of His word went out into the more glorious Light of his presence."[18] "She is rejoicing," said her son Rolf, "with Our Savior."[19]

In addition to authority over and appreciation from their congregations, the women also attained their goal of spreading their brand of Pentecostal revivalism. Woodworth-Etter and McPherson's followers took up their leaders' mission and industriously set out to convert others to the Pentecostal message. The fruit of their labors was expansive. Pentecostal revivalism, the movement that both women helped to found, now has approximately 500 million practitioners.[20] The Assemblies of God now boasts 60 million worshippers, and McPherson's own denomination has nearly 8 million worldwide.[21] For Pentecostal revivalists there could be no greater evidence for the authority of their work than an increase in numbers.[22]

In addition to institutional growth, one of the most telling indicators of McPherson's success over time was the number of her imitators. Woodworth-Etter's desexualized motherly image had limited staying power in celebrity revivalist circles, but McPherson's blend of sexy intimacy with Jesus and her love for harnessing mass media in service to her message resonated with subsequent female revivalists. Several famous 1920s, 1930s, and 1940s women evangelists, such as Rheba Crawford the "Angel of Broadway" and Uldine Utley the "Girl Evangelist," looked to McPherson as a mentor.[23] Young women who attended her Bible college dressed in Foursquare uniforms, styled their hair like McPherson and self-consciously adopted her gestures.[24] Women who graduated from L.I.F.E. preached across the country with methods "a la McPherson."[25] Men and well as women followers preached on her favorite topic: the bride and the bridegroom.[26] Female graduates such as Ione Jefferies, Bessie Bruffet, Alice Parham, Alice LaMar, and Evelyn Thompson, although married, took the lead in their ministries and were the featured pastor in their respective churches.[27] Many lesser-known women followed McPherson's lead, some left their husbands behind, took their children to L.I.F.E. Bible College, and went on to pastor around the country. For example, in 1929 42-year-old Rosa M. Phillippi brought her children to California, received her degree, and was later appointed as a pastor in Hood River, Oregon.[28]

McPherson's influence lingers in celebrity revivalist circles. Kathryn Kuhlman, a popular female televangelist who followed in McPherson's footsteps with a healing ministry and preaching career that spanned the 1940s–1970s, was open about her admiration for McPherson and her desire to imitate her ministry.[29] "No one in the whole world living today appreciates this woman more than [me]," she said during a broadcast dedicated to McPherson's memory.[30] Her flowing, feminine gowns, her soothing, friendly voice, her use of mass media, her lack of sustainable marital relationships, her adoration of Jesus as her life partner, and her massive, adoring audiences show that McPherson's method of ministering had continued relevance in the generation after her death.

Kuhlman was just one of many female celebrity ministers who imitated McPherson's approach. Televangelists like Tammy Faye Bakker and Jan Crouch carried the ultra-feminine brand of female minister with murky sexual histories into the 1970s and 1980s.[31] Bakker and Crouch became famous for their ability to charm television audiences as well as their affinity for cosmetics. The ministers had daily contact with their followers who adored them for their beauty and femininity as much as they loved their message. Similarly, contemporary female ministers like Juanita Bynum and Paula White have had enormous success taking on the role of female ministers with a good dose of sex appeal and very little success in marriage.[32] As was the case with their predecessor, their scandals have not stopped them from cultivating loyal followers.

McPherson's influence is not limited to female revivalists. Famous male ministers such as fellow Californian Robert Schuller, Baptist Billy Graham, (now defrocked) Assemblies of God minister Jimmy Swaggart, and countless others followed in McPherson's media-friendly footsteps. Like McPherson, they combined revivalism with mass media, and enjoyed spectacular results. In many cases, they created equally spectacular scandals. Thus, McPherson's influence was not limited to female revivalists in her generation, and in this way her work transgressed (and continues to transgress) gender boundaries.

In addition to their influence on Pentecostal revivalism, the women's stories provide several insights into the study of gender and revivalism. First, Woodworth-Etter and McPherson's revivalist ministries illustrate the claim that the "misfirings"[33] of ritualized acts create opportunities to resist the norms that they ostensibly uphold.[34] Woodworth-Etter and McPherson performed acts such as the altar call that in typical revivalist services signaled the masculinity of the minister and the femininity of the congregation. But instead of being masculine-feminine exchanges, Woodworth-Etter's altar calls were mother–child encounters, and McPherson's were romantic meetings between the bridegroom and bride. The women's services repeated this typically masculine act, but also changed it slightly to accommodate their womanliness. Therefore, through the ritualized act of revivalist preaching, the women were able to use practices that were typically used to *restrain* women from the institution to *resist* gender and ministerial norms.

Second, Woodworth-Etter and McPherson's stories illuminate how the movement as a whole negotiated race and class during the 1890s–1920s. Iain MacRobert's *The Black Roots and White Racism of Early Pentecostalism in the USA* discusses the racial tensions behind theological divisions in the interracial first generation and increasingly segregated second generation of the movement.[35] Woodworth-Etter and McPherson's story shows that class and racial divisions were facilitated through programming and architectural choices, as well as theological disagreements. McPherson's shift from the "not of this world," rural austere holiness of the Woodworth-Etter tabernacle to the urban, opulent, media-savvy Pentecostal temple was a popular innovation that has been repeated in many revivalist circles. McPherson's partitioned areas for ecstatic expression, programmed services, and distinction between herself and African-American worshippers ushered her church, and the many who imitated her in Pentecostal circles, into the mainstream middleclass of revivalism.

Third, Woodworth-Etter and McPherson's careers demonstrate the power of practice in Pentecostalism. They were credible ministers, in spite of their gender, scandal, and lack of conventional qualifications, in large part because of their ability to *do* Pentecostal revivalism effectively. The minister's gender, even in the masculinized field of revivalist ministry, was subordinate to the ability to perform well.

Fourth, the fact that Woodworth-Etter and McPherson could stretch the boundaries of their womanliness so far and still maintain credibility with their followers shows that gender binaries during this period were not as set as 1890s–1920s Americans or even historians have thought. The historiography of women and public authority in the late nineteenth and early twentieth centuries is typically told with a rise–fall narrative structure. Women made extraordinary gains in the public sphere through improvements in education, healthcare, and suffrage, the narrative goes, only to lose ground as gender roles resolidified during the prosperous Roaring Twenties when women's political prowess gave way to consumerist ideals, and sexuality gave way to sexiness.[36] In other words, women went from political players to household spenders.[37] This fall continued during the Depression era, historians argue, as women were asked to relinquish public authority roles in the wake of an increasingly dire job market.[38]

Students of American revivalism have largely accepted this narrative. Female church leaders, according to many, made strides during the 1890s–1910s alongside female lawyers, doctors, and professors, but, the story goes, they then backslid.[39] Margaret Bendroth's *Fundamentalism and Gender* supports this story by claiming that while the post-Civil War years brought about an "emancipation of women," gender anxieties in fundamentalist revivalism caused the movement to restrict women's leadership roles and masculinize the movement in the 1920s and 1930s.[40] Similarly, Anthea Butler's work argues that in the Progressive era, African-American women in Pentecostalism had significant institutional authority.[41] This authority diminished over time, according to Butler, as the Church of God in Christ (COGIC) reconfigured holiness from a corporate ecclesial goal to a personal one, and as COGIC women moved from the working to middle classes and took on more traditional gender roles.[42]

Woodworth-Etter and McPherson's stories show that at least for some revivalists, this narrative was not applicable in all cases. Woodworth-Etter embodied the holiness ideals (modesty, plainness, etc.) that Butler credited with empowering women in the Church of God in Christ and enjoyed a powerful holiness career. McPherson's larger, more influential, and more mainstream ministry played into many aspects that historians have argued limited women. She was overtly sexy and embodied some of the consumerist ideals bemoaned by scholars of the era. She wore expensive clothes, makeup, and hairstyles. She did not promote feminist ideals like suffrage or the entrance of women into the professions. McPherson was nevertheless powerful. She exchanged one kind of femininity for another, found authority there, and many more followed suit. In the so-called devolvement into sexiness and consumerism, Pentecostal revivalist women like McPherson and her followers found (and continue to find) power to lead. No matter how "instinctively" male the office of the ministry, gender, divorce, single motherhood, and public scandal were no match for Woodworth-Etter and McPherson's co-opted versions of ideal womanhood displayed in ministerial identities through classic revivalist methods.

In addition, Woodworth-Etter and McPherson's stories reveal an emerging hermeneutic that helped to define Pentecostalism. The biblically literate literature of Woodworth-Etter and McPherson demonstrates that the Bible was every bit as important to Pentecostal revivalists as it was to other Protestants of the era. True, the women did not use the Bible in the same manner as their fundamentalist or modernist counterparts, but that did not mean that it was not central to their message. Woodworth-Etter's biblical mother and McPherson's biblical bride was soaked in biblical references.

Woodworth-Etter and McPherson's work with the Bible concerning their authority as female ministers displays an emerging Pentecostal hermeneutic that was an alternative to the fundamentalist-modernist battles raging around them. As self-proclaimed fundamentalists and other sympathetic conservative evangelicals traded barbs with liberal, modernist Protestants in the mainline over historical critical readings of Pauline texts that were read as prohibitive to women ministers,

Woodworth-Etter and McPherson rarely even addressed the texts at the center of these arguments. In addition, they almost never used the same approach to the text.

Their approach was experiential; the women found their stories in biblical archetypes, not through exegesis. It was this biblical hermeneutic and their evolving relationship with the world that contributed to the creation of a distinctly Pentecostal identity. Pentecostals were certainly not mainline; they shared with their revivalist siblings an anti-Catholic aversion to the liturgical traditions of mainliners and shared with their fundamentalist brothers and sisters a fear of the "modernist" methods employed by the emerging liberals therein. They were not quite fundamentalist; Pentecostals were too removed from the academic approach to the scriptures inherent within early fundamentalism to be fundamentalist and the fundamentalists were determined to exclude their ecstatic neighbors from their version of orthodoxy. They were also not exactly holiness; Pentecostals were moving away from the other-wordliness of the holiness movement and toward an active engagement with the world through mass media. By the time McPherson reached her zenith as a celebrity minister, she represented a movement with holiness roots that was slowly leaving them behind. Thus, Woodworth-Etter and McPherson's efforts to create a space for themselves as ministers give insight into how Pentecostals have been (and perhaps will continue to be) distinct from their revivalist counterparts: experience-oriented, but biblically centered. Biblically centered, but not fundamentalist. Interested in holiness codes, but not so much that it would get in the way of communicating through mass media.

Additional questions remain regarding the staying power of performance in Pentecostalism and Pentecostal hermeneutics. How are institutions shaped by performances like those of Woodworth-Etter and McPherson? Are polity and policy an outgrowth of dynamism in the pulpit? In what ways do Woodworth-Etter and McPhersons's approaches to the Bible continue to shape Pentecostal groups? Woodworth-Etter and McPherson's hermeneutics shared in common a lack of engagement with fundamentalist-modernist arguments, but Woodworth-Etter's holiness eschatology and McPherson's divine romance set the stage for differing approaches to the Bible that might explain why some Pentecostal denominations continue to cling to holiness codes while others have long left them behind. These remaining avenues of research show us that even though they are silent, Maria Woodworth-Etter and Aimee Semple McPherson continue to speak.

NOTES

INTRODUCTION

1. "The Malcontent Woman by a Discontent Man," *The Review of Reviews* 11 (1895). The *Review of Reviews* was a collection of journalistic offerings from top magazines in the United Kingdom, Australia, and the United States. The American version was a forerunner to the *Literary Digest* and enjoyed a large circulation in the 1890s–1920s.
2. Ibid.
3. Ibid.
4. Maria B. Woodworth-Etter, *Signs and Wonders God Wrought in the Ministry for Forty Years* (Indianapolis, IN: Mrs. M. B. W. Wetter, 1916), 20.
5. Ibid., 19.
6. Ibid., 20.
7. Ibid., 21.
8. Ibid.
9. M. B. Woodworth-Etter, *Spirit-Filled Sermons* (Indianapolis, IN: Mrs. M. B. Woodworth-Etter, 1921), 8.
10. Maria Beulah Woodworth-Etter, *Marvels and Miracles God Wrought in the Ministry for Forty-Five Years* (Indianapolis, IN: Mrs. M. B. W. Etter, 1922), 6–7.
11. Maria Beulah Woodworth-Etter, *Signs and Wonders* (New Kensington, PA: Whitaker House, 1997), 9.
12. "She Will Be Tried," *St. Louis Post-Dispatch*, September 2, 1890, 4.
13. Wayne Warner, *The Woman Evangelist: The Life and Times of Charismatic Evangelist Maria B. Woodworth-Etter*, vol. 8, Studies in Evangelicalism (Metuchen, NJ: Scarecrow Press, 1986), 136.
14. "An Insane Female Evangelist Declares Herself in Communion with the Blessed Trinity and the Devil," *The Quebec Saturday Budget*, September 1, 1890, 10.
15. The female ministers she did appoint usually shared the pulpit with their husbands was in the case of Thomas and Lyda Paino or Herbert W. Thomas "and Wife." Woodworth-Etter, *Marvels and Miracles*, 402.
16. Ibid., 501.
17. Warner, *The Woman Evangelist*, 159.

18. Aimee Semple McPherson, "The Story of My Life," *The Bridal Call Foursquare* 8, no. 10 (1925): 19.
19. Aimee Semple McPherson, *Aimee: Life Story of Aimee Semple McPherson* (Los Angeles, CA: Foursquare Publications, 1979), 23.
20. Ibid., 24.
21. Ibid.
22. Ibid., 4.
23. Ibid., 70.
24. Ibid.
25. Ibid., 73.
26. Ibid.
27. Aimee Semple McPherson, *This Is That: Personal Experiences, Sermons and Writings of Aimee Semple McPherson* (Los Angeles, CA: Echo Park Evangelistic Association, 1923), 213.
28. Edith Waldvogel Blumhofer, *Aimee Semple McPherson: Everybody's Sister*, Library of Religious Biography (Grand Rapids, MI: W. B. Eerdmans, 1993), 127.
29. Mark Chaves, *Ordaining Women: Culture and Conflict in Religious Organizations* (Cambridge, MA: Harvard University Press, 1997), 187–8.
30. Edith Waldvogel Blumhofer, *Restoring the Faith: The Assemblies of God, Pentecostalism, and American Culture* (Urbana: University of Illinois Press, 1993), 24.
31. Matthew Avery Sutton, *Aimee Semple McPherson and the Resurrection of Christian America* (Cambridge, MA: Harvard University Press, 2007), 41–2.
32. "Aver They Are Cured: One Threw Her Brace Away Holy Rollers Fail to Help Blind Boy," *The Boston Globe*, August 27, 1913; "The Medical Critic and Guide," *Journal of Sociology and Humanity* 28–29 (1930): 12. Male ministers were also accused of quackery during this period, but chapter 6 will argue that the punishment for female faith healers was more severe than for their male counterparts.
33. Charles W. Wendite, "Voodoo Priestess," *Oakland Tribune*, November 30, 1889, in Wayne Warner, *The Woman Evangelist: The Life and Times of Charismatic Evangelist Maria B. Woodworth-Etter* (Metuchen, NJ: Scarecrow Press, 1986), 79; Sutton, *Aimee Semple McPherson and the Resurrection of Christian America*, 31.
34. "Victims of Hypnotism; Religious Frenzy Inspired by an Insane Revivalist," *The New York Times*, September 1, 1890; "Aimee's Sanity Aired in Trial," *The Windsor Daily Star*, October 29, 1937.
35. George H. Beale, "Aimee Bride for Third Time; Weds 250 Pound Preacher," *Modesto News-Herald*, September 14, 1931.
36. McPherson, *Aimee: Life Story of Aimee Semple McPherson*, 238.
37. Frances B. Cogan, *All-American Girl: The Ideal of Real Womanhood in Mid-Nineteenth-Century America* (Athens, GA: University of Georgia Press, 1989), 103.

38. Chaves, *Ordaining Women: Culture and Conflict in Religious Organizations*, 84–129.

39. In contrast, scholarship flourishes in fields dedicated to women, gender, and Protestantism from the Puritan era through the nineteenth century. See, for example, Catherine A. Brekus, *Strangers and Pilgrims: Female Preaching in America, 1740–1845*, Gender and American Culture (Chapel Hill, NC: University of North Carolina Press, 1998); Ruth H. Bloch, *Gender and Morality in Anglo-American Culture, 1650–1800* (Berkeley: University of California Press, 2003); Marilyn J. Westerkamp, *Women and Religion in Early America, 1600–1850: The Puritan and Evangelical Traditions*, Christianity and Society in the Modern World (New York: Routledge, 1999); Carroll Smith-Rosenberg, *Disorderly Conduct: Visions of Gender in Victorian America*, 1st ed. (New York: A.A. Knopf, 1985); Nancy F. Cott, *The Bonds of Womanhood: "Woman's Sphere" In New England, 1780–1835*, 2nd ed. (New Haven, CT: Yale University Press, 1997).

40. Susan Hill Lindley, *You Have Stept out of Your Place: A History of Women and Religion in America*, 1st ed. (Louisville, KY: Westminster John Knox Press, 1996).

41. Margaret Lamberts Bendroth and Virginia Lieson Brereton, *Women and Twentieth-Century Protestantism* (Urbana: University of Illinois Press, 2002).

42. Catherine Wessinger, *Religious Institutions and Women's Leadership: New Roles Inside the Mainstream*, Studies in Comparative Religion (Columbia: University of South Carolina Press, 1996).

43. Chaves, *Ordaining Women: Culture and Conflict in Religious Organizations*.

44. Margaret Lamberts Bendroth, *Fundamentalism and Gender, 1875 to the Present* (New Haven: Yale University Press, 1993), 54–72; Betty A. DeBerg, *Ungodly Women: Gender and the First Wave of American Fundamentalism* (Macon, GA: Mercer University Press, 2000), 75–98.

45. Grant Wacker, *Heaven Below: Early Pentecostals and American Culture* (Cambridge, MA: Harvard University Press, 2001), 158–76.

46. Catherine Wessinger, *Women's Leadership in Marginal Religions: Explorations Outside the Mainstream* (Urbana, IL: University of Illinois Press, 1993), 10.

47. Cynthia Grant Tucker, *Prophetic Sisterhood: Liberal Women Ministers of the Frontier, 1880–1930*, 1st Indiana University Press ed. (Bloomington, IN: Indiana University Press, 2000), 1.

48. See, for example, Chaves, *Ordaining Women*, 1–13; Paula D. Nesbitt, *Feminization of the Clergy in America: Occupational and Organizational Perspectives* (New York: Oxford University Press, 1997), 10–11.

49. Chaves, *Ordaining Women*, 1–13.

50. Ibid.

51. Ibid., 5.
52. Maria Beulah Woodworth-Etter and Roberts Liardon, *Maria Woodworth-Etter: The Complete Collection of Her Life Teachings* (Tulsa, OK: Albury, 2000).
53. Daniel Mark Epstein, *Sister Aimee: the Life of Aimee Semple McPherson* (Orlando: Harcourt Brace and Company, 1993).
54. Blumhofer, *Aimee Semple McPherson*, 1–21.
55. Sutton, *Aimee Semple McPherson*, 212–36.
56. Richard W. Etulain, *Western Lives: A Biographical History of the American West* (Albuquerque, NM: University of New Mexico Press, 2004), 312.
57. Peter Gardella, *Innocent Ecstasy: How Christianity Gave America an Ethic of Sexual Pleasure* (New York: Oxford University Press, 1985), 83.
58. Ibid.
59. Douglas G. Jacobsen, *A Reader in Pentecostal Theology: Voices from the First Generation* (Bloomington: Indiana University Press, 2006), 20.
60. Sutton, *Aimee Semple McPherson*, 37–65.
61. D. W. Bebbington, *The Dominance of Evangelicalism: The Age of Spurgeon and Moody*, A History of Evangelicalism (Downers Grove, IL: InterVarsity Press, 2005), 23; Lynn Bridgers, *The American Religious Experience: A Concise History* (Lanham, MD: Rowman and Littlefield Publishers, 2006), 59; Wacker, *Heaven Below: Early Pentecostals and American Culture*, 26.
62. Woodworth-Etter, *Marvels and Miracles*, 1.
63. Blumhofer, *Aimee Semple McPherson*, 191.
64. See, for example, Michael James McClymond, *Embodying the Spirit: New Perspectives on North American Revivalism* (Baltimore, MD: Johns Hopkins University Press, 2004), 2; William Gerald McLoughlin, *Revivals, Awakenings, and Reform: An Essay on Religion and Social Change in America, 1607–1977*, Chicago History of American Religion (Chicago, IL: University of Chicago Press, 1978), 1. Leigh Eric Schmidt traces the roots of this style of worship to post-Reformation Scotland in Leigh Eric Schmidt, *Holy Fairs: Scotland and the Making of American Revivalism*, 2nd ed. (Grand Rapids, MI: W.B. Eerdmans Publishing, 2001).
65. McClymond, *Embodying the Spirit: New Perspectives on North American Revivalism*, 6.
66. William H. Cooper, *The Great Revivalists in American Religion, 1740–1944: The Careers and Theology of Jonathan Edwards, Charles Finney, Dwight Moody, Billy Sunday and Aimee Semple Mcpherson* (Jefferson, NC: McFarland and Company, 2010), 32; Mark A. Noll, *America's God: From Jonathan Edwards to Abraham Lincoln* (New York: Oxford University Press, 2002), 295.
67. George M. Marsden, *Fundamentalism and American Culture*, 2nd ed. (New York: Oxford University Press, 2006), 11; Edith Waldvogel

Blumhofer and Randall Herbert Balmer, *Modern Christian Revivals* (Urbana: University of Illinois Press, 1993), xi.

68. Randall Herbert Balmer, "Matthews, Mark (Allison)," in *Encyclopedia of Evangelicalism*, ed. Randall Herbert Balmer (Waco, TX: Baylor University Press, 2004), 430; Albert E. Thompson, *The Life of A. B. Simpson* (Brooklyn, NY: The Christian Alliance Publishing Company, 1920), 42.

69. Lyle W. Dorsett, *Billy Sunday and the Redemption of Urban America*, Library of Religious Biography (Grand Rapids, MI: W.B. Eerdmans 1991), 75.

70. William Kostlevy, *Holy Jumpers: Evangelicals and Radicals in Progressive Era America*, Religion in America Series (New York: Oxford University Press, 2010), 18.

71. Richard E. Wentz, *American Religious Traditions: The Shaping of Religion in the United States* (Minneapolis: Fortress, 2003), 201; Thomas A. Robinson and Lanette R. Ruff, *Out of the Mouths of Babes: Girl Evangelists in the Flapper Era* (New York: Oxford University Press, 2011), 100.

72. Robinson and Ruff, 100.

73. Ibid.

74. Henry Trawick, *Modern Revivalism* (Nashville, TN: Barbee and Smith, 1898), 30.

75. Charles Price, "Letters from the Foreign Field," *Golden Grain* 1 (3): 21.

76. See, for example, Allan Anderson, *An Introduction to Pentecostalism: Global Charismatic Christianity* (New York: Cambridge University Press, 2004), 273; Ruth Tucker and Walter L. Liefeld, *Daughters of the Church: Women and Ministry from New Testament Times to the Present* (Grand Rapids, MI: Academie Books, 1987), 359; Glenn C. Altschuler and Jan M. Saltzgaber, *Revivalism, Social Conscience, and Community in the Burned-over District: The Trial of Rhoda Bement* (Ithaca, NY: Cornell University Press, 1983), 76–7.

77. Blumhofer, *Restoring the Faith*, 24.

78. Sutton, *Aimee Semple McPherson and the Resurrection of Christian America*, 12.

79. Margaret M. Poloma and John Clifford Green, *The Assemblies of God: Godly Love and the Revitalization of American Pentecostalism* (New York: New York University Press, 2010), 91, 160; Lisa P. Stephenson, *Dismantling the Dualisms for American Pentecostal Women in Ministry: A Feminist-Pneumatological Approach*, Global Pentecostal and Charismatic Studies (Boston, MA: Brill, 2012), 2; Lawless, "Not So Different a Story after All: Pentecostal Women in the Pulpit," 41; Wacker, *Heaven Below: Early Pentecostals and American Culture*, 158.

80. Stephenson, *Dismantling the Dualisms for American Pentecostal Women in Ministry: A Feminist-Pneumatological Approach*, 2; Lawless, "Not So Different a Story after All: Pentecostal Women in the Pulpit," 41.

81. Cooper, *The Great Revivalists in American Religion*, 172; Phyllis D. Airhart, *Serving the Present Age: Revivalism, Progressivism, and the Methodist Tradition in Canada*, Mcgill-Queen's Studies in the History of Religion (Montreal: McGill-Queen's University Press, 1992), 81.

82. William Bell Riley, *The Perennial Revival; a Plea for Evangelism*, 2nd ed. (Philadelphia, PA: American Baptist Publication Society, 1916), 114.

83. See, for example, Thomas Steven Molnar, *Authority and Its Enemies* (New Brunswick, NJ: Transaction, 1995); Bruce Lincoln, *Authority: Construction and Corrosion* (Chicago, IL: University of Chicago Press, 1994); Yves René Marie Simon, *A General Theory of Authority* (Notre Dame, IN: University of Notre Dame Press, 1980); Richard Sennett, *Authority*, 1st Vintage Books ed. (New York: Vintage Books, 1981); Max Weber, Hans Heinrich Gerth, and C. Wright Mills, *From Max Weber: Essays in Sociology*, Routledge Classics in Sociology (New York: Routledge, 2009).

84. For example, William H. Cooper Jr.'s *The Great Revivalists in American Religion: 1740–1944* refers to "traditional authority of the churches," the authority of the Bible or reason, but does not necessarily give a theoretical definition of the term. See Cooper, *The Great Revivalists in American Religion, 1740–1944: The Careers and Theology of Jonathan Edwards, Charles Finney, Dwight Moody, Billy Sunday and Aimee Semple McPherson*, 46, 167.

85. Anthony T. Kronman, *Max Weber*, Jurists Profiles in Legal Theory (London: E. Arnold, 1983), 43.

86. Ibid., 39.

87. Ibid.

88. C. K. Ansell, "Legitimacy," in *International Encyclopedia of the Social and Behavioral Sciences*, ed. Neil J. Smelser and Paul B. Baltes (New York: Elsevier, 2001), 8705.

89. Ibid.

90. Ibid.

91. Ibid.

92. See, for example, McClymond, *Embodying the Spirit*, 97; Cooper, *The Great Revivalists in American Religion*, 167; Wessinger, *Women's Leadership in Marginal Religions*, 1; Nesbitt, *Feminization of the Clergy in America*, 11–17.

93. See, for example, Ira L. Mandelker, *Religion, Society, and Utopia in Nineteenth-Century America* (Amherst: University of Massachusetts Press, 1984), 19; Westerkamp, *Women and Religion in Early America*, 1; Derek Davis and Barry Hankins, *New Religious Movements and Religious Liberty in America*, 1st ed. (Waco, TX: J.M. Dawson Institute of Church-State Studies: Baylor Univerisity Press, 2002), 93; Eugene V. Gallagher and W. Michael Ashcraft, *Introduction to New and Alternative Religions in America*, 5 vols. (Westport, CT: Greenwood Press, 2006), 192; Anthea D. Butler, *Women in the Church*

of God in Christ: Making a Sanctified World (Chapel Hill: University of North Carolina Press, 2007), 6; Wessinger, *Religious Institutions and Women's Leadership: New Roles Inside the Mainstream*, 5.

94. E. Brooks Holifield, *God's Ambassadors: A History of the Christian Clergy in America*, Pulpit and Pew (Grand Rapids, MI: William B. Eerdmans, 2007), 69; James R. Goff and Grant Wacker, *Portraits of a Generation: Early Pentecostal Leaders* (Fayetteville: University of Arkansas Press, 2002), 400.

95. See Margaret Poloma's influential discussion of Pentecostal revivalist authority in Weberian terms: argaret M. Poloma, *The Assemblies of God at the Crossroads: Charisma and Institutional Dilemmas*, 1st ed. (Knoxville: University of Tennessee Press, 1989). Many subsequent discussions of Pentecostal authority rely heavily on Poloma's analysis; see, for example, Elaine Lawless, "Not So Different a Story after All: Pentecostal Women in the Pulpit," in *Women's Leadership in Marginal Religions: Explorations Outside the Mainstream*, ed. Catherine Wessinger (Urbana: University of Illinois Press, 1993), 41. See also Grant Wacker's discussion of Woodworth-Etter and McPherson's charisma in Wacker, *Heaven Below: Early Pentecostals and American Culture*, 114–15.

96. "Religion: Fosdick," *Time*, October 13, 1924; "'Who Is City's Greatest Preacher?' Here's Pen Picture of Popular One," *New York Tribune*, March 10, 1919.

97. Catherine M. Bell, *Ritual Theory, Ritual Practice* (New York: Oxford University Press, 1992), 216.

98. Amy Hollywood, "Performativity, Citationality, Ritualization," *History of Religions* 42, no. 2 (2002): 101.

99. Hollywood argues that bodily acts are subject to the same slippages and misfirings that Austin and Derrida identify in speech acts in: Ibid., 110.

100. Ibid., 115.

101. McPherson's existing records, preserved by her denomination, are more numerous than those from the non-denominational Woodworth-Etter. In addition, McPherson's ministry utilized more media forms (e.g., film, radio) than did her predecessor.

102. See, for example, Janet Saltzman Chafetz, *Handbook of the Sociology of Gender*, Handbook of Sociology, Social Research (New York: Springer, 2006); James A. Winders, *Gender, Theory, and the Canon* (Madison: University of Wisconsin Press, 1991); Ellen T. Armour and Susan M. St. Ville, *Bodily Citations: Religion and Judith Butler*, Gender, Theory, and Religion (New York: Columbia University Press, 2006); Judith Squires, *Gender in Political Theory* (Malden, MA: Polity Press Blackwell Publishers, 1999); Paula England, *Theory on Gender/Feminism on Theory*, Social Institutions and Social Change (New York: A. de Gruyter, 1993).

103. Daniel Boyarin, "Gender," in *Critical Terms for Religious Studies*, ed. Mark C. Talor (Chicago, IL: University of Chicago Press, 1998), 117.

104. Joan Wallach Scott, *Gender and the Politics of History*, Gender and Culture (New York: Columbia University Press, 1988), 42–4.
105. Richard King, *Orientalism and Religion: Postcolonial Theory, India and 'the Mystic East'* (New York: Routledge, 1999), 13.
106. Judith Butler, *Gender Trouble: Feminism and the Subversion of Identity*, Thinking Gender (New York: Routledge, 1990), xi–xiv.
107. Adapted from Richard King's table on the dichotomies of Enlightenment thought: King, *Orientalism and Religion*, 13.
108. William LaFleur, "Body," in *Critical Terms for Religious Studies*, ed. Mark C. Taylor (Chicago, IL: University of Chicago Press, 1998), 37.

1 "TRULY MANLY": THE IDEAL AMERICAN MINISTER

1. As J. Z. Smith has noted, context is key for any comparative enterprise. Therefore, this chapter begins by providing context for this study of gender and American revivalism. Jonathan Z. Smith, *Drudgery Divine: On the Comparison of Early Christianities and the Religions of Late Antiquity*, Jordan Lectures in Comparative Religion 14 (Chicago: University of Chicago Press, 1990), 17, 25, 33.
2. See Paula Nesbitt's brief outline of the history of the male institution in: Nesbitt, *Feminization of the Clergy in America: Occupational and Organizational Perspectives*, 9–18.
3. For a history of obstacles facing the few American women who "stept out" of their place and into ministerial leadership, see Lindley, *You Have Stept out of Your Place: A History of Women and Religion in America*. For a survey of the obstacles facing female ministers from the biblical era to the twentieth century, see Barbara J. MacHaffie, *Her Story: Women in Christian Tradition*. (Minneapolis, MN: Fortress Press, 2003).
4. Steven J. Diner, *A Very Different Age: Americans of the Progressive Era*, 1st ed. (New York: Hill and Wang, 1998), 5.
5. American first-wave feminism can be traced to the eighteenth-century liberal thought of John Stuart Mill and Harriet Taylor, although it gained traction in American political circles during the abolitionist movement in the mid-nineteenth century. First-wave feminists were defined in large part by their desire for female suffrage (as well as temperance, labor, education, and health care reform) during the years between 1890 and 1920. See James P. Sterba, *Controversies in Feminism*, Studies in Social, Political, and Legal Philosophy (Lanham, MD: Rowman and Littlefield, 2001), 173–6.
6. Barbara Miller Solomon, *In the Company of Educated Women: A History of Women and Higher Education in America* (New Haven, CT: Yale University Press, 1985), 78–93.
7. Robyn Muncy, *Creating a Female Dominion in American Reform, 1890–1935* (New York: Oxford University Press, 1991), xii–xiii.

8. Ibid., xiv; Karen Graves, *Girls' Schooling during the Progressive Era: From Female Scholar to Domesticated Citizen*, Garland Reference Library of Social Science (New York: Garland, 1998), 56–7.

9. Nancy Schrom Dye, "Introduction," in *Gender, Class, Race, and Reform in the Progressive Era*, ed. Noralee Frankel and Nancy Schrom Dye (Lexington, KY: University Press of Kentucky, 1991), 4.

10. Mark Chaves, "External Pressures," in *Ordaining Women*, 38–63.

11. Chaves, *Ordaining Women*, 16.

12. Euphemia Drysdale, "Woman and the Ministry," *The Homiletic Review* 5, no. 83 (1922): 349.

13. Glenn T. Miller, *Piety and Profession: American Protestant Theological Education, 1870–1970* (Grand Rapids, MI: William B. Eerdmans, 2007), 178.

14. Bendroth, *Fundamentalism and Gender*, 73–96.

15. Ibid., 63–72.

16. Ibid., 67–70.

17. H. B. Taylor, "New Testament Restrictions of Women," *Western Recorder* 85, no. 27 (1910): 2.

18. Bendroth, *Fundamentalism and Gender*, 64.

19. Clifford Putney, *Muscular Christianity: Manhood and Sports in Protestant America, 1880–1920* (Cambridge, MA: Harvard University Press, 2001), 81.

20. Ibid., 9–10.

21. Ibid., 43; Janet Forsythe Fishburn, "Walter Rauschenbusch and The 'Woman Movement': A Gender Analysis," in *Gender and the Social Gospel*, ed. Wendy J. Deichmann Edwards and Carolyn De Swarte (Urbana, IL: University of Illinois Press, 2003), 73.

22. Susan Hill Lindley, "Gender and the Social Gospel Novel," in *Gender and the Social Gospel*, ed. Wendy J. Deichmann Edwards and Carolyn De Swarte Gifford (Urbana: University of Illinois Press, 2003), 185–201.

23. Bendroth, *Fundamentalism and Gender*, 27; Gail Bederman, "'The Women Have Had Charge of the Church Work Long Enough': The Men and Religion Forward Movement of 1911–1912 and the Masculinization of Middle-Class Protestantism," *American Quarterly* 41 (1989): 121–2.

24. Wacker, *Heaven Below*, 160–71.

25. A. B. Simpson, *The Holy Spirit* (New York: Christian Alliance Publishing, 1895), 392.

26. Billy Sunday, *Get on the Water Wagon* (William Ashley Sunday, 1915), 14.

27. E. Anthony Rotundo, *American Manhood: Transformations in Masculinity from the Revolution to the Modern Era* (New York: BasicBooks, 1993), 274–9.

28. Newton Marshall Hall, "The Laborer and Her Hire," *The Outlook* 123, no. 4 (1919): 134.

29. William A. Quale, "The Gospel of Mastery," *The Advance* 51, no. 2108 (1906): 424.

30. Rotundo, *American Manhood*, 277.

31. Hall, "The Laborer and Her Hire," 134.

32. Putney, *Muscular Christianity*, 5.

33. Ibid.

34. Gail Bederman, *Manliness and Civilization: A Cultural History of Gender and Race in the United States, 1880–1917*, Women in Culture and Society (Chicago, IL: University of Chicago Press, 1995), 17.

35. Rotundo, *American Manhood*, 254, 268.

36. Martin E. Marty, *Modern American Religion* (Chicago, IL: University of Chicago Press, 1986), 10.

37. The bibliography for this period of American history is lengthy. The following volumes have sustaining interpretive power: Marsden, *Fundamentalism and American Culture*; William R. Hutchison, *The Modernist Impulse in American Protestantism* (Durham: Duke University Press, 1992); Ferenc Morton Szasz, *The Divided Mind of Protestant America, 1880–1930* (Tuscaloosa, AL: University of Alabama Press, 1982); George Cotkin, *Reluctant Modernism: American Thought and Culture, 1880–1900*, Twayne's American Thought and Culture Series (New York: Twayne Publishers, 1992).

38. Bederman, *Manliness and Civilization*, 87.

39. Ibid., 88.

40. Angela Marie Smith, "Monsters in the Bed: Horror-Film Eugenics of Dracula and *Frankenstein*," in *Popular Eugenics: National Efficiency and American Mass Culture in the 1930s*, ed. Susan Currell and Christina Cogdell (Athens: Ohio University Press 2006), 348.

41. "Colleges Must Be Modern," *The New York Times*, June 4, 1909.

42. Rotundo, *American Manhood*, 248.

43. Daniel Eli Burnstein, *Next to Godliness: Confronting Dirt and Despair in Progressive Era New York City* (Urbana: University of Illinois Press, 2006), 1–8.

44. Bethan Benwell, *Masculinity and Men's Lifestyle Magazines*, Sociological Review Monographs (Oxford: Blackwell/Sociological Review, 2003), 65.

45. Ibid.

46. Gaylyn Studlar, *This Mad Masquerade: Stardom and Masculinity in the Jazz Age*, Film and Culture (New York: Columbia University Press, 1996), 13.

47. Benwell, *Masculinity and Men's Lifestyle Magazines*, 65.

48. "Davidson's Life Story Reads Like Fiction," *New York Times*, May 7, 1922.

49. Rotundo, *American Manhood*, 258.

50. Ibid., 248

51. Even after railroads supposedly closed the Western frontier, taming the American West was a chief concern for late-nineteenth- and

early-twentieth-century Americans. Novels recounting the adventures of Western figures like Wyatt Earp and Calamity Jane as well as traveling shows like Buffalo Bill's Wild West Show (1883–1916) piqued interest around the country in taming the "primitive" (albeit closed) frontier. See Susan Kollin, "The Global West: Temporality, Spatial Politics, and Literary Production," in *A Companion to the Literature and Culture of the American West*, ed. Nicolas S. Witschi, *Blackwell Companions to Literature and Culture* (Malden, MA: Wiley-Blackwell, 2011), 523.

52. Rotundo, *American Manhood*, 259.
53. "Roosevelt Boomers Issue Statement," *Reading Eagle*, February 11, 1912.
54. Rotundo, *American Manhood*, 258.
55. Bederman, *Manliness and Civilization*, 91.
56. Rotundo, *American Manhood*, 222–83.
57. Putney, *Muscular Christianity*, 5.
58. Jennifer Smith Maguire, *Fit for Consumption: Sociology and the Business of Fitness* (New York: Routledge, 2008), 36.
59. Anthony Synnott, *Re-Thinking Men: Heroes, Villains and Victims* (Burlington, VT: Ashgate, 2009), 262.
60. Benwell, *Masculinity and Men's Lifestyle Magazines*, 71.
61. Leonard Keene Hirshberg, "'That Tired Feeling' Best Cured by Physical Culture," *Evening Tribune*, September 19, 1917.
62. David R. Roediger, *Working toward Whiteness: How America's Immigrants Became White—the Strange Journey from Ellis Island to the Suburbs* (New York: Basic Books, 2005), 21.
63. "South African Question," *The New York Times*, January 4, 1904; Bederman, *Manliness and Civilization*, 30.
64. Jeanne D. Petit, *The Men and Women We Want: Gender, Race, and the Progressive Era Literacy Test Debate*, Gender and Race in American History (Rochester, NY: University of Rochester Press, 2010), 2, 11.
65. Ibid., 19.
66. Petit, *The Men and Women We Want*, 1; Wendy Kline, *Building a Better Race: Gender, Sexuality, and Eugenics from the Turn of the Century to the Baby Boom* (Berkeley: University of California Press, 2001), 9; Kevin P. Murphy, *Political Manhood: Red Bloods, Mollycoddles, and the Politics of Progressive Era Reform* (New York: Columbia University Press, 2008), 202; Graves, *Girls' Schooling During the Progressive Era*, 48.
67. Kline, *Building a Better Race*, 9.
68. Petit, *The Men and Women We Want*, 4, 39.
69. This project treats whiteness as a social construct. Anglo-Saxons and Western Europeans were the standard for ideal whiteness, but many European Protestants, if they had been in the country long enough and had adopted enough Anglo-Saxon cultural norms (signaled often by anglicizing given names and surnames), had potential to be considered "white," at the turn of the century. In this project, I use "white"

to refer to those Americans of European descent who fit into this category. Roediger, *Working toward Whiteness*, 2–9.

70. Petit, *The Men and Women We Want*, 37.

71. Bederman, *Manliness and Civilization*, 170–215

72. Ibid., 204

73. Ibid., 205.

74. The adjective "red-blooded" came to be associated with all things virile and sexually potent, as well as all things quintessentially American
during the late nineteenth and early twentieth centuries. See Kevin
P. Murphy's discussion of the sexual connotations of the term and its
relationship to Americanness in Murphy, *Political Manhood*, 1–10.

75. Bederman, *Manliness and Civilization*, 170–216; Rotundo, *American
Manhood*, 222–46; Ileen A. DeVault, "'Give the Boys a Trade': Gender
and Job Choice," in *Work Engendered: Toward a New History of
American Labor*, ed. Ava Baron (Ithaca, NY: Cornell University Press,
1991), 191–216.

76. Murphy, *Political Manhood*, 3.

77. "Get Manhood in a Week," *The San Francisco Call*, February 17,
1898; "American Manhood," *The Conservative*, November 1, 1900;
"Political Pot-Pie," *The Seattle Republican*, January 13, 1905; "The
Manhood of Men," *The Evening Missourian*, November 6, 1917;
P. S. Gage, "American 'Boys' Find Manhood in Untamed Wilds as
Members of Forest Conservation Groups," *Christian Science Monitor*,
November 23, 1933; Leonard Merrill, "Millions in Manhood," *Los
Angeles Herald*, June 1, 1905.

78. "Two Fine Specimens of Physical Manhood," *The Deseret News*,
February 13, 1900.

79. Bederman, *Manliness and Civilization*, 16; Varda Burstyn, *The Rites of
Men: Manhood, Politics, and the Culture of Sport* (Toronto: University
of Toronto Press, 1999), 62.

80. Jay Mechling, *On My Honor: Boy Scouts and the Making of American
Youth* (Chicago, IL: University of Chicago Press, 2001), 40.

81. "Our Own Opinion," *Public Opinion: A Comprehensive Summary
of the Press throughout the World on All Important Current Topics* 39
(1905): 523; *Official Proceedings of the Grand Lodge, Free and Accepted
Masons* (Macon, GA: Smith and Watson, 1908).

82. Putney, *Muscular Christianity*, 2. There were those opposed to the
muscular Christianity movement. For example, Christian Church minister Dr. A. F. Moore's article critiquing the new American masculinity
as the "strongest possible exercise of the human will," (See Dr. A. F.
Moore, "Spirituality," *Herald of Gospel Liberty* 103, no. 27–52 (1911)).
Harry Fosdick, although at first a strong proponent of the movement, also rejected it after the Great War. As Putney, Bederman, and
Bendroth demonstrate, these dissenting voices were in the minority.

83. Putney, *Muscular Christianity*, 1.

84. Although Protestants were particularly fond of muscular Christianity, muscular Catholicism also surfaced during this period. See Ibid., 174.

85. Bederman, *Manliness and Civilization*, 17; Rotundo, *American Manhood*, 222–83; Putney, *Muscular Christianity*, 4.

86. Gerald Roberts, *The Strenuous Life: The Cult of Manliness in the Era of Theodore Roosevelt* (East Lansing: Michigan State University Press, 1977), 51; Charles H. Lippy, *Do Real Men Pray?: Images of the Christian Man and Male Spirituality in White Protestant America*, 1st ed. (Knoxville: University of Tennessee Press, 2005), 81.

87. Dr. John Watson, *Church Folks: Being Practical Studies in Congregational Life* (New York: Doubleday, Page, 1900), 166.

88. Putney, *Muscular Christianity: Manhood and Sports in Protestant America, 1880–1920*, 82.

89. Ibid., 82–83.

90. Woodbridge Riley, "Esoteric Cults," *The Saturday Review of Literature* 5, no. 20 (1928).

91. Margaret Bendroth, "Why Women Loved Billy Sunday: Urban Revivalism and Popular Entertainment in Early Twentieth-Century American Culture," *Religion and American Culture: A Journal of Interpretation* 14, no. 2 (2004): 263–4.

92. Charles Reynolds Brown, *The Art of Preaching* (New York: The MacMillan Company, 1922), 158.

93. Harold Pattison, *For the Work of the Ministry: For the Classroom, the Study and the Street* (Philadelphia, PA: American Baptist Publication Society, 1907), 36.

94. Ibid.

95. Arthur Stephen Hoyt, *The Work of Preaching: A Book for the Class-Room and Study* (New York: The Macmillan Company, 1917), 320; Pattison, *For the Work of the Ministry*, 39, 366.

96. Pattison, *For the Work of the Ministry*, 168.

97. James Farrah, "The Work of a Pastor," *Homiletic Review: An International Monthly Magazine of Current Religious Thought, Sermonic Literature and Discussion of Practical Issues* 63 (1912): 202.

98. Bendroth, *Fundamentalism and Gender, 1875 to the Present*, 20–22.

99. "What Do the People of Lewiston and Auburn Think of Sunday and His Boston Campaign," *Lewiston Evening Journal*, November 25, 1916, 5.

100. Frederick M. Barton, *One Hundred Revival Sermons and Outlines* (Cleveland, OH: George H. Doran Company, 1908), 134.

101. Riley, *The Perennial Revival: a Plea for Evangelism*, 103.

102. J. H. MacDonald et al., *The Revival: A Symposium* (Cincinnati, OH: Jennings and Graham, 1905), 38.

103. R. A. Torrey, *Revival Addresses* (Chicago, IL: Fleming H. Revell Company, 1903), 153.

104. R. A. Torrey, *Talks to Men about the Bible and the Christ of the Bible* (New York: F. H. Revell, 1904).

105. Michael S. Kimmel and Amy Aronson, *Men and Masculinities: A Social, Cultural, and Historical Encyclopedia* (Santa Barbara, CA: ABC-CLIO, 2004), 54–55.

106. Bendroth, "Why Women Loved Billy Sunday," 251.

107. "Takes Manhood to Live for Christ, Billy Sunday Says," *Boston Daily Globe*, January 20, 1917, 2.

108. Bishop Thomas Benjamin Neely, *The Minister in the Itinerant System* (New York: Fleming H. Revell Company, 1914), 186.

109. Karin E. Gedge, *Without Benefit of Clergy: Women and the Pastoral Relationship in Nineteenth-Century American Culture*, Religion in America Series (Oxford: Oxford University Press, 2003), 13.

110. Ibid., 198–9.

111. Bederman, *Manliness and Civilization*, 17; Rotundo, *American Manhood*, 222–83; Putney, *Muscular Christianity*, 4. Some male revivalists who toured perpetually like Billy Sunday spent fewer hours doing home visitations, but other prominent revivalists like A. B. Simpson and J. Frank Norris did home visitations regularly.

112. Mrs. Burnett, "Mrs. Burnett Outlines Woman's Sphere," *The New York Times*, September 29, 1907; "Centenary of Trousers Rouses an Ancient Debate," *The New York Times*, January 5, 1913.

113. Bederman, *Manliness and Civilization*, 87.

114. Harriet Abbot, "What the Newest New Woman Is," in *The American New Woman Revisted: A Reader, 1894–1930*, ed. Martha H. Patterson (New Brunswick, NJ: Rutgers University Press, 2008), 222.

115. Graves, *Girls' Schooling during the Progressive Era*, 49.

116. Trisha Franzen, *Spinsters and Lesbians: Independent Womanhood in the United States*, The Cutting Edge (New York: New York University Press, 1996), 48; Stephanie Coontz, *Marriage, a History: From Obedience to Intimacy or How Love Conquered Marriage* (New York: Viking, 2005), 195.

117. "The New Woman: What She Is Saying, Thinking and Doing," *Mansfield Daily Shield*, December 9, 1904.

118. Karen Graves, *Girls' Schooling during the Progressive Era*, 49.

119. Ibid.

120. Carolyn L. Kitch, *The Girl on the Magazine Cover: The Origins of Visual Stereotypes in American Mass Media* (Chapel Hill: University of North Carolina Press, 2001), 24, 113, 117, 188.

121. Kitch identifies several alternative visions of womanhood to the mainstream models in Ibid., 75–100.

122. Sharon Hays, *The Cultural Contradictions of Motherhood* (New Haven, CT: Yale University Press, 1996), 39–54.

123. Ibid.

124. Elizabeth Macfarlane Sloan Chesser, *Woman, Marriage, and Motherhood* (New York: Funk and Wagnalls, 1913), 6.

125. Hays, *The Cultural Contradictions of Motherhood*, 39–54.
126. "Woman's Part in Life as Dr. Adler Sees It," *New York Times*, January 13, 1913, 116; "Urges Occupation for Every Woman," *New York Times*, February 28, 1915; Edward Marshall, "This School Teaches Women How to Be Good Mothers," *New York Times*, June 9, 1912; Dye, "Introduction," 3.
127. Amber E. Kinser, *Motherhood and Feminism*, Seal Studies (Berkeley, CA: Seal Press, 2010), 41.
128. Marshall, "This School Teaches Women How to Be Good Mothers."
129. Sarah Comstock, *Mothercraft* (New York: Hearst's International Library, 1915); *Mothercraft: A Selection of Courses of Lectures on Infant Care Delivered under the Auspices of the National Association for the Prevention of Infant Mortality* (London: National League for Physical Education and Improvement, 1916).
130. Petit, *The Men and Women We Want*, 28.
131. "Woman's Part in Life as Dr. Adler Sees It"; "Urges Occupation for Every Woman"; "Woman and Home," *Washington Reporter*, November 11, 1892.
132. Anna Freelove Betts, *The Mother-Teacher of Religion*, ed. D. G. Downey and G. H. Betts, The Abingdon Religious Education Texts (New York: The Abingdon Press, 1922), 15.
133. Betts, *The Mother-Teacher of Religion*, 4.
134. Mrs. L. E. Corlett, "Educated Motherhood," *The Iowa Year Book of Agriculture* 11 (1910): 690.
135. Sherrie A. Inness, "'It Is Pluck, but—Is It Sense?': Athletic Student Culture in Progressive-Era Girls' College Fiction," in *The Girl's Own: Cultural Histories of the Anglo-American Girl, 1830–1915*, ed. Claudia Nelson and Lynne Vallone (Athens: University of Georgia Press, 1994), 221.
136. By the late nineteenth century, a majority of women were educated in co-educational colleges and universities. Leslie Miller-Bernal and Susan L. Poulson, *Challenged by Coeducation: Women's Colleges since the 1960s*, 1st ed. (Nashville, TN: Vanderbilt University Press, 2006), 3.
137. Inness, "'It Is Pluck, but—Is It Sense?': Athletic Student Culture in Progressive-Era Girls' College Fiction," 221.
138. Edward Marshall, "This School Teaches Women How to Be Good Mothers," *New York Times*, June 9, 1912.
139. Wendy Kline, *Building a Better Race*, 19.
140. Marshall, "This School Teaches Women How to Be Good Mothers"; "Plan Nation-Wide Eugenics Society," *New York Times*, November 16, 1913.
141. Nancy Schrom Dye, "Introduction," in *Gender, Class, Race, and Reform in the Progressive Era*, ed. Noralee Frankel and Nancy Schrom Dye (Lexington: University Press of Kentucky, 1991), 3.
142. Ibid., 3–5.
143. Chesser, *Woman, Marriage, and Motherhood*, 6.

144. Lynne Vallone, "'The True Meaning of Dirt': Putting Good and Bad Girls in Their Place(s)," in *The Girl's Own: Cultural Histories of the Anglo-American Girl, 1830–1915*, ed. Claudia Nelson and Lynne Vallone (Athens: University of Georgia Press, 1994), 259–84.

145. Trisha Franzen, *Spinsters and Lesbians: Independent Womanhood in the United States*, 6.

146. "Is Motherhood Crime," *The Pittsburg Press*, November 14, 1913; Rima D. Apple, *Perfect Motherhood: Science and Childrearing in America* (New Brunswick, NJ: Rutgers University Press, 2006), 47.

147. Hays, *The Cultural Contradictions of Motherhood*, 41; Apple, *Perfect Motherhood: Science and Childrearing in America*, 47–9; "Is Motherhood Crime."

148. Christine Bolt, *The Women's Movements in the United States and Britain from the 1790s to the 1920s* (Amherst: University of Massachusetts Press, 1993), 43; Christina Simmons, *Making Marriage Modern: Women's Sexuality from the Progressive Era to World War II*, Studies in the History of Sexuality (New York: Oxford University Press, 2009), 105–37; Lori J. Kenschaft, *Reinventing Marriage: The Love and Work of Alice Freeman Palmer and George Herbert Palmer*, Women in American History (Urbana: University of Illinois Press, 2005), 1.

149. Simmons, *Making Marriage Modern: Women's Sexuality from the Progressive Era to World War II*, 20, 159; Julia Kirk Blackwelder, *Now Hiring: The Feminization of Work in the United States, 1900–1995*, 1st ed. (College Station: Texas A&M University Press, 1997), 90–1.

150. Kenschaft, *Reinventing Marriage: The Love and Work of Alice Freeman Palmer and George Herbert Palmer*, 8.

151. Ibid., 1.

152. Samuel J. Holmes, *The Trend of the Race: A Study of Present Tendencies in the Biological Development of Civilized Mankind* (New York: Harcourt Brace and Company, 1921), 227.

153. Arthur Crabb, "The Superwoman," *Good Housekeeping*, May 1922, 29.

154. Ibid., 197.

155. Lori Kenschaft traces the celebration of a marriage characterized by intimacy and friendship as far back as ancient Greek mythology. See Kenschaft, *Reinventing Marriage: The Love and Work of Alice Freeman Palmer and George Herbert Palmer*, 8.

156. Ibid., 9.

157. Ibid.

158. Christina Simmons argues that 1920s Americans created a mythical period of sexual repression in the Victorian era and then rebelled against this largely imaginary past with more supposedly liberal sexual mores. This was expressed properly within the confines of the heterosexual marriage relationship. See Christina Simmons, "Modern Sexuality and the Myth of Victorian Repression," in *Passion and Power: Sexuality in History*, ed. Kathy Lee Peiss, Christina Simmons, and Robert A. Padgug (Philadelphia, PA: Temple University Press, 1989), 168–9.

159. Vallone, "'The True Meaning of Dirt': Putting Good and Bad Girls in Their Place(s)," 259.

160. Ibid.

161. Simmons, "Modern Sexuality and the Myth of Victorian Repression," 165.

162. Kathleen Anne McHugh, *American Domesticity: From How-to Manual to Hollywood Melodrama* (New York: Oxford University Press, 1999), 111–18.

163. Simmons, "Modern Sexuality and the Myth of Victorian Repression," 165.

164. See analysis of the pros and cons of flappers in women's college circles in Margaret A. Lowe, *Looking Good: College Women and Body Image, 1875–1930*, Gender Relations in the American Experience (Baltimore, MD: Johns Hopkins University Press, 2003), 113, 121.

165. Angela Schlater, "Flaming Youth: Gender in 1920s Hollywood" (PhD dissertation, Loyola University, 2008), 177.

166. Simmons, *Making Marriage Modern: Women's Sexuality from the Progressive Era to World War II*, 143.

167. Kenschaft, *Reinventing Marriage: The Love and Work of Alice Freeman Palmer and George Herbert Palmer*, 215.

168. Ibid.

169. Kitch, *The Girl on the Magazine Cover: The Origins of Visual Stereotypes in American Mass Media*, 54.

170. Thomas Jackson Woofter, *Studies in Citizenship*, vol. 23 (Athens: University of Georgia School of Education, 1920), 72.

171. Simmons, *Making Marriage Modern: Women's Sexuality from the Progressive Era to World War II*, 219.

172. Mary E. Odem, *Delinquent Daughters: Protecting and Policing Adolescent Female Sexuality in the United States, 1885–1920*, Gender & American Culture (Chapel Hill: University of North Carolina Press, 1995), 52.

173. Ibid., 168–9.

174. Wessinger, *Religious Institutions and Women's Leadership: New Roles inside the Mainstream*, 7–12.

175. Catherine M. Prelinger, *Episcopal Women: Gender, Spirituality, and Commitment in an American Mainline Denomination*, Religion in America Series (New York: Oxford University Press, 1992), 24.

176. Kendal P. Mobley, "The Ecumenical Woman's Missionary Movement: Helen Barrett Montgomery and *the Baptist*, 1920–30," in *Gender and the Social Gospel*, ed. Wendy J. Deichmann Edwards and Carolyn De Swarte Gifford (Urbana: University of Illinois Press, 2003), 167–79.

177. Tomeiko Ashford Carter, *Virginia Broughton: The Life and Writings of a Missionary* (Knoxville: University of Tennessee Press, 2010), xxxvii; Bendroth and Brereton, *Women and Twentieth-Century Protestantism*, 174.

178. Mobley, "The Ecumenical Woman's Missionary Movement: Helen Barrett Montgomery and *the Baptist*, 1920–30."

179. "For More Women Pastors," *St. Joseph News-Press*, August 30, 1923.

180. Estrelda Alexander, *The Women of Azusa Street* (Cleveland, OH: Pilgrim Press, 2005), 164; Butler, *Women in the Church of God in Christ: Making a Sanctified World*, 62.

181. Anna W. Prosser, "Wedding Bells," *Triumphs of Faith* 10, no. 6 (1890).

182. Ibid.

183. Cheryl J. Sanders, "History of Women in the Pentecostal Movement," *Cyberjournal for Pentecostal-Charismatic Research* 2, no. 2 (1997).

184. Diane H. Winston, *Red-Hot and Righteous: The Urban Religion of the Salvation Army* (Cambridge, MA: Harvard University Press, 1999), 151.

185. Edith Waldvogel Blumhofer, "'A Little Child Shall Lead Them': Child Evangelist Uldine Utley," in *The Contentious Triangle: Church, State, and University: A Festschrift in Honor of Professor George Huntston Williams*, ed. George Huntston Williams, Rodney Lawrence Petersen, and Calvin Augustine Pater (Kirksville, MO: Thomas Jefferson University Press, 1999), 315, 317.

186. Wallace D. Best, *Passionately Human, No Less Divine: Religion and Culture in Black Chicago, 1915–1952* (Princeton, NJ: Princeton University Press, 2005), 157–60.

187. Anna Howard Shaw and Elizabeth Garver Jordan, *The Story of a Pioneer*, National American Woman Suffrage Association Collection (New York: Harper and Brothers, 1915), 193.

188. Ibid., 130.

189. Gail Bederman, *Manliness and Civilization*, 17; E. Anthony Rotundo, *American Manhood*, 222–83; Clifford Putney, *Muscular Christianity*, 4.

190. Steven J. Diner, *A Very Different Age: Americans of the Progressive Era*, 177; Bruce A. Kimball, *The "True Professional Ideal" In America: A History* (Cambridge, MA: Blackwell, 1992), 98, 287; Glenn T. Miller, *Piety and Profession: American Protestant Theological Education, 1870–1970* (Grand Rapids, MI: William B. Eerdmans, 2007), 314–39, 81–403. E. Brooks Holifield challenges this narrative of decline, citing historians' tendency to romanticize a nonexistent pious American past as well as simplistic analysis of the kinds of authority wielded by ministers in American society. Holifield argues that in many ways American clergy maintained much of their authority over congregation members even as they relinquished certain areas of their dominion to social scientists and mental health professionals (E. Brooks Holifield, *God's Ambassadors: A History of the Christian Clergy in America*, Pulpit and Pew (Grand Rapids, MI: William B. Eerdmans, 2007), 4.). In this project, I side with scholars on this topic who argue that the loss of jurisdiction to psychology and social science, as well as loss of salary, and public esteem is tantamount to decline.

191. Diner, *A Very Different Age: Americans of the Progressive Era*, 177; Kimball, *The "True Professional Ideal" in America: A History*, 198–300; Nathan O. Hatch, *The Professions in American History* (Notre Dame, IN: University of Notre Dame Press, 1988), 24.

192. Historians provide several possible explanations for the changing status of late-nineteenth- and early-twentieth-century American ministers. Steven K. Green argues that the nineteenth century's gradual "second disestablishment" undermined the authority of historic American religious institutions; Steven K. Green, *The Second Disestablishment: Church and State in Nineteenth-Century America* (New York: Oxford University Press, 2010), 388. Glenn T. Miller and E. Anthony Rotundo blame the changing status, in part, on a profession-wide talent vacuum as the best and brightest chose between more profitable careers in medicine or the law and less prestigious service to the church; Miller, *Piety and Profession: American Protestant Theological Education, 1870–1970*, xxiii; Rotundo, *American Manhood*, 172. Charles Lippy contends that competition from various men's organizations such as fraternal lodges and the Young Men's Christian Association (YMCA) seduced young men away from their ecclesiastical commitments; Charles H. Lippy, *Do Real Men Pray?*, 81. Bruce Kimball points to the marginalization of theological reflection, preference for scientific inquiry, and a corresponding skepticism about religious authority claims as causes for the decline of American clergy; Kimball, *The "True Professional Ideal" in America: A History*, 287.

193. For a chart comparing ministers' salary increases with that of other full-time employees, see table 4.3 in Ibid., 259.

194. Viscount James Bryce, *The American Commonwealth*, vol. 2 (New York: The MacMillan Company, 1910), 777.

195. Miller, *Piety and Profession: American Protestant Theological Education, 1870–1970*, 382.

196. P. R. Hayward and Merle N. English, "What the Depression Is Doing to the Cause of Religious Education," *Religious Education* 27, no. 10 (1932); Sydney E. Ahlstrom, *A Religious History of the American People*, 2nd ed. (New Haven, CT: Yale University Press, 2004), 895; Robert T. Handy, *The American Religious Depression, 1925–1935*, Facet Books. Historical Series 9 (Philadelphia, PA: Fortress Press, 1968).

197. Sydney E. Ahlstrom, *A Religious History of the American People*, 895; P. R. Hayward and Merle N. English, "What the Depression Is Doing to the Cause of Religious Education," *Religious Education* 27, no. 10 (1932).

198. Miller, *Piety and Profession: American Protestant Theological Education, 1870–1970*, 710.

199. Milton O. Nelson, "The Church and the Critic: A Few of the Comments from the Independent Readers on the Article by Dr. Franklin H. Giddings, 'Can the Churches Be Saved?'" *The Independent* 106, no. 3784 (1921): 153.

200. Karin E. Gedge, *Without Benefit of Clergy: Women and the Pastoral Relationship in Nineteenth-Century American Culture*, Religion in America Series (Oxford: Oxford University Press, 2003), 13, 99.

201. Edgar Sheffield Brightman, *Religious Values* (New York: The Abingdon Press, 1925), 83.

202. "New York Letter—By 'Stylus'," *The Christian Advocate* 75, no. 6 (1900): 24.

203. "Ordination of Rev. George Fuller," *The Pacific Unitarian* 10, no. 1 (1901): 230.

204. Charles B. Hershey, "Wiping Off Boundary Lines," *Herald of Gospel Liberty* 102, no. 14 (1910).

2 "Walking Bibles": Narrating Female Pentecostal Ministry

1. Nathan O. Hatch and Mark A. Noll, *The Bible in America: Essays in Cultural History* (New York: Oxford University Press, 1982), 4.

2. Sally K. Gallagher, *Evangelical Identity and Gendered Family Life* (New Brunswick, NJ: Rutgers University Press, 2003), 36.

3. Paula D. Nesbitt, *Feminization of the Clergy in America: Occupational and Organizational Perspectives*, 10.

4. In this monograph I use the King James Version of every text because this was the version used by most revivalists in the 1890s–1920s. American Bible Society, *The Holy Bible, Containing the Old and New Testaments* (New York: American Bible Society, 1901).

5. Nesbitt, *Feminization of the Clergy in America: Occupational and Organizational Perspectives*, 15.

6. Bendroth, *Fundamentalism and Gender, 1875 to the Present*, 35.

7. Ibid., 36–9.

8. Nesbitt, *Feminization of the Clergy in America: Occupational and Organizational Perspectives*, 21.

9. Lois A. Boyd and R. Douglas Brackenridge, *Presbyterian Women in America: Two Centuries of a Quest for Status*, 2nd ed., Contributions to the Study of Religion (Westport, CT: Greenwood Press, 1996), 101; Nesbitt, *Feminization of the Clergy in America: Occupational and Organizational Perspectives*, 21.

10. Louisa M. Woosley, *Shall Woman Preach? Or, the Question Answered* (Caneyville, KY: Cumberland Presbyterian Church, 1891).

11. W. T. Stead, *Life of Mrs. Booth, the Founder of the Salvation Army* (New York: Fleming H. Revell Company, 1900), 92.

12. Betty A. DeBerg, *Ungodly Women: Gender and the First Wave of American Fundamentalism* (Macon, GA: Mercer University Press, 2000), 77.

13. F. Godet, "Women's Share in the Ministry of the Word," *The Contemporary Review* 45 (1884).

14. Juergen Ludwig Neve, "Shall Women Preach in the Congregation? An Exegetical Treatise," *Lutheran Quarterly* 23, no. 3 (1903).

15. Benjamin L. Hartley, *Evangelicals at a Crossroads: Revivalism and Social Reform in Boston, 1860–1910*, 1st ed., Revisiting New England: The New Regionalism (Durham: University of New Hampshire Press, 2011), 119–20.

16. Ibid.

17. W. M. C. Ladd, "George Adam Smith and Others," *The American Friend* 6, no. 42 (1899): 997.

18. Bendroth, *Fundamentalism and Gender, 1875 to the Present*, 36, 40.

19. Priscilla Pope-Levinson, "Revivalism," in *Encyclopedia of Women and Religion in North America*, ed. Rosemary Skinner Keller, Rosemary Radford Ruether, and Marie Cantlon (Bloomington: Indiana University Press, 2006), 422.

20. Ibid.

21. Katherine Caroline Bushnell, *God's Word to Women: One Hundred Bible Studies on Women's Place in the Divine Economy*, 2d ed. (Oakland, CA: K.C. Bushnell, 1930), 231. See also Alma White, *The New Testament Church* (Denver, CO: Pillar of Fire, 1907), 218.

22. See, for example, Carrie Judd Montgomery, "The Fulness of the Spirit," *Triumphs of Faith* 49, no. 9 (1929); Bushnell, *God's Word to Women: One Hundred Bible Studies on Women's Place in the Divine Economy*, 260; Society, *The Holy Bible, Containing the Old and New Testaments*; White, *The New Testament Church*, 223; Henry Eyster Jacobs, *A Summary of the Christian Faith* (Philadelphia, PA: General Council Publication House, 1905), 592.

23. Alma White, *The New Testament Church* (Bound Brook, NJ: The Pentecostal Union, 1912), 223.

24. DeBerg, *Ungodly Women: Gender and the First Wave of American Fundamentalism*, viii–viv.

25. Miller, *Piety and Profession: American Protestant Theological Education, 1870–1970*, 189.

26. Frederick E. Taylor, "The Gospel for This Age," *The Bible Magazine by Bible Teachers Training School* 1, no. 7 (1913): 518.

27. Billy Sunday and William T. Ellis, *"Billy" Sunday, the Man and His Message, with His Own Words Which Have Won Thousands for Christ*, Authorized ed. (Philadelphia, PA: The John C. Winston Company, 1914), 77.

28. Stroh, "Women as Pastors," 25.

29. Kendra Irons, "Madeline Southard (1877–1967) on 'Ecclesial Suffrage'," *Methodist History* 45, no. 1 (2006): 16.

30. Maria Beulah Woodworth-Etter, "Woman's Privilege in the Gospel," in *Marvels and Miracles God Wrought in the Mnistry for Forty-Five Years* (Indianapolis, IN: Mrs. M. B. W. Etter, 1922), 552–61.

31. Maria Beulah Woodworth-Etter, *Marvels and Miracles God Wrought in the Ministry for Forty-Five Years* (Indianapolis, IN: Mrs. M. B. W. Etter, 1922), 13–14.

32. Aimee Semple McPherson, *Aimee: Life Story of Aimee Semple McPherson*, 25–6.

33. Ibid., 27.

34. Aimee Semple McPherson, *This Is That: Personal Experiences, Sermons and Writings of Aimee Semple McPherson* (Los Angeles, CA: Echo Park Evangelistic Association, 1923), 57.

35. Ibid., 102.

36. Maria Beulah Woodworth, *The Life, Work, and Experience of Mariah Beulah Woodworth* (St. Louis, MO: Commercial Printing Company, 1894), 439.

37. Woodworth-Etter, *Marvels and Miracles God Wrought in the Ministry for Forty-Five Years*, 9.

38. Ibid.

39. Woodworth-Etter, *Marvels and Miracles God Wrought in the Ministry for Forty-Five Years*, 7.

40. Ibid.

41. Ibid., 12.

42. Ibid., 13.

43. Ibid.

44. Etter, *Signs and Wonders God Wrought in the Ministry for Forty Years*, 30; Woodworth-Etter, *Marvels and Miracles God Wrought in the Ministry for Forty-Five Years*, 13–14; Maria Beulah Woodworth-Etter, *Life and Testimony of Mrs. M. B. Woodworth-Etter* (Indianapolis, IN: August Feick, 1925), 180–1; Maria Beulah Woodworth-Etter, *Acts of the Holy Ghost* (Dallas, TX: John P. Worley Printing, 1912), 34, 480.

45. Etter, *Signs and Wonders God Wrought in the Ministry for Forty Years*, 212.

46. Woodworth-Etter, *Marvels and Miracles God Wrought in the Ministry for Forty-Five Years*, 101.

47. Ibid.

48. Maria Beulah Woodworth-Etter, *The Life, Work, and Experience of Maria Woodworth, Evangelist, Written by Herself*, 227; Maria Beulah Woodworth-Etter, *Signs and Wonders* (New Kensington, PA: Whitaker House, 1997), 106.

49. Sharon Hays, *The Cultural Contradictions of Motherhood* (New Haven, CT: Yale University Press, 1996), 39–54; Maria Beulah Woodworth-Etter, *Spirit Filled Sermons*, 10.

50. In addition to its mainstream Protestant usage, many different groups used Mother in Israel in the Progressive era. The term appears in Jewish, Latter Day Saint, Christian Science, and Theosophical publications of the period. See, for example, Charles W. Penrose, "Death of Mrs. E. H. Cannon," *Deseret News Weekly*, February 1882; Wilford Woodruff, "Talks to the Sisters," *Deseret News*, February 24, 1894; Hugh Ireland, "Mother," *Liahona The Elders' Journal* 14, no. 1 (1916); Hjalmar Hjorth Boyesen, "A Mother in Israel," *New Era Illustrated Magazine*, July 1905; I. M. Haldeman, *Christian Science in the Light*

of Holy Scripture (New York: F. H. Revell Company, 1909); Nurho de Manhar, "The Sepher Ha-Zohar or Book of Light," *The Word* 7, no. 1 (1907).

51. Emily Oliver Gibbes, *The Origin of Sin, and Dotted Words in the Hebrew Bible* (New York: C.T. Dillingham, 1893), 300–1.

52. "A Mother in Israel," *Baltimore Sun*, October 19, 1909.

53. William Mackintosh Mackay, *The Woman of Tact, and Other Bible Types of Modern Women* (New York: Hodder and Stoughton, 1912), 79–80.

54. Ibid.

55. G. Selikowitsch, "Flats and Sharps," *The Advocate: America's Jewish Journal* 37, no. 1 (1909): 15.

56. W. M. Flinders Petrie, *Egypt and Israel* (New York: Society for Promoting Christian Knowlegde; E. S. Gorham, etc., 1911), 26.

57. Ibid.

58. "Miss Couzins on Law and Women," *The New York Times*, March 27, 1894.

59. J. Glentworth Butler, *The Bible-Work* (New York: The Butler Bible-Work Company, 1892), 191.

60. Joseph Barber Lightfoot, *Leaders in the Northern Church: Sermons Preached in the Diocesse of Durham* (New York: Macmillan, 1890), 59.

61. Grace Aguilar, *The Women of Israel* (New York: D. Appleton and Company, 1888), 210.

62. William Pringle Livingston, *Mary Slessor of Calabar* (New York: Hodder and Stoughton, 1916), 170.

63. Aguilar, *The Women of Israel*, 212.

64. Frank K. Sims, "A Model Mother and a Father Who Failed," *Expositor and Current Anecdotes* 11, no. 1 (1909): 507; Dinsdale T. Young, *The Crimson Book* (New York: A. C. Armstrong and Son, 1903), 283.

65. Maria Beulah Woodworth-Etter, *Trials and Triumphs of the Evangelist Mrs. M. B. Woodworth Written by Herself* (St. Louis, MO: Mrs. M. B. Woodworth, 1885), 50.

66. Ibid.

67. Woodworth-Etter, *Signs and Wonders*, 15.

68. Woodworth-Etter, *The Life, Work, and Experience of Maria Woodworth, Evangelist, Written by Herself*, 227; Woodworth-Etter, *Signs and Wonders*, 106.

69. Woodworth, *The Life, Work, and Experience of Mariah Beulah Woodworth*, 308.

70. Woodworth-Etter, *Marvels and Miracles God Wrought in the Ministry for Forty-Five Years*, 113.

71. Woodworth-Etter, *Acts of the Holy Ghost*, 12.

72. Ibid., 538.

73. Woodworth-Etter, *Marvels and Miracles God Wrought in the Ministry for Forty-Five Years*, 568.

74. Woodworth-Etter, *The Life, Work, and Experience of Maria Woodworth, Evangelist, Written by Herself*, 164.

75. Ibid., 581.
76. Woodworth-Etter, *Marvels and Miracles God Wrought in the Ministry for Forty-Five Years*, 164.
77. Woodworth-Etter, *Signs and Wonders God Wrought in the Ministry for Forty Years*, 212.
78. Woodworth-Etter, *Marvels and Miracles God Wrought in the Ministry for Forty-Five Years*, iii.
79. Woodworth-Etter, *The Life, Work, and Experience of Maria Woodworth, Evangelist, Written by Herself*, 164.
80. Woodworth-Etter, *Signs and Wonders God Wrought in the Ministry for Forty Years*, 28.
81. Woodworth-Etter, *Trials and Triumphs of the Evangelist Mrs. M. B. Woodworth Written by Herself*, 148.
82. Woodworth, *The Life, Work, and Experience of Mariah Beulah Woodworth*, 36.
83. Woodworth-Etter, *Trials and Triumphs of the Evangelist Mrs. M. B. Woodworth Written by Herself*, 175.
84. Woodworth, *The Life, Work, and Experience of Mariah Beulah Woodworth*, 325.
85. Woodworth-Etter, *Signs and Wonders*, 235; Woodworth, *The Life, Work, and Experience of Mariah Beulah Woodworth*, 125.
86. Woodworth-Etter, *Trials and Triumphs of the Evangelist Mrs. M. B. Woodworth Written by Herself*, 152.
87. Maria Beulah Woodworth-Etter, *Holy Ghost Sermons by Mrs. M. B. Woodworth-Etter* (Indianapolis, IN: Mrs. M. B. Woodworth-Etter, 1918), 66.
88. Woodworth, *The Life, Work, and Experience of Mariah Beulah Woodworth*, 30, 42, 49; Woodworth-Etter, *Acts of the Holy Ghost*, 37.
89. Warner, *The Woman Evangelist: The Life and Times of Charismatic Evangelist Maria B. Woodworth-Etter*, 86.
90. Woodworth-Etter, *Acts of the Holy Ghost*, 32.
91. Woodworth-Etter, *Life and Testimony of Mrs. M. B. Woodworth-Etter*, 12.
92. Woodworth-Etter, *Signs and Wonders God Wrought in the Ministry for Forty Years*, 310.
93. Woodworth-Etter, *Holy Ghost Sermons by Mrs. M. B. Woodworth-Etter*, 124.
94. Woodworth-Etter, *Acts of the Holy Ghost*, 339.
95. Ibid.
96. Etter assisted his wife by writing many of her personal correspondences.
97. Woodworth-Etter, *Acts of the Holy Ghost*, 339.
98. Woodworth-Etter, *Signs and Wonders God Wrought in the Ministry for Forty Years*, 138.
99. Warner, *The Woman Evangelist: The Life and Times of Charismatic Evangelist Maria B. Woodworth-Etter*, 88, 233, 39.

100. Woodworth-Etter, *Marvels and Miracles God Wrought in the Ministry for Forty-Five Years*, 102–3.

101. Woodworth-Etter, *Signs and Wonders God Wrought in the Ministry for Forty Years*, 323.

102. A. B. Simpson, *Wholly Sanctified*, On Cover: The Alliance Colportage Series (New York: Christian Alliance Publishing, 1890), 7.

103. A. B. Simpson, *A Larger Christian Life* (New York: Christian Alliance Publishing, 1889), 89.

104. William Kostlevy, *Holy Jumpers: Evangelicals and Radicals in Progressive Era America*, 21.

105. Aimee Semple McPherson, *Aimee: Life Story of Aimee Semple McPherson*, 23.

106. Ibid., 23.

107. Ibid., 32.

108. Ibid., 34.

109. Ibid., 70.

110. Aimee Semple McPherson, "The Temple of the Word: Dome of Revelations," *The Bridal Call Foursquare* 11, no. 3 (1927): 15.

111. Ibid., 8–10.

112. Ibid., 11.

113. Aimee Semple McPherson, "The Temple of the Word: Dome of Revelations," *The Bridal Call Foursquare* 11, no. 3 (1927): 11.

114. Aimee Semple McPherson, "The Story of My Life," *The Bridal Call Foursquare* 8, no. 10 (1925): 18.

115. Aimee Semple McPherson, "The Vacant Chair," *The Bridal Call Foursquare* 8, no. 10 (1925): 14.

116. Aimee Semple McPherson, "They Have Taken My Lord Away," *The Bridal Call Foursquare* 12, no. 4 (1928).

117. Aimee Semple McPherson, "They Have Taken My Lord Away," *The Bridal Call Foursquare* 12, no. 4 (1928).

118. Ibid.

119. McPherson, *Aimee: Life Story of Aimee Semple McPherson*, 76.

120. Aimee Semple McPherson, "Drops from Ye Editorial Brow," *The Bridal Call Foursquare* 15, no. 5 (1931): 2.

121. McPherson, "The Temple of the Word: Dome of Revelations," 11.

122. Ibid.

123. McPherson, "The Temple of the Word: Dome of Revelations," 11.

124. Ibid.

125. Schlater, "Flaming Youth: Gender in 1920s Hollywood," 106.

126. Joanne J. Meyerowitz, *Women Adrift: Independent Wage Earners in Chicago, 1880–1930*, Women in Culture and Society (Chicago, IL: University of Chicago Press, 1988), 129; Schlater, "Flaming Youth: Gender in 1920s Hollywood," 106.

127. Richard Dyer MacCann, *Films of the 1920s*, American Movies (Lanham, MD: Scarecrow Press, 1996), 44.

128. Aimee Semple McPherson, "When Is He Coming," *The Bridal Call* 4, no. 6 (1920): 2; Aimee Semple McPherson, "The Holy Spirit: Who Is He and Why to Receive Him?," *The Bridal Call* 4, no. 6 (1920); Aimee Semple McPherson, "As a Bride Adorned: Glowing Sermon on the Glorious Second Coming of Christ," *The Bridal Call* 9, no. 9 (1926): 14.

129. McPherson, "When Is He Coming."

130. McPherson, "As a Bride Adorned: Glowing Sermon on the Glorious Second Coming of Christ," 13.

131. Aimee Semple McPherson, "As a Bride Adorned: Glowing Sermon on the Glorious Second Coming of Christ," 13.

132. Aimee Semple McPherson, "Four Mountain Peaks of Glory from the Book of Ruth," *The Bridal Call* 6, no. 5 (1922): 8.

133. Ibid; McPherson, "They Have Taken My Lord Away."

134. Aimee Semple McPherson, "The Foursquare Gospel," *The Bridal Call Foursquare* 2, no. 2 (1929): 4.

135. See, for example, "Evangelist to End Services Tomorrow," *The Owosso Argus-Press*, March 22, 1930, 145; J. Pressler Barrett, "Brethren, Can This Be Possible?," *The Herald of Gospel Liberty* 110, no. 48 (1918); J. Corson Miller, "A Bride of Christ," *Catholic World* 112, no. 667 (1920); Elizabeth Randolph, "Young People's Work," *The Sabbath Recorder* 89, no. 1 (1920); Church of God (Cleveland), *The Book of Doctrines: Issued in the Interest of the Church of God* (Cleveland, TN: Church of God Publishing House, 1922), 145; Keith L. Brooks, *Sermon Illustrations of the Bible, Topically Arranged* (Los Angeles: Bible Institute of Los Angeles, 1920), 14; Clarence Larkin, *Rightly Dividing the Word* (Philadelphia, PA: Fox Chase, 1921), 47; James Moore Hickson, *The Healing of Christ in His Church* (New York: E. S. Gorham, 1919), 43; Jonathan Ritchie Smith, *The Wall and the Gates* (Philadelphia, PA: The Westminster Press, 1919), 186; Alanson Wilcox, *A History of the Disciples of Christ* (Cincinnati, OH: The Standard Publishing Company, 1918), 140.

136. Harold L. Lundquist, "Sunday School Lesson," *Farmer's Advocate*, February 4, 1938.

137. "Large Audience Hears Evangelist on Lord's Return," *The Evening Independent*, December 5, 1928.

138. Douglas G. Jacobsen, *Thinking in the Spirit: Theologies of the Early Pentecostal Movement* (Bloomington: Indiana University Press, 2003), 102–3.

139. A. T. Lange, "The Glory That Excelleth," *Triumphs of Faith* 29, no. 11 (1909): 255.

140. William Seymour, "Behold the Bridegroom Cometh," *The Apostolic Faith* 1, no. 5 (1907): 2.

141. William Seymour, "The Holy Ghost and His Bride," in *The Azusa Street Revival* (Shippensburg, PA: Destiny Image Publishers, 2006): 129.

142. George Floyd Taylor, *The Spirit and the Bride: A Scriptural Presentation of the Operations, Manifestations, Gifts and Fruit of the Holy Spirit in His Relation to the Bride with Special Reference to The "Latter Rain" Revival* (Dunn, NC, 1907).

143. G. T. Haywood, "Baptized into the Body" (Christian Outlook: Pentecostal Assemblies of the World, circa 1925).

144. Seymour, "The Holy Ghost and His Bride," 129.

145. McPherson, "As a Bride Adorned: Glowing Sermon on the Glorious Second Coming of Christ," 14.

146. In many ways, McPherson's erotic treatment of the relationship between the bridegroom and the bride of Christ resembled Medieval interpretations of the figure. See Dyan Elliott, "The Eroticized Bride of Hagiography," in *The Bride of Christ Goes to Hell: Metaphor and Embodiment in the Lives of Pious Women, 200–1500, The Middle Ages Series* (Philadelphia, PA: University of Philadelphia Press, 2012), 174–233.

147. Aimee Semple McPherson, "The Song of Songs: An Exposition of the Song of Solomon by Aimee Semple McPherson," *The Bridal Call Foursquare* 8, no. 7 (1929): 13.

148. McPherson, *This Is That: Personal Experiences, Sermons and Writings of Aimee Semple McPherson*, 653–5.

149. Ibid.

150. Ibid.

151. Aimee Semple McPherson, "The Song of Songs: An Exposition of the Song of Solomon by Aimee Semple McPherson," 13.

152. Aimee Semple McPherson, *Aimee: Life Story of Aimee Semple McPherson*, 101.

153. Aimee Semple McPherson, *This Is That*, 653–5.

154. Aimee Semple McPherson, "The Holy Spirit in Old Testament Types and Shadows," *The Bridal Call Foursquare* 11, no. 2 (1927): 30.

155. Ibid., 30

156. McPherson, *Aimee: Life Story of Aimee Semple McPherson*, 112.

157. Aimee Semple McPherson, "This Is That," *The Bridal Call* 2, no. 11 (1920): 1.

158. Aimee Semple McPherson, *This Is That: Personal Experiences, Sermons, Writings of Aimee Semple McPherson* (Los Angeles: Foursquare Publications, 1979): 251–252.

159. Aimee Semple McPherson, "Lost and Restored: Or the Dispensation of the Holy Spirit from the Ascension of the Lord Jesus to His Coming Descension," *The Bridal Call* 1, no. 2 (1918): 1.

160. Ibid.

161. Aimee Semple McPherson, "God's David," *The Bridal Call* 8, no. 1 (1924): 27.

162. McPherson, *Aimee: Life Story of Aimee Semple McPherson*, 211.

163. Ibid., 157.

164. Ibid., 221.

165. Aimee Semple McPherson, "Rebekah at the Well," *The Bridal Call Foursquare* 15, no. 5 (1926): 9.
166. Aimee Semple McPherson, "The Story of My Life," *The Bridal Call* 8, no. 10 (1925).
167. Ibid.
168. McPherson, *Aimee: Life Story of Aimee Semple McPherson*, 238–9.
169. Blumhofer, *Aimee Semple McPherson: Everybody's Sister*, 368–9.
170. Ibid., 374.
171. See, for example, Aimee Semple McPherson, "My Journeylog," *The Bridal Call Foursquare* 10, no. 2 (1926): 18; Aimee Semple McPherson, "There Was an Old Woman Who Lived in a Shoe," *The Bridal Call Foursquare* 12, no. 6 (1928): 25; Aimee Semple McPherson, "The British Isles Call Sister," *The Bridal Call Foursquare* 12, no. 7 (1928): 30.
172. McPhersons listed her parenting duties alongside other business and, unlike Woodworth-Etter, she did not write about her responsibility to them as a part of her calling to ministry. See, for example, the following discussion of her ministry chores: "There were all the diplomas to be signed; two payrolls to get out for the workmen, missionaries, Temple and field staffs; the pay roll to keep this great work moving is between five and seven thousand dollars per month. Teachers, stenographers, artists, writers, musicians, announcers for radio, janitors, office force, printers, editorial staff, and a host of others are needed for wheels to carry the work along. There was unfinished business to complete; my own darling Roberta and Rolf to plan and care for. There was teaching in the big school and the closing of school for the holidays, and the plans for the immediate opening of the Summer School...." in Aimee Semple McPherson, "Drops from Ye Editorial Brow," *The Bridal Call Foursquare* 12, no. 7 (1928): 3; Aimee Semple McPherson, "The Story of My Life: The Story So Far," *The Bridal Call Foursquare* 9, no. 8 (1926): 21.
173. Aimee Semple McPherson, "Roberta Star Semple," *The Bridal Call Foursquare* 12, no. 4 (1928): 10.

3 "PANTS DON'T MAKE PREACHERS": THE IMAGE OF A FEMALE PENTECOSTAL MINISTER

1. William LaFleur, "Body," in *Critical Terms for Religious Studies*, 37.
2. David Morgan and Sally M. Promey, "Introduction," in *The Visual Culture of American Religions*, ed. David Morgan and Sally M. Promey (Berkeley, CA: University of California Press, 2001), 12.
3. Ibid., 1–26.
4. LaFleur, "Body," 37.
5. Ibid., 38.
6. Ibid.

7. Ibid.

8. Ibid., 37.

9. In this project, no subject is a proponent of the unmodified body (strictly defined), because every person wore clothing. This chapter argues that Woodworth-Etter believed that the body should be modified as little as possible in contrast to McPherson who modified her appearance freely for the sake of communicating her message.

10. Barnard, "One Picture Is Worth a Thousand Words."

11. Kitch, *The Girl on the Magazine Cover: The Origins of Visual Stereotypes in American Mass Media*, 17.

12. Karen Sternheimer, *Celebrity Culture and the American Dream: Stardom and Social Mobility* (New York: Routledge, 2011), 2–3.

13. Kitch, *The Girl on the Magazine Cover: The Origins of Visual Stereotypes in American Mass Media*, 17.

14. "Pulpit Sex Given Blow," *Los Angeles Times*, January 8, 1936.

15. Kelly J. Baker, "Religious Dress," in *Material Culture in America*, ed. Helen Sheumaker and Shirley Teresa Wajda (Santa Barbara, CA: ABC-CLIO, 2008), 388.

16. Ibid.

17. Ibid.

18. Kitch, *The Girl on the Magazine Cover: The Origins of Visual Stereotypes in American Mass Media*, 11.

19. Gayle V. Fischer, *Pantaloons and Power: Nineteenth-Century Dress Reform in the United States* (Kent, OH: Kent State University Press, 2001), 22.

20. Miller, *Piety and Profession: American Protestant Theological Education, 1870–1970*, 385; Diner, *A Very Different Age: Americans of the Progressive Era*, 165; Fischer, *Pantaloons and Power: Nineteenth-Century Dress Reform in the United States*, 22.

21. Jacob Fry, *The Pastor's Guide: Or, Rules and Notes in Pastoral Theology* (Philadelphia, PA: General Council Publication House, 1915), 73.

22. J. B. A., "A Commercial Traveler's Plea for a Better-Salaried Clergy," *The Fortnightly Review* 24, no. 1 (1917): 274.

23. William E. Barton, "What Laymen Wish Ministers Knew," *The Expositor* 8, no. 3 (1906).

24. Ibid; George Henry Gerberding, *The Lutheran Pastor* (Philadelphia, PA: Lutheran Publication Society, 1902), 153; Fry, *The Pastor's Guide: Or, Rules and Notes in Pastoral Theology*, 73; A., "A Commercial Traveler's Plea for a Better-Salaried Clergy," 274; Herman Joseph Heuser, *The American Ecclesiastical Review: A Monthly Publication for the Clergy* 83 (1930): 139; C. Abbetmeyer, "Some Externals of Worship," *Homiletic Magazine* 42, no. 1 (1918): 45; "The American Lutheran," *The American Lutheran* 11–12, no. 1 (1928): 622; A. W. Pegues, "The Necessity of a Trained Ministry," in *The United Negro: His Problems and His Progress*, ed. Irvine Garland Penn and John Wesley Edward Bowen (Atlanta, GA: D. E. Luther Publishing, 1902),

120; Albert Josiah Lyman, *The Christian Pastor in the New Age* (New York: Thomas Y. Crowell, 1909), 118.

25. Albert E. Thompson, *The Life of A. B. Simpson*, 1, 237.

26. Ibid., 272.

27. Elijah Brown, *The Real Billy Sunday: The Life and Work of Rev. William Ashley Sunday, D.D., the Baseball Evangelist* (New York: Fleming H. Revell Company, 1914), 227.

28. Seth Dowland, "Defending Manhood: Gender, Social Order and the Rise of the Christian Right in the South" (Dissertation, Duke University, 2007), 7.

29. Lee Grieveson, Esther Sonnet, and Peter Stanfield, *Mob Culture: Hidden Histories of the American Gangster Film* (New Brunswick, NJ: Rutgers University Press, 2005), 167.

30. Kitch, *The Girl on the Magazine Cover: The Origins of Visual Stereotypes in American Mass Media*, 12–16.

31. Ibid.

32. Kristina Harris, "Introduction," in *Turn-of-the-Century Fashion Patterns and Tailoring Techniques* (New York: Dover Publications, 2000), iv.

33. Fischer, *Pantaloons and Power: Nineteenth-Century Dress Reform in the United States*, 176.

34. Ibid., 3.

35. Fred Lohmann, "God Visiting San Antonio with Mighty Power," *Word and Witness*, February 20, 1913.

36. "Visions in Trances," *Warsaw Daily Times*, May 18, 1885.

37. "Took Her Child to See Christ, She Tells Judge," *Topeka Daily Capital*, August 13, 1915, in *Maria Woodworth-Etter: The Complete Collection of Her Life Teachings*, ed. Roberts Liardon (Tulsa, OK: Albury, 2000).

38. Martha H. Patterson, *Beyond the Gibson Girl: Reimagining the American New Woman, 1895–1915* (Urbana: University of Illinois Press, 2005), 43–4.

39. Sherrie A. Inness, *Intimate Communities: Representation and Social Transformation in Women's College Fiction, 1895–1910* (Bowling Green, OH: Bowling Green State University Popular Press, 1995), 100.

40. Ibid.

41. Kitch, *The Girl on the Magazine Cover: The Origins of Visual Stereotypes in American Mass Media*, 133.

42. John E. Main, *The Booze Route; a Reform Book* (Los Angeles: Commercial Printing House, 1907), 154.

43. "Said to Be Religion: Strange Scenes At "Revival Meetings" Held in Indiana," *New York Times*, January 23, 1885; "Visions in Trances."

44. "Aver They Are Cured: One Threw Her Brace Away Holy Rollers Fail to Help Blind Boy"; "Minors Take Part in Holy-Roller Services," *The Topeka Daily Capitol*, August 29, 1913, in *Maria Woodworth-Etter: The Complete Collection of Her Life Teachings*, ed. Roberts Liardon (Tulsa, OK: Albury, 2000).

45. "Visions in Trances."
46. Butler, *Women in the Church of God in Christ: Making a Sanctified World*, 80–1; Vinson Synan, *The Holiness-Pentecostal Tradition: Charismatic Movements in the Twentieth Century*, 2nd ed. (Grand Rapids, MI: W.B. Eerdmans Publishing Company, 1997), 34–5.
47. Main, *The Booze Route; a Reform Book*, 154.
48. Susie Cunningham Stanley, *Holy Boldness: Women Preachers' Autobiographies and the Sanctified Self*, 1st ed. (Knoxville: University of Tennessee Press, 2002), 82–5.
49. Butler, *Women in the Church of God in Christ: Making a Sanctified World*, 69–71. See also Percy Given, "Deets Pacific Bible College," *Nazarene Messenger* 12, no. 1 (1907).
50. Main, *The Booze Route; a Reform Book*, 154.
51. Charles Brougher Jernigan, *Pioneer Days of the Holiness Movement in the Southwest* (Kansas City, MO: Pentecostal Nazarene Publishing House, 1919), 7–8.
52. Stanley, *Holy Boldness: Women Preachers' Autobiographies and the Sanctified Self*, 82–5.
53. Anthea D. Butler, *Women in the Church of God in Christ: Making a Sanctified World*, 79.
54. Woodworth-Etter, *Marvels and Miracles God Wrought in the Ministry for Forty-Five Years*, 558.
55. Woodworth-Etter, *Trials and Triumphs of the Evangelist Mrs. M. B. Woodworth Written by Herself*, 110.
56. Woodworth-Etter, *Acts of the Holy Ghost*, 243.
57. Woodworth-Etter, *Signs and Wonders*, 129.
58. Ibid., 537; Woodworth-Etter, *Marvels and Miracles God Wrought in the Ministry for Forty-Five Years*, 49.
59. Burnstein, *Next to Godliness: Confronting Dirt and Despair in Progressive Era New York City*, 4.
60. Woodworth-Etter, *Marvels and Miracles God Wrought in the Ministry for Forty-Five Years*.
61. Woodworth-Etter, *Signs and Wonders*, 116.
62. Putney, *Muscular Christianity: Manhood and Sports in Protestant America, 1880–1920*, 82, 83.
63. "Aimee McPherson Starts Battle with Voliva for Souls," *The Deseret News*, September 6, 1929, 1.
64. "Dedication to the Memory of Aimee Semple McPherson," in *I Believe in Miracles, Vol. 5* (USA 1973).
65. Ibid.
66. Janet Lee, *War Girls: The First Aid Nursing Yeomanry in the First World War* (New York: Manchester University Press 2005), 80.
67. Jonathan H. Ebel, *Faith in the Fight: Religion and the American Soldier in the Great War* (Princeton, NJ: Princeton University Press, 2010), 141–3.

68. Kitch, *The Girl on the Magazine Cover: The Origins of Visual Stereotypes in American Mass Media*, 121–81; Lee, *War Girls: The First Aid Nursing Yeomanry in the First World War*, 64.

69. Kitch, *The Girl on the Magazine Cover: The Origins of Visual Stereotypes in American Mass Media*, 122.

70. Ibid., 136–59.

71. Ibid., 164.

72. Kitch, *The Girl on the Magazine Cover: The Origins of Visual Stereotypes in American Mass Media*, 121.

73. DeBerg, *Ungodly Women: Gender and the First Wave of American Fundamentalism*, 99–118; Robert Moats Miller, *Harry Emerson Fosdick: Preacher, Pastor, Prophet* (New York: Oxford University Press, 1985), 425–8.

74. Robinson and Ruff, *Out of the Mouths of Babes: Girl Evangelists in the Flapper Era*, 58, 157.

75. Journalist and historian Carey McWilliams wrote that McPherson embraced many aspects of Roaring Twenties culture, including flapper sensibilities. See Carey McWilliams, "Sunlight in My Soul," in *The Aspirin Age, 1919–1941*, ed. Isabel Leighton (New York: Simon and Schuster, 1949), 60.

76. "Aimee Sails South Lauding New York," *Boston Daily Globe*, March 4, 1927.

77. Grover Cleveland Loud, *Evangelized America* (Freeport, NY: Books for Libraries Press, 1928), 325.

78. Frank Sibley, "Aimee Arrives for Big Revival," *Daily Boston Globe*, 1931.

79. Blumhofer, *Aimee Semple McPherson: Everybody's Sister*, 293.

80. Robinson and Ruff, *Out of the Mouths of Babes: Girl Evangelists in the Flapper Era*, 58.

81. Ibid.

82. "Religion: Disappearance," in *Time* (Time Warner, 1926).

83. United Press, "Angelus Temple Funds Tied up by Mrs. Kennedy," *Berkeley Daily Gazette*, July 30, 1927.

84. Beale, "Aimee Bride for Third Time; Weds 250 Pound Preacher."

85. "A Slipping Sister," *The Miami News*, May 5, 1927.

86. "Aimee Bobs Her Hair: Followers Secede," *Lawrence Daily Journal—World*, April 25, 1927.

87. Ibid.

88. Charles Price, "Make Me a Blessing," *Golden Grain* 10, no. 11 (1936): 15.

89. Ibid.

90. McPherson, "Four Mountain Peaks of Glory from the Book of Ruth."; McPherson, "They Have Taken My Lord Away."

91. "Aimee Semple McPherson in Costume of Palestinian Woman, Which She Wore during the Recounting of Her "Journeylog," *The Bridal Call Foursquare* 10, no. 2 (1926).

92. Thomas Fish, "Sister Aimee's Dutch Swan Song: A Study of the Illustrated Sermon," *Journal of Religion and Theatre* 8, no. 1 (2009): 48–70.

93. Kate Douglas Wiggin, Pickford Film Corporation, and Artcraft Pictures Corporation, *Rebecca of Sunnybrook Farm* (Los Angeles, CA: Pickford Film Corporation Released by Artcraft Pictures Corporation, 1917), Motion Picture.

94. Fred Niblo et al., "Ben-Hur: A Tale of the Christ" (United States: Metro-Goldwyn-Mayer, 1925).

95. Henry James Forman, "New Faiths, and the Men and Women Who Follow Them," *The New York Times*, December 1, 1946.

96. "Cold Fails to Halt M'pherson Crowds," *The New York Times*, February 20, 1927.

97. "Thousands Wait Many Hours for Pastor's Resurrection," *The Atlanta Constitution*, May 24, 1926.

98. "Sure She Is Dead," *Berkeley Daily Gazette*, June 4, 1926; Alma Whitaker, "Aimee Semple M'pherson," *The Los Angeles Times*, June 13, 1926; "Woman Pastor Found, Canada Dispatch Says; Aimee Semple McPherson Reported in Alberta by Detectives," *Miami Daily News*, June 5, 1926.

99. "Religion: Disappearance."

100. "Religion: Return," in *Time* (Time Warner, 1926).

101. "Cheering Throngs Hail Aimee M'pherson Here: Crowd of 30,000 Showers Pastor with Flowers as She Returns; Appreciation Expressed," *Los Angeles Times*, June 27, 1926.

102. "Man Sought in McPherson Case, Reappears," *The Atlanta Constitution* May 28, 1926.

103. "Keyes Will Listen to Miss 'X' Story; Woman Was to Get $5,000 from Aimee M'pherson, She States," *Telegraph-Herald*, September 13, 1926.

104. "Five in M'Pherson Case Swear Pastor in Carmel; Cheers and Hisses Greet Evangelist as Dramatic Hearing Starts; Sharp Clashes Mark Day," *Los Angeles Times*, September 28, 1926.

105. Licoln Quarberg, "Aimee Ordered Held over for Perjury Trial," *Berkeley Daily Gazette*, September 2, 1926.

106. "Keyes Will Listen to Miss 'X' Story; Woman Was to Get $5,000 from Aimee M'pherson, She States."

107. "Evangelist Cool as Trial Starts," *Boston Daily Globe*, September 28, 1926.

108. "At Aimee McPherson's Counsel Table," *The Evening Independent*, October 8, 1926.

109. "Aimee's Mother under Arrest," *The Morning Leader*, September 18, 1926.

110. "Kidnaped Evangelist before Jury," *Warsaw Union*, July 8, 1926.

111. Gaston Leroux et al., *The Phantom of the Opera* (Universal Pictures Corp, 1925).

112. James Oliver Curwood and Charles Livingston Bull, *Nomads of the North: A Story of Romance and Adventure under the Open Stars* (Garden City, NY: Doubleday, 1919).

113. "Caught Evangelist in Falsehood, Is Claim of Former Boston Pastor," *The Morning Leader*, October 12, 1926.

114. Don Roberts, "Sister Aimee and Ma," *The Pittsburg Press*, September 24, 1930.

115. "Religion: Sisters V. Satan," in *Time* (Time Warner, 1937).

4   "A GLORIOUS SYMBOL": BUILDING A FEMALE PENTECOSTAL WORSHIP SPACE

1. Jeanne Halgren Kilde, *When Church Became Theatre: The Transformation of Evangelical Architecture and Worship in Nineteenth-Century America* (New York: Oxford University Press, 2002), 11.

2. Ibid., 3.

3. Ibid., 19–21.

4. Ibid., 149.

5. Ibid., 195–6.

6. Ibid., 159.

7. "The Decoration of Trinity Church, Boston," *The American Architect and Building News* 5, no. 178 (1879).

8. Annette Benert, *The Architectural Imagination of Edith Wharton: Gender, Class, and Power in the Progressive Era* (Madison, NJ: Fairleigh Dickinson University Press, 2007), 52.

9. Thompson, *The Life of A. B. Simpson*, 57.

10. Ibid., 96.

11. Russell Sturgis, "The Revival of Cathedral Building: Great Christian Houses of Worship Which Have Been Erected in Recent Years or Are Now in Process of Construction—Their Effectiveness and Artistic Meaning," *Munsey's Magazine*, April 1907, 192.

12. Ralph Adams Cram, *Church Building: A Study of the Principles of Architecture in Their Relation to the Church* (Boston, MA: Small, Maynard and Company, 1901), 83.

13. Ibid.

14. Kilde, *When Church Became Theatre: The Transformation of Evangelical Architecture and Worship in Nineteenth-Century America*, 110–1.

15. Ibid., 219.

16. Jeanne Halgren Kilde, "Church Architecture and the Second Great Awakening," in *Embodying the Spirit: New Perspectives on North American Revivalism*, ed. Michael James McClymond (Baltimore, MD, 2004), 84.

17. Ann Taves, "The Camp Meeting and the Paradoxes of Evangelical Protestant Ritual," in *Teaching Ritual*, ed. Catherine M. Bell, *Teaching Religious Studies Series* (New York: Oxford University Press, 2007), 123.

18. See Michael McClymond's description of a typical revivalist altar/ pulpit in Michael James McClymond, *Embodying the Spirit: New Perspectives on North American Revivalism* (Baltimore, MD: Johns Hopkins University Press, 2004), ix.

19. Fisher Humphreys, "Altar Call," in *Encyclopedia of Religion in the South*, ed. Charles H. Lippy, Samuel S. Hill, and Charles Reagan Wilson (Macon, GA: Mercer University Press, 2005), 50–1.

20. Mark K. George, *Israel's Tabernacle as Social Space*, Society of Biblical Literature: Ancient Israel and Its Literature (Atlanta, GA: Society of Biblical Literature, 2009), 85.

21. James F. White, *Protestant Worship: Traditions in Transition*, 1st ed. (Louisville, KY: Westminster John Knox Press, 1989), 231.

22. Humphreys, "Altar Call," 50–1.

23. Rodger M. Payne, *The Self and the Sacred: Conversion and Autobiography in Early American Protestantism*, 1st ed. (Knoxville: University of Tennessee Press, 1998), 74.

24. Ibid., 75.

25. "Advanced Lines of Church Activity," *Western Christian Advocate*, March 3, 1915, 16.

26. Anne C. Loveland and Otis B. Wheeler, *From Meetinghouse to Megachurch: A Material and Cultural History* (Columbia: University of Missouri Press, 2003), 82–3.

27. J. O. Peck, *The Revival and the Pastor* (New York: Cranston and Curtis, 1894), 180.

28. Loveland and Wheeler, *From Meetinghouse to Megachurch: A Material and Cultural History*, 15.

29. Douglas Carl Abrams, *Selling the Old-Time Religion: American Fundamentalists and Mass Culture, 1920–1940* (Athens: University of Georgia Press, 2001), 21.

30. Theodore Thomas Frankenberg, *Billy Sunday: His Tabernacles and Sawdust Trails* (Columbus, OH: F. J. Heer Printing, 1917): 80.

31. A. C. B., "The Albert Hall Revival," *The Speaker* 11 (1905): 607–8.

32. Kilde, *When Church Became Theatre: The Transformation of Evangelical Architecture and Worship in Nineteenth-Century America*, 6, 34.

33. R. A. Torrey, *Revival Addresses* (Chicago, IL: Fleming H. Revell Company, 1903), 103.

34. Maria Beulah Woodworth-Etter, "Woodworth-Etter Campaign in Indianapolis," *The Christian Evangel* 242, no. 308 (1918).

35. Woodworth-Etter, *Marvels and Miracles God Wrought in the Ministry for Forty-Five Years*, 48.

36. Ibid.

37. Ibid., 352.

38. Ibid.

39. Ibid., 353.

40. Woodworth-Etter, *Life and Testimony of Mrs. M. B. Woodworth-Etter*, 97.

41. Warner, *The Woman Evangelist: The Life and Times of Charismatic Evangelist Maria B. Woodworth-Etter*, 53.

42. Woodworth-Etter, *Life and Testimony of Mrs. M. B. Woodworth-Etter*, 97.

43. Woodworth-Etter, *Marvels and Miracles God Wrought in the Ministry for Forty-Five Years*, 412.

44. Woodworth, *The Life, Work, and Experience of Mariah Beulah Woodworth*, 201.

45. Woodworth-Etter, *Marvels and Miracles God Wrought in the Ministry for Forty-Five Years*, 27.

46. Maria Beulah Woodworth-Etter, *Acts of the Holy Ghost, or the Life, Work, and Experience of Mrs. M. B. Woodworth-Etter, Evangelist* (Dallas, TX: John F. Worley Printing, 1915), 108.

47. Woodworth-Etter, *Spirit Filled Sermons*, 202.

48. Ibid; Warner, *The Woman Evangelist: The Life and Times of Charismatic Evangelist Maria B. Woodworth-Etter*, 264; Woodworth-Etter, *Marvels and Miracles God Wrought in the Ministry for Forty-Five Years*, 352–3.

49. Woodworth-Etter, *Acts of the Holy Ghost, or the Life, Work, and Experience of Mrs. M. B. Woodworth-Etter, Evangelist*, 555.

50. Maria Beulah Woodworth-Etter, *Life and Experience Including Sermons and Visions of Mrs. M. B. Woodworth-Etter* (St. Louis, MO: Commercial Printing, 1904), 58.

51. Woodworth-Etter, *Acts of the Holy Ghost, or the Life, Work, and Experience of Mrs. M. B. Woodworth-Etter, Evangelist*, 11.

52. Kevin Kuzma, "The Presence of the Past," Echo Park Historical Society, accessed June 10, 2012, http://historicechopark.org/id37.html.

53. Lyle W. Dorsett, *Billy Sunday and the Redemption of Urban America*, Library of Religious Biography (Grand Rapids, MI: W.B. Eerdmans 1991), 65.

54. Aimee Semple McPherson, "Bringing Back the Ark," *The Bridal Call* 5, no. 2 (1921): 5.

55. Aimee Semple McPherson, *The Personal Testimony of Aimee Semple McPherson* (Los Angeles, CA: Heritage Department of the International Church of the Foursquare Gospel, 1998), 56.

56. McPherson, *Aimee: Life Story of Aimee Semple McPherson*, 123.

57. McPherson, *The Personal Testimony of Aimee Semple McPherson*, 56.

58. Ibid., 45.

59. R. S. Fanning, "The Mystery of the Ionic Volute," *Architectural Record* 40 (1916): 288.

60. Irving K. Pond, *The Meaning of Architecture; an Essay in Constructive Criticism* (Boston, MA: Marshall Jones Company, 1918), 96.

61. Fanning, "The Mystery of the Ionic Volute," 288.

62. James Fergusson, *History of the Modern Styles of Architecture*, Volume 1 (London: J. Murray, 1902), 311; Lucy Fischer, *Designing Women:*

Cinema, Art Deco, and the Female Form, Film and Culture (New York: Columbia University Press, 2003), 27.

63. Fergusson, *History of the Modern Styles of Architecture,* 172. This criticism did not acknowledge that in fact *Style Modern* included angular patterns and geometrical designs as well as rounded edges.

64. Janet Simonsen, director of the Foursquare Heritage Center, interviewed by the author, at the Foursquare Heritage Center, 2008.

65. See, for example, Aimee Semple McPherson, "The Echo Park Revival Tabernacle News," *The Bridal Call* 5, no. 11 (1922): 20.

66. McPherson, *Aimee: Life Story of Aimee Semple McPherson,* 122.

67. McPherson, *The Personal Testimony of Aimee Semple McPherson,* 58.

68. McPherson, *Aimee: Life Story of Aimee Semple McPherson,* 124.

69. Ibid.

70. Simonsen, director of the Foursquare Heritage Center, 2008.

71. McPherson, *Aimee: Life Story of Aimee Semple McPherson,* 123. According to the United States Department of Labor's Consumer Price Index, Angelus Temple's construction would cost $3,465,964.91 in 2014. "CPI Inflation Calculator," ed. Bureau of Labor Statistics (Washington, DC: United States Department of Labor, 2014). The value of the land itself would be exponentially greater in 2015 than its value in the 1920s.

72. Aimee Semple McPherson, *Aimee: Life Story of Aimee Semple McPherson,* 123.

73. Ibid., 121.

74. Sternheimer, *Celebrity Culture and the American Dream: Stardom and Social Mobility,* 2–3.

75. Tona J. Hangen, *Redeeming the Dial: Radio, Religion and Popular Culture in America* (Chapel Hill: University of North Carolina Press, 2002), 68.

76. Dr. Page Putnam Miller, Jill S. Topolski, and Vernon Horn, "National Historic Landmark Nomination Form," ed. Department of the Interior National Park Service (Washington, DC: National Register of Historic Places, 1991).

77. Daniel Mark Epstein, *Sister Aimee: The Life of Aimee Semple McPherson,* 266.

78. McPherson, *Aimee: Life Story of Aimee Semple McPherson,* 126.

79. Blumhofer, *Aimee Semple McPherson: Everybody's Sister,* 250.

80. Simonson, director of the Foursquare Heritage Center, 2008.

81. Ibid.

82. Ibid.

83. Sutton, *Aimee Semple McPherson and the Resurrection of Christian America,* 189–96.

84. "Angelus Temple Gives Aid to Thousands of Needy: Free Dining Hall Has Also Been Opened," *The Florence Times,* March 18, 1932.

5 "Thunder" and "Sweetness": Authority and Gender in Pentecostal Performance

1. Bell, *Ritual Theory, Ritual Practice*, 205.
2. David Chidester and Edward Tabor Linenthal, *American Sacred Space*, Religion in North America (Bloomington: Indiana University Press, 1995), 10.
3. Bell, *Ritual Theory, Ritual Practice*, 205.
4. Ibid., 216.
5. Woodworth-Etter, "Woodworth-Etter Campaign in Indianapolis."
6. McPherson, *Aimee: Life Story of Aimee Semple McPherson*, 126.
7. R. M. Patterson, "Revival Preaching," *The Presbyterian Banner* 88, no. 29 (1902): 12.
8. Emil Hirsch, "A Case with a Difference," *The Advocate* 49, no. 10 (1915): 301.
9. Robinson and Ruff, *Out of the Mouths of Babes: Girl Evangelists in the Flapper Era*, 111–19.
10. Grant Wacker, *Heaven Below: Early Pentecostals and American Culture* (Cambridge, MA: Harvard University Press, 2001), 113.
11. Mark A. Noll, *A History of Christianity in the United States and Canada* (Grand Rapids, MI: W.B. Eerdmans, 1992), 176.
12. See C. P. McIlvaine et al., *Revivals: How to Promote Them*, ed. Walter P. Doe (New York: E. B. Treat, 1895), 444; W. A. Tyson, *The Revival* (Nashville, TN: Cokesbury Press, 1925), 187; Peck, *The Revival and the Pastor*, 264; Barton, *One Hundred Revival Sermons and Outlines*, viii; Riley, *The Perennial Revival; a Plea for Evangelism*, 50; Frank Grenville Beardsley, *A Mighty Winner of Souls: Charles G. Finney, a Study in Evangelism* (New York: American Tract Society, 1937), 35.
13. J. H. MacDonald et al., *The Revival: A Symposium* (Cincinnati, OH: Jennings and Graham, 1905), 9.
14. Committee on the War and Religious Outlook, *Christian Unity: Its Principles and Possibilities* (New York: Association Press, 1921), 262.
15. Robinson and Ruff, *Out of the Mouths of Babes: Girl Evangelists in the Flapper Era*, 118; Hartley, *Evangelicals at a Crossroads: Revivalism and Social Reform in Boston, 1860–1910*, 16.
16. J. O. Peck, *The Revival and the Pastor* (New York: Cranston and Curts, 1894), 118.
17. See Marsden, *Fundamentalism and American Culture*, 73; Bridgers, *The American Religious Experience: A Concise History*, 8; Wentz, *American Religious Traditions: The Shaping of Religion in the United States*, 201; Donald Charles Swift, *Religion and the American Experience: A Social and Cultural History, 1765–1997* (Armonk, NY: M.E. Sharpe, 1998), 4; Marianne Perciaccante, *Calling Down Fire: Charles Grandison Finney and Revivalism in Jefferson County*,

New York, 1800–1840 (Albany: State University of New York Press, 2003), 66.

18. William H. Cooper, *The Great Revivalists in American Religion, 1740–1944*, 32; Mark A. Noll, *America's God: From Jonathan Edwards to Abraham Lincoln* (New York: Oxford University Press, 2002), 295.

19. Noll, *America's God: From Jonathan Edwards to Abraham Lincoln*, 295.

20. Peck, *The Revival and the Pastor*, 12–13.

21. William Bell Riley, *The Perennial Revival; a Plea for Evangelism*, 49–50.

22. Bell, *Ritual Theory, Ritual Practice*, 216.

23. Amy Hollywood, "Performativity, Citationality, Ritualization," *History of Religions* 42, no. 2 (2002): 101.

24. Bendroth, *Fundamentalism and Gender, 1875 to the Present*, 13.

25. Peck, *The Revival and the Pastor*, 40.

26. Thomas D. Morison, "The Evangelical Repository" (Philadelphia, PA: W.S. Young, 1883), 90.

27. William Henry Young, *How to Preach with Power*, 3rd ed. (Athens, GA: The How Publishing, 1909), 276.

28. Roxanne Mountford, *The Gendered Pulpit: Preaching in American Protestant Spaces*, Studies in Rhetorics and Feminisms (Carbondale: Southern Illinois University Press, 2003), 45–7; Wallace D. Best, *Passionately Human, No Less Divine: Religion and Culture in Black Chicago, 1915–1952* (Princeton, NJ: Princeton University Press, 2005), 155.

29. William T. Ellis, *Billy Sunday: The Man and His Message* (Philadelphia, PA: The John C. Winston Company, 1914), 138.

30. Ellis, *Billy Sunday*, 139.

31. Billy Sunday, *Easter*, film (United States, April 8, 1917).

32. "'I Am Too Tired!' Billy Sunday Cries," *The New York Times*, May 30, 1917.

33. Ibid.

34. The offertory was probably the most mobile of all revivalist service elements. Sometimes a preacher would give the offertory before the altar call and sometimes the offertory closed the service.

35. William Edward Biederwolf, *Evangelism: Its Justification, Its Operation, and Its Value* (New York: Fleming H. Revell Company, 1921), 195–202.

36. Peck, *The Revival and the Pastor*, 109.

37. Torrey, *Revival Addresses*, 219.

38. William Bell Riley, *Revival Sermons; Essentials in Effective Evangelism* (New York: Fleming H. Revell Company, 1929), 24, 32, 81; MacDonald et al., *The Revival: A Symposium*, 36, 123, 34, 41; Riley, *The Perennial Revival; a Plea for Evangelism*, 37, 70–2, 81, 87, 117,

46, 55; Evan Roberts et al., *The Story of the Welsh Revival as Told by Eyewitnesses: Together with a Sketch of Evan Roberts and His Message to the World* (New York: F.H. Revell, 1905), 13, 69; Torrey, *Revival Addresses*, 83, 140, 91, 201, 70; J. Wilbur Chapman, *Revival Sermons* (New York: Fleming H. Revell Company, 1911), 135, 91, 211; Peck, *The Revival and the Pastor*, 30, 61, 68–9, 80, 122, 64, 66–7, 99, 244, 62; Frederick M. Barton, *One Hundred Revival Sermons and Outlines* (New York: Hodder and Stoughton, 1906), 89, 128, 68, 80, 209, 38, 49, 361, 79, 427, 33, 47–8, 51; Len G. Broughton, *The Revival of a Dead Church*, vol. 5, The Colportage Library (Chicago, IL: The Bible Institute Colportage Association, 1900), 11–12, 23–4, 46, 53, 60, 101; Orrin Philip Gifford, *Honest Debtors; Sermons and Addresses* (Philadelphia, PA: The Judson Press, 1922), 25–6, 48–9, 69, 85–6, 89, 114–15, 27–9, 48, 54, 71, 215; Frederick Watson Hannan, *Evangelism* (New York: The Methodist Book Concern, 1921), 162, 84, 229; Alfred E. Garvie, *The Christian Preacher*, International Theological Library (Edinburgh: T. & T. Clark, 1920), 102, 83, 287, 315, 96, 441.

39. Torrey, *Revival Addresses*, 247.
40. Riley, *The Perennial Revival; a Plea for Evangelism*, 81.
41. MacDonald et al., *The Revival: A Symposium*, 134.
42. McClymond, *Embodying the Spirit: New Perspectives on North American Revivalism*, 33–4.
43. Peck, *The Revival and the Pastor*, 261.
44. "Faith-Healing, Christian Science, and Kindred Phenomena," *The Popular Science Monthly* 43, no. 2 (1893): 271.
45. Heather D. Curtis, *Faith in the Great Physician: Suffering and Divine Healing in American Culture, 1860–1900*, Lived Religions (Baltimore, MD: Johns Hopkins University Press, 2007), 106.
46. Gipsy Smith, *Real Religion; Revival Sermons Delivered during His Twentieth Visit to America* (New York: George H. Doran Company, 1922), 102.
47. Ibid., 102.
48. In this case, the show of manhood was in reference to men abstaining from alcohol. Brown, *The Real Billy Sunday: The Life and Work of Rev. William Ashley Sunday, D.D., the Baseball Evangelist*, 214; Robert Francis Martin, *Hero of the Heartland: Billy Sunday and the Transformation of American Society, 1862–1935* (Bloomington: Indiana University Press, 2002), 128.
49. Evan Roberts et al., *The Story of the Welsh Revival as Told by Eyewitnesses*, 31.
50. "Pledges for Missions," *New York Times*, October 15, 1900.
51. Ibid.
52. "The Malcontent Woman by a Discontent Man," *The Review of Reviews* 11 (1895).
53. Young, *How to Preach with Power*, 276.

54. Woodworth-Etter, *Signs and Wonders*, 100.

55. Stanley Frodsham, "Spiritual Life Must Precede Her Cures: Alleged Divine Healer Says That Her Successes Are Due to Spirit of the Lord Working through Her," *The Indianapolis Star*, September 10, 1904.

56. Woodworth-Etter, *Marvels and Miracles God Wrought in the Ministry for Forty-Five Years*, 454.

57. "Woodworth-Etter Goes into a Trance," *The Indianapolis Star*, October 2, 1904, in *Maria Woodworth-Etter: The Complete Collection of Her Life Teachings*, ed. Roberts Liardon (Tulsa, OK: Albury, 2000).

58. "Woodworth-Etter Goes into a Trance," *The Indianapolis Star*, October 2, 1904.

59. Theodore Diller, "Hypnotism in a Religious Meeting," *The Medical News* 57, no. 13 (1890): 303.

60. Frodsham, "Spiritual Life Must Precede Her Cures: Alleged Divine Healer Says That Her Successes Are Due to Spirit of the Lord Working through Her."

61. "Woodworth-Etter Goes into a Trance."

62. Ibid.

63. Woodworth-Etter, *Marvels and Miracles God Wrought in the Ministry for Forty-Five Years*, 10.

64. "An Insane Female Evangelist Declares Herself in Communion with the Blessed Trinity and the Devil."

65. Ibid.

66. Woodworth-Etter, *Marvels and Miracles God Wrought in the Ministry for Forty-Five Years*, 65.

67. Woodworth-Etter, *Signs and Wonders*, 66.

68. Ibid., 100.

69. Woodworth-Etter, *Marvels and Miracles God Wrought in the Ministry for Forty-Five Years*, 252.

70. Ibid.

71. Woodworth-Etter, *Life and Experience Including Sermons and Visions of Mrs. M. B. Woodworth-Etter*, 63; Seeley D. Kinne, "God's Deeds of Mercy and Power in Chicago," *Word and Witness* 9, no. 8 (1913).

72. Stanley Frodsham, "Glorious Victories of God in Dallas, Texas," *Word and Witness* 9, no. 1 (1913).

73. Zenas Dane, "Useless Knowledge," *Good Housekeeping*, March 1888, 280; Wilbur Fisk Tillett, "Southern Womanhood," *The Century Illustrated Monthly Magazine*, November 1891, 16.

74. Maria Beulah Woodworth-Etter and Roberts Liardon, *Maria Woodworth-Etter: The Complete Collection of Her Life Teachings*, 495.

75. Ibid., 97–102.

76. Woodworth-Etter, *Marvels and Miracles God Wrought in the Ministry for Forty-Five Years*, 31.

77. Ibid., 412.

78. Curtis, *Faith in the Great Physician: Suffering and Divine Healing in American Culture, 1860–1900*, 106.

79. "The Day of God's Visitation: The Lame Walk, the Blind See, the Deaf Hear," *The Latter Rain Evangel* 5, no. 11 (1913): 4.

80. "Indiana State News: Happenings Throughout the State During the Past Week," *Bluffton Weekly Chronicle*, September 17, 1885, in *Maria Woodworth-Etter: The Complete Collection of Her Life Teachings*, ed. Roberts Liardon (Tulsa, OK: Albury, 2000).

81. "Made Whole by Faith," *Chicago Herald*, October 20, 1887.

82. Woodworth-Etter, *Life and Testimony of Mrs. M. B. Woodworth-Etter*, 128. For additional examples of testimonies to Woodworth-Etter's healing act, see: Woodworth-Etter, *Marvels and Miracles God Wrought in the Ministry for Forty-Five Years*, 432–5; Woodworth-Etter, *Life and Experience Including Sermons and Visions of Mrs. M. B. Woodworth-Etter*, 97–102.

83. Woodworth-Etter, *Marvels and Miracles God Wrought in the Ministry for Forty-Five Years*, 402.

84. Ibid., 286.

85. Ibid., 268.

86. Woodworth-Etter, *Signs and Wonders*, 167.

87. Woodworth-Etter, *Marvels and Miracles God Wrought in the Ministry for Forty-Five Years*, 84.

88. "Very Latest," *The Clinton Age*, June 22, 1888.

89. "Indiana State News: Happenings Throughout the State During the Past Week."

90. Woodworth-Etter, *Marvels and Miracles God Wrought in the Ministry for Forty-Five Years*, 183.

91. Ibid., 95.

92. Woodworth-Etter, *Life and Experience Including Sermons and Visions of Mrs. M. B. Woodworth-Etter*, 125.

93. Woodworth-Etter, *Acts of the Holy Ghost, or the Life, Work, and Experience of Mrs. M. B. Woodworth-Etter, Evangelist*, 397.

94. Ibid.

95. Wayne Warner, *Maria Woodworth-Etter: For Such a Time as This* (Alachua, FL: Bridge-Logos, 2009), 287.

96. Carrie Judd Montgomery, "The Work and the Workers," *Triumphs of Faith* 10, no. 1 (1890): 22.

97. Woodworth-Etter, *Signs and Wonders God Wrought in the Ministry for Forty Years*, 160.

98. The difference in racial and class makeup was not necessarily due to Simpson, Chapman and Sunday's prejudice or Woodworth-Etter's lack of it. It is possible that the two male ministers, as representatives of white, middleclass manliness and by extension the dominant culture, were less appealing to those who did not resemble them. Perhaps a female counterpart, who, by virtue of her femaleness, was outside the hegemony of middleclass white American revivalism, was more inviting to people of color or persons in the working/poor classes. Another explanation

could have been that the emerging Pentecostal movement had interracial roots and as an early Pentecostal architect Woodworth-Etter attracted more African-American attendees. In addition, there could have been more diversity in Simpson and Chapman's meetings that went unseen by reporters. Woodworth-Etter, as part of the Pentecostal revivalist movement, was known for an association with African-American Protestantism and so reporters could have been expecting to see greater diversity in her meetings.

99. F. H., "Billy Sunday," *The New Republic* 2, no. 20 (1915): 173; "Big Missionary Gifts," *New York Times*, October 13, 1902.

100. "Crowds Give $70,000 to Dr. Simpson's Fund," *The New York Times*, October 10, 1904.

101. Frederick William Betts, *Billy Sunday, the Man and Method* (Boston, MA: The Murray Press, 1916), 14.

102. "Big Missionary Gifts," *The New York Times*, October 13, 1902.

103. "Crowds Give $70,000 to Dr. Simpson's Fund."

104. Bendroth, "Why Women Loved Billy Sunday," 256; William T. Ellis, *Billy Sunday, the Man and His Message* (Philadelphia, PA: The John C. Winston Company, 1914), 165.

105. See, for example, accounts of Moses Foreford and Jim Barby, two African American attendees: "Paralyzed Negro Becomes Athlete: Moses Foreford Takes Treatment of Mrs. Woodworth-Etter at Revival Meeting," *The Indianapolis Star*, September 28, 1904, in *Maria Woodworth-Etter: The Complete Collection of Her Life Teachings*, ed. Roberts Liardon (Tulsa, OK: Albury, 2000).
    Warner, *The Woman Evangelist: The Life and Times of Charismatic Evangelist Maria B. Woodworth-Etter*, 79.

106. "Evangelist Mrs. Woodworth: Who She Is, Where She Came Frome, and What She Is Doing at Salem," *Daily Statesman*, May 29, 1892, in *Maria Woodworth-Etter: The Complete Collection of Her Life Teachings*, ed. Roberts Liardon (Tulsa, OK: Albury, 2000).

107. "Faithful Believe She Can Cure All Ills," *The Atlanta Journal*, April 4, 1914, in *Maria Woodworth-Etter: The Complete Collection of Her Life Teachings*, ed. Roberts Liardon (Tulsa, OK: Albury, 2000).

108. "The Tipton Revival," *Indianian-Republican*, May 14, 1885

109. Paul Harvey, *Freedom's Coming: Religious Culture and the Shaping of the South from the Civil War through the Civil Rights Era* (Chapel Hill: University of North Carolina Press, 2005), 109–10; David Edwin Harrell, *Varieties of Southern Evangelicalism* (Macon, GA: Mercer University Press, 1981), 52.

110. Woodworth-Etter, *Marvels and Miracles God Wrought in the Ministry for Forty-Five Years*, 57–9.

111. "Trance Religion," *Kokomo Dispatch*, May 28, 1885.

112. "Took No Money for Healing: Mrs. Etter Gave God Credit for Cures," *Boston Daily Globe*, August 29, 1913.

113. Wendite, "Voodoo Priestess," 79.

114. "Aver They Are Cured: One Threw Her Brace Away Holy Rollers Fail to Help Blind Boy"; "Minors Take Part in Holy-Roller Services," in, *Maria Woodworth-Etter: The Complete Collection of Her Life Teachings*, ed. Roberts Liardon (Tulsa, OK: Albury, 2000).

115. Warner, *The Woman Evangelist: The Life and Times of Charismatic Evangelist Maria B. Woodworth-Etter*, 90–3.

116. "Took No Money for Healing: Mrs. Etter Gave God Credit for Cures."

117. "Tells How She Got "Power," *Boston Globe*, August 30, 1913.

118. Woodworth-Etter, *Marvels and Miracles God Wrought in the Ministry for Forty-Five Years*, 103–4.

119. Ibid.

120. "Victims of Hypnotism; Religious Frenzy Inspired by an Insane Revivalist," *The New York Times*, September 1, 1890.

121. Don Roberts, "Sister Aimee and Ma," *The Pittsburgh Press*, September 24, 1930.

122. Sarah Comstock, "Aimee Semple McPherson: Prima Donna of Revivalism," *Harper's Magazine*, December 1927.

123. McPherson, "As a Bride Adorned: Glowing Sermon on the Glorious Second Coming of Christ."

124. Aimee Semple McPherson, "Second Coming of Christ," *The Bridal Call Foursquare* 12, no. 12 (1929): 8.

125. McPherson, *This Is That: Personal Experiences, Sermons and Writings of Aimee Semple Mcpherson*, 653–5.

126. Comstock, "Aimee Semple McPherson: Prima Donna of Revivalism."

127. "Aimee to Settle Down, Hutton Says," *The Leader-Post*, June 30, 1933.

128. Aimee Semple McPherson, "The Year of Jubilee," *The Bridal Call Foursquare* 11, no. 4 (1927): 32.

129. "Mrs. Aimee Hutton Home," *New York Times*, August 2, 1933; Amy Lawrence, *Echo and Narcissus: Women's Voices in Classical Hollywood Cinema* (Berkeley: University of California Press, 1991), 88.

130. Lawrence, *Echo and Narcissus: Women's Voices in Classical Hollywood Cinema*, 88.

131. Allene Sumner, "Prison Bars Will Not Dim Ardor of Aimee McPherson's Faithful," *Milwaukee Journal*, September 25, 1926.

132. Aimee Semple McPherson, "Fighting His Way to Hell," *The Bridal Call Foursquare* 8, no. 3 (1924): 29.

133. Charles S. Price, "The Opening," *The Bridal Call* 6, no. 8 (1923): 16.

134. Ibid.

135. Anthony Quinn, *The Original Sin: A Self-Portrait*, 1 ed. (Boston: Little, Brown and Company, 1972), 125–6.

136. McPherson, *This Is That: Personal Experiences, Sermons and Writings of Aimee Semple McPherson*, 73.

137. McPherson, "The Story of My Life," 12.

138. Aimee Semple McPherson, "The Story of My Life," *The Bridal Call* 8, no. 10 (1925): 12.

139. Ibid.

140. Quinn, *The Original Sin: A Self-Portrait*, 125–6.

141. W. E. Waggoner, "Noted Wichita Journalist Reviews Revival," *The Bridal Call* 6, no. 1 (1922): 17.

142. Ibid.

143. "Mrs. Aimee McPherson, Noted Evangelist, Dead," *The Milwaukee Journal*, September 28, 1944.

144. Anthony Quinn, *The Original Sin, a Self-Portrait*, 125–6.

145. Loud, *Evangelized America*, 328.

146. Sumner, "Prison Bars Will Not Dim Ardor of Aimee McPherson's Faithful."

147. "Atheist Fog-Bound on Way to Debate," *Berkeley Daily Gazette*, January 17, 1934.

148. Loud, *Evangelized America*, 322.

149. "Bishop Rice Wants Aimee to Be 38th Spiritual Wife," *The Pittsburgh Press*, 1930.

150. Ibid.

151. Ibid.

152. Ibid.

153. "A Tribute to Aimee Semple McPherson from Her Elders, Workers and Members in Honor of Her Birthday," *The Bridal Call Foursquare* 12, no. 5 (1928).

154. Ibid.

155. Ibid.

156. James M. Grey, "What About Mrs. Aimee Semple McPherson?," *Moody Bible Institute Monthly* 22, no. 3 (1921).

157. Edith Waldvogel Blumhofer, *Aimee Semple McPherson: Everybody's Sister*, 263.

158. Ibid., 16.

159. McPherson, *Aimee: Life Story of Aimee Semple McPherson*, 67.

160. Simonsen, director of the Foursquare Heritage Center, 2008.

161. Comstock, "Aimee Semple McPherson: Prima Donna of Revivalism."

162. Ibid.

163. Blumhofer, *Aimee Semple McPherson: Everybody's Sister*, 219.

164. McPherson did not give any details as to the ethnicity of the people whom she called "Gypsies" (e.g., Roma, Sinti, or Irish Travelers). Anthropologist Albert Thomas Sinclair noted in 1917 that Roma lived in California: Albert Thomas Sinclair, *American Gypsies* (New York: The New York Public Library, 1917), 13.

165. In 1920s film and radio, the term "Sambo" referred to an African American who behaved in a stereotypically cheerful, comical, and submissive manner. See Joseph Boskin, *Sambo: The Rise and Demise of an American Jester* (New York: Oxford University Press, 1986), 148–97.

166. Aimee Semple McPherson, "The Conquering Host," *The Bridal Call Foursquare* 10, no. 3 (1926): 5; Aimee Semple McPherson, "Satan's Master Stroke," *The Bridal Call Foursquare* 10, no. 4 (1926): 21; Aimee Semple McPherson, "The Need of the Hour," *The Bridal Call Foursquare* 11, no. 3 (1927): 31.
167. Aimee Semple McPherson, "Mamoth Divine Healing Services," *The Bridal Call Foursquare* 5, no. 3 (1921): 9.
168. Elizabeth C. Collier, "My Church," *The Bridal Call Foursquare* 8, no. 3 (1924): 28.

6   "A Regular Jezebel": Female Ministry, Pentecostal Ministry on Trial

1. C. H. Forney, *History of the Churches of God in the United States of North America* (Harrisburg, PA: The Churches of God Publishing House, 1914), 237.
2. John Alexander Dowie, "Elijah's Restoration Messages," *Leaves of Healing* 13, no. 12 (1903): 374; John Alexander Dowie, "Trance Evangelist," *Leaves of Healing* 1, no. 24 (1895): 381.
3. John Alexander Dowie, "Trance Evangelism," 381.
4. Dowie, "Elijah's Restoration Messages," 374.
5. Ibid.
6. John Bunyan Campbell, *Spirit Vitapathy; a Religious Scientific System of Health and Life for Body and Soul* (Cincinnati, OH: H. Watkin, 1891), 348.
7. Orville Coats, "The Ordination of Mrs. McPherson," *Moody Bible Institute Monthly* 22, no. 9 (1922): 1027.
8. Robert Shuler, *"Fighting Bob" Shuler of Los Angeles* (Indianapolis, IN: Dog Ear Publishing, 2011), 174–84.
9. Ibid., 184.
10. "Police Check Hoodlumism. Pentacostal [Sic] Meeting at Montwait Interrupted Many Times Last Evening," *Framingham Daily Tribune*, August 7, 1913, in *Maria Woodworth Etter: The Complete Collection of Her Life Teachings*, ed. Roberts Liardon (Tulsa, OK: Albury, 2000).
11. "Has the Day of Miracles Past?," *Framingham Daily Tribune*, August 7, 1913, in *Maria Woodworth Etter: The Complete Collection of Her Life Teachings*, ed. Roberts Liardon (Tulsa, OK: Albury, 2000).
12. "Police Check Hoodlumism."
13. Ibid.
14. "Aver They Are Cured: One Threw Her Brace Away Holy Rollers Fail to Help Blind Boy"; "Minors Take Part in Holy-Roller Services," in *Maria Woodworth-Etter: The Complete Collection of Her Life Teachings*, ed. Roberts Liardon (Tulsa, OK: Albury, 2000).
15. "Took No Money for Healing: Mrs. Etter Gave God Credit for Cures."

16. Ibid.
17. "Tells How She Got 'Power'."
18. "Took No Money for Healing: Mrs. Etter Gave God Credit for Cures."
19. "Tells How She Got 'Power'."
20. See "More Hypnotism on Women," *Lewiston Morning Tribune*, 1913; "Hypnotism Overcame Her: Begged Husband to Keep Dead Man Away as Unable to Resist His Power," *Lewiston Morning Tribune*, April 5, 1913; "Swindled by an Adventuress," *The Star*, December 24, 1904; "Hypnotism Did It All," *New York Times*, February 15, 1907; "Hypnotism Not a Factor," *New York Times*, April 15, 1895.
21. Fred Nadis, *Wonder Shows: Performing Science, Magic, and Religion in America* (New Brunswick, NJ: Rutgers University Press, 2005), 85–112.
22. See "Student of Occult Sciences Falls Unconscious after Experiments," *New York Times*, May 29, 1908.
23. See, for example, "Couldn't Awaken Hynotist's Subject: Friend Cries in Vain to the Man Dead in the Morgue That His Heart Is Beating," *New York Times*, November 10, 1909; "Hypnotism Is Fatal: Subject's Support Gives Way and His Head Is Crushed," *Aurora Daily Express*, May 17, 1901.
24. See, for example, "Victims of Hypnotism; Religious Frenzy Inspired by an Insane Revivalist." See also "Woodworth-Etter Goes into a Trance"; "Driven Crazy by Religion; Victims of Mrs. Woodworth's Revivals in St. Lewis," *The New York Times*, April 12, 1891, in *Maria Woodworth-Etter: The Complete Collection of Her Life Teachings*, ed. Roberts Liardon (Tulsa, OK: Albury, 2000); "Sees Visions of Heaven: Strange Reports from Mrs. Woodworth's Meetings," *Chicago Daily Tribune*, December 21, 1890."
25. "Steals Men's Wits Away. Male and Female Bipeds in Frenzied Prayer. They Cry, Shout and Swing Their Arms in Air Till Exhausted. Woman Evangelist Charged with Hypnotizing Her Hearers," *Boston Daily Globe*, September 1, 1890.
26. "A Hypnotic Revivalist Disappears: Mrs. Maria B. Woodworth Shakes the Dust of St. Louis from Her Feet," *Chicago Tribune*, April 24, 1891.
27. "Driven Crazy by Religion; Victims of Mrs. Woodworth's Revivals in St. Lewis."
28. "The Malcontent Woman by a Discontent Man."
29. Woodworth-Etter's methods were questioned in many cities where she pitched her revival tent. Worries over the safety of Woodworth-Etter's methods resulted in a Probate Judge ordering minors to be excluded from her meetings in Topeka, Kansas. See "Boy Cured by Miracle Is Taken from Meeting," *Topeka Daily Capital*, August 12, 1915. Others in Fremont, Nebraska voiced concern for "tragedies enacted by those who hope for relief from suffering." See "Hundreds Crowd Tent of The "Divine Healer.""
30. Warner, *The Woman Evangelist: The Life and Times of Charismatic Evangelist Maria B. Woodworth-Etter*, 232.

31. "Find Second Trunk in M'pherson Case," *New York Times*, November 2, 1926.

32. Dan Campbell, "Aimee's Captivity Traced through Various Hotels," *The Evening Independent*, October 2, 1926.

33. Sutton, *Aimee Semple McPherson and the Resurrection of Christian America*, 135.

34. Dan Campbell, "Aimee Apparently at End of Her Kidnaping Romance," *The Evening Independent*, September 16, 1926.

35. Mayme Peak, "Mrs. McPherson Wrings Sobs from Congregation," *Boston Daily Globe*, September 20, 1926; "Aimee's Followers Believe She Is a Christian Martyr," *The Evening Independent*, September 20, 1926; "Martyr Show Given by Mrs. M'Pherson," *New York Times*, October 3, 1926.

36. "Aimee's Followers Believe She Is a Christian Martyr."

37. Schlater, "Flaming Youth: Gender in 1920s Hollywood," 109; Beth L. Bailey, *From Front Porch to Back Seat: Courtship in Twentieth-Century America* (Baltimore, MD: Johns Hopkins University Press, 1988), 101.

38. Sumner, "Prison Bars Will Not Dim Ardor of Aimee McPherson's Faithful."

39. "Mrs. M'pherson, Evangelist, Faces Probe," *Beddeford Weekly Journal*, October 1, 1926.

40. "Keyes Drops Case against Aimee," *Telegraph-Herald*, January 10, 1927.

41. Ibid. In *Aimee Semple McPherson and the Resurrection of Christian America*, Matthew Sutton speculates that McPherson may have blackmailed newspaper mogul William Randolph Hearst in order to turn the tide of public opinion (and then her case) in her favor (Sutton, *Aimee Semple McPherson and the Resurrection of Christian America*, 139).

42. Even in death, McPherson was known primarily for her famous disappearance. See, for example, "Death Comes to the Evangelist," *The Baltimore Sun*, September 28, 1944; "Autopsy Ordered on Body of Evangelist," *The Evening Independent*, September 28, 1944; "Aimee Semple McPherson Dead," *Beaver County Times*, September 29, 1944.

43. Betts, *Billy Sunday, the Man and Method*, 31–2.

44. Aimee Semple McPherson, "Christ, Our Spiritual Gibraltar," *The Bridal Call Foursquare* 10, no. 4 (1929): 4.

45. Loud, *Evangelized America*, 322; "Membership Doubled in Few Months," *Pittsburgh Post-Gazette*, January 18, 1927; Sumner, "Prison Bars Will Not Dim Ardor of Aimee McPherson's Faithful"; "Judge Issues Warning in Temple Scrap," *Lawrence Journal-World*, April 24, 1937; Comstock, "Aimee Semple McPherson: Prima Donna of Revivalism," 11.

46. "Simpson Will Explain; He Is to Address the Christian Alliance Camp Meeting, Answering Charges of Misuse of Funds," *New York Times*, August 13, 1899.

47. "Turns on Sunday: Evangelist's Former Secretary to Reveal 'Inside Workings'," *The Daily Star*, June 15, 1915.
48. "Billy Sunday's Son Is Arrested," *The Miami News*, November 25, 1929.
49. "Texas Minister Kills Man in Church; the Rev. J. Frank Norris, Fundamentalist, Shoots Fort Worth Lumberman," *New York Times*, July 18, 1926.
50. See "Norris Acquitted in Swift Trial," *New York Times*, January 26, 1927; "Norris, Amid Sobs, Tells of Killing," *New York Times*, January 22, 1927; "Preacher Slayer Ready for Trial," *New York Times*, October 31, 1926.

CONCLUSION

1. Edith Waldvogel Blumhofer, "Women in Pentecostalism," in *Encyclopedia of Women and Religion in North America*, ed. Rosemary Skinner Keller, Rosemary Radford Ruether, and Marie Cantlon (Bloomington: Indiana University Press, 2006), 404.
2. Technically, Thomas and Lyda Paino succeeded Woodworth-Etter after her death at the Maria B. Woodworth-Etter Taberbacle, but Thomas assumed primary leadership responsibilities.
3. Nathaniel M. Van Cleave and Ronald D. Williams, *The Vine and the Branches: A History of the International Church of the Foursquare Gospel* (Los Angeles, CA: Foursquare Publishing, 1992), 41.
4. Bill Shepson, "More Female Senior Pastors Than Ever Before," *Foursquare*, 2010.
5. Margaret M. Poloma and John Clifford Green, *The Assemblies of God: Godly Love and the Revitalization of American Pentecostalism*, 109.
6. The Foursquare Church, "Tammy Dunahoo Accepts VP Role," last modified February 25, 2009, http://www.foursquare.org/news/article/tammy_dunahoo_accepts_vp_role.
7. Lucy Stone et al., *Friends and Sisters: Letters between Lucy Stone and Antoinette Brown Blackwell, 1846–93*, Women in American History (Urbana: University of Illinois Press, 1987), 228.
8. Boyd and Brackenridge, *Presbyterian Women in America: Two Centuries of a Quest for Status*, 104.
9. Woodworth-Etter, *Life and Testimony of Mrs. M. B. Woodworth-Etter*, 126.
10. Ibid., 127–8.
11. Ibid., 129.
12. Ibid., 134.
13. "Sea Did Not Give up Dead," *The Evening Independent*, May 24, 1924.
14. Ibid.
15. "Aimee Semple McPherson: Thousands Mourn at Famed Evangelist's Funeral," *LIFE*, October 30, 1944, 85.

16. Ibid., 86.

17. Ibid., 85.

18. Judge Carlos S. Hardy, "Carry on," *The Bridal Call Foursquare* 10, no. 2 (1926): 27.

19. "Aimee Semple McPherson: Thousands Mourn at Famed Evangelist's Funeral," *LIFE*, October 30, 1944, 85.

20. "Pentecostal Resource Page," in *The Pew Forum on Religion & Public Life* (Pew Research Center, 2006).

21. "U.S. Religious Landscape Survey," in *Pew Forum on Religion and Public Life* (Pew Research Center, 2007).

22. Cooper, *The Great Revivalists in American Religion, 1740–1944*, 172; Airhart, *Serving the Present Age: Revivalism, Progressivism, and the Methodist Tradition in Canada*, 81.

23. One-time Angelus Temple staff pastor Rheba Crawford and well-known evangelist Uldine Utley are examples of this trend. Crawford cultivated a McPherson-like ministry preaching on Broadway in New York. Her white dresses, fresh-faced beauty, and dynamic preaching earned her a reputation as the "Angel of Broadway," and also a later homage in the form of the character Sarah Brown in the 1933 short story and 1950 musical, *Guys and Dolls*. See Damon Runyon, *Guys and Dolls* (New York: Frederick A. Stokes, 1931). Crawford hoped to inherit the Temple from McPherson, but the Angel and the Bride ultimately parted ways acrimoniously. See "Mrs. Hutton's Flock Uneasy over Control," *Chicago Tribune*, June 10, 1933. Utley converted at a McPherson service and copied her taste for flowing dresses and flowers. Utley preached about Jesus as her "Rose of Sharon" and "Lilly of the Valley." See "Religion: Terror's Troth," *Time Magazine*, January 10, 1938.

24. Simonsen, director of the Foursquare Heritage Center, 2008.

25. *Time Magazine* described Ester Locy's McPherson-esque meetings as "lusty revival meetings," "a la McPherson." "Religion: McPherson V. Voliva," *Time Magazine*, September 16, 1929.

26. See, for example, Dr. Charles A. Shreve, "A Beautiful Bride," *The Bridal Call Foursquare* 14, no. 13 (1931).

27. Van Cleave and Williams, *The Vine and the Branches: A History of the International Church of the Foursquare Gospel*, 42.

28. Rosa M. Phillippi, "Application for Admission Lighthouse of International Foursquare Evangelism," ed. LIFE Bible College (Echo ParkLos Angeles: Angelus Temple, 1929).

29. "Dedication to the Memory of Aimee Semple McPherson."

30. Ibid.

31. Kathryn Irene Sheffield, "The Creation of Female Gender Identity on Evangelical Television: Old Wine in New Bottles" (PhD dissertation, Arizona State University, ProQuest LLC, 2009), 34, 36.

32. "Megachurch Pastors Put Marriage Asunder," *Deseret News*, September 1, 2007; "Lawyer: Televangelist Juanita Bynum Files for Divorce," *Fox News*, September 11, 2007.

33. Hollywood, "Performativity, Citationality, Ritualization," 115.

34. Ibid.

35. Iain MacRobert, *The Black Roots and White Racism of Early Pentecostalism in the USA* (New York: St. Martin's Press, 1988).

36. See, for example, Pamela Robertson, "Feminist Camp in *Gold Diggers of 1933*," in *Hollywood Musicals, the Film Reader*, ed. Steven Cohan (New York: Routledge, 2002), 137; Kitch, *The Girl on the Magazine Cover: The Origins of Visual Stereotypes in American Mass Media*, 12; Christina Simmons, *Making Marriage Modern: Women's Sexuality from the Progressive Era to World War II*, 1st ed. (New York: Oxford University Press, 2009), 149.

37. Kitch, *The Girl on the Magazine Cover: The Origins of Visual Stereotypes in American Mass Media*, 133.

38. Robertson, "Feminist Camp in *Gold Diggers of 1933*," 138.

39. Chaves, *Ordaining Women*, 109–10; Catherine M. Prelinger, *Episcopal Women: Gender, Spirituality, and Commitment in an American Mainline Denomination*, 24.

40. Bendroth, *Fundamentalism and Gender, 1875 to the Present*, 3, 14–19.

41. Butler, *Women in the Church of God in Christ: Making a Sanctified World*, 157–66.

42. Ibid., 157–66.

BIBLIOGRAPHY

A., J. B. "A Commercial Traveler's Plea for a Better-Salaried Clergy." *The Fortnightly Review* 24, no. 1 (1917): 274.

Abbetmeyer, C. "Some Externals of Worship." *Homiletic Magazine* 42, no. 1 (1918): 44–8.

Abbot, Harriet. "What the Newest New Woman Is." In *The American New Woman Revisted: A Reader, 1894–1930*, edited by Martha H. Patterson, pp. 221–26. New Brunswick, NJ: Rutgers University Press, 2008.

"Advanced Lines of Church Activity." *Western Christian Advocate*, March 3, 1915, 16–17.

Aguilar, Grace. *The Women of Israel*. New York: D. Appleton and Company, 1888.

Ahlstrom, Sydney E. *A Religious History of the American People*, 2nd ed. New Haven, CT: Yale University Press, 2004.

"Aimee Bobs Her Hair: Followers Secede." *Lawrence Journal—World*, April 25, 1927.

"Aimee McPherson Starts Battle with Voliva for Souls." *The Deseret News*, September 6, 1929, 1.

"Aimee Sails South Lauding New York." *Boston Daily Globe*, March 4, 1927.

"Aimee Semple McPherson Dead." *Beaver County Times*, September 29, 1944, 12.

"Aimee Semple McPherson in Costume of Palestinian Woman, Which She Wore during the Recounting of Her "Journeylog." *The Bridal Call Foursquare* 10, no. 2 (1926): Coverplate.

"Aimee Semple McPherson: Thousands Mourn at Famed Evangelist's Funeral." *LIFE*, October 30, 1944, 85–89.

"Aimee to Settle Down, Hutton Says." *The Leader-Post*, June 30, 1933, 6.

"Aimee's Followers Believe She Is a Christian Martyr." *The Evening Independent*, September 20, 1926, 6.

"Aimee's Mother under Arrest." *The Morning Leader*, September 18, 1926, 1.

"Aimee's Sanity Aired in Trial." *The Windsor Daily Star*, October 29, 1937, 23.

Airhart, Phyllis D. *Serving the Present Age: Revivalism, Progressivism, and the Methodist Tradition in Canada*, Mcgill-Queen's Studies in the History of Religion. Montreal: McGill-Queen's University Press, 1992.

Alexander, Estrelda. *The Women of Azusa Street*. Cleveland, OH: Pilgrim Press, 2005.

Altschuler, Glenn C. and Jan M. Saltzgaber. *Revivalism, Social Conscience, and Community in the Burned-over District: The Trial of Rhoda Bement.* Ithaca, NY: Cornell University Press, 1983.

"American Manhood." *The Conservative*, November 1, 1900, 1.

"An Insane Female Evangelist Declares Herself in Communion with the Blessed Trinity and the Devil." *The Quebec Saturday Budget*, September 1, 1890, 10.

Anderson, Allan. *An Introduction to Pentecostalism: Global Charismatic Christianity.* New York: Cambridge University Press, 2004.

"Angelus Temple Gives Aid to Thousands of Needy: Free Dining Hall Has Also Been Opened." *The Florence Times*, March 18, 1932, 2.

Ansell, C. K. "Legitimacy." In *International Encyclopedia of the Social & Behavioral Sciences*, edited by Neil J. Smelser and Paul B. Baltes, pp. 8704–6. New York: Elsevier, 2001.

Apple, Rima D. *Perfect Motherhood: Science and Childrearing in America.* New Brunswick, NJ: Rutgers University Press, 2006.

Armour, Ellen T. and St. Susan M. Ville. *Bodily Citations: Religion and Judith Butler*, Gender, Theory, and Religion. New York: Columbia University Press, 2006.

"At Aimee McPherson's Counsel Table." *The Evening Independent*, October 8, 1926, 11.

"Atheist Fog-Bound on Way to Debate." *Berkeley Daily Gazette*, January 17, 1934, 18.

"Autopsy Ordered on Body of Evangelist." *The Evening Independent*, September 28, 1944.

"Aver They Are Cured: One Threw Her Brace Away Holy Rollers Fail to Help Blind Boy." *The Boston Globe*, August 27, 1913.

B., A. C. "The Albert Hall Revival." *The Speaker* 11 (1905): 607–8.

Bailey, Beth L. *From Front Porch to Back Seat: Courtship in Twentieth-Century America.* Baltimore, MD: Johns Hopkins University Press, 1988.

Balmer, Randall Herbert. "Matthews, Mark (Allison)." In *Encyclopedia of Evangelicalism*, edited by Randall Herbert Balmer, pp. 358–59. Waco, TX: Baylor University Press, 2004.

Barnard, Fred R. "One Picture Is Worth a Thousand Words." *Printer's Ink* 10 (1927): 114.

Barrett, J. Pressler. "Brethren, Can This Be Possible?" *The Herald of Gospel Liberty* 110, no. 48 (1918): 1139.

Barton, Frederick M. *One Hundred Revival Sermons and Outlines.* New York: Hodder and Stoughton, 1906.

———. *One Hundred Revival Sermons and Outlines.* Cleveland, OH: George H. Doran Company, 1908.

Barton, William E. "What Laymen Wish Ministers Knew." *The Expositor* 8, no. 3 (1906): 105–6.

Beale, George H. "Aimee Bride for Third Time; Weds 250 Pound Preacher." *Modesto News-Herald*, September 14, 1931.

Beardsley, Frank Grenville. *A Mighty Winner of Souls: Charles G. Finney, a Study in Evangelism.* New York: American Tract Society, 1937.

Bebbington, D. W. *The Dominance of Evangelicalism: The Age of Spurgeon and Moody,* A History of Evangelicalism. Downers Grove, IL: InterVarsity Press, 2005.

Bederman, Gail. "The Women Have Had Charge of the Church Work Long Enough": The Men and Religion Forward Movement of 1911–1912 and the Masculinization of Middle-Class Protestantism." *American Quarterly* 41 (1989): 432–65.

———. *Manliness and Civilization: A Cultural History of Gender and Race in the United States, 1880–1917,* Women in Culture and Society. Chicago, IL: University of Chicago Press, 1995.

Bell, Catherine M. *Ritual Theory, Ritual Practice.* New York: Oxford University Press, 1992.

Bendroth, Margaret. "Why Women Loved Billy Sunday: Urban Revivalism and Popular Entertainment in Early Twentieth-Century American Culture." *Religion and American Culture: A Journal of Interpretation* 14, no. 2 (2004): 251–71.

Bendroth, Margaret Lamberts. *Fundamentalism and Gender, 1875 to the Present.* New Haven, CT: Yale University Press, 1993.

Bendroth, Margaret Lamberts and Virginia Lieson Brereton. *Women and Twentieth-Century Protestantism.* Urbana, IL: University of Illinois Press, 2002.

Benert, Annette. *The Architectural Imagination of Edith Wharton: Gender, Class, and Power in the Progressive Era.* Madison, NJ: Fairleigh Dickinson University Press, 2007.

Benwell, Bethan. *Masculinity and Men's Lifestyle Magazines,* Sociological Review Monographs. Oxford: Blackwell/Sociological Review, 2003.

Best, Wallace D. *Passionately Human, No Less Divine: Religion and Culture in Black Chicago, 1915–1952.* Princeton, NJ: Princeton University Press, 2005.

Betts, Anna Freelove. *The Mother–Teacher of Religion,* The Abingdon Religious Education Texts. New York: The Abingdon Press, 1922.

Betts, Frederick William. *Billy Sunday, the Man and Method.* Boston, MA: The Murray Press, 1916.

Biederwolf, William Edward. *Evangelism: Its Justification, Its Operation, and Its Value.* New York: Fleming H. Revell Company, 1921.

"Big Missionary Gifts." *The New York Times,* October 13, 1902.

"Billy Sunday's Son Is Arrested." *The Miami News,* November 25, 1929, 3.

"Bishop Rice Wants Aimee to Be 38th Spiritual Wife." *The Pittsburgh Press,* 1930, 8.

Blackwelder, Julia Kirk. *Now Hiring: The Feminization of Work in the United States, 1900–1995,* 1st ed. College Station, TX: Texas A&M University Press, 1997.

Bloch, Ruth H. *Gender and Morality in Anglo-American Culture, 1650–1800*. Berkeley, CA: University of California Press, 2003.

Blumhofer, Edith Waldvogel. *Aimee Semple McPherson: Everybody's Sister*, Library of Religious Biography. Grand Rapids, MI: W.B. Eerdmans Publishing Company, 1993.

————. *Restoring the Faith: The Assemblies of God, Pentecostalism, and American Culture*. Urbana, IL: University of Illinois Press, 1993.

————. "'A Little Child Shall Lead Them': Child Evangelist Uldine Utley." In *The Contentious Triangle: Church, State, and University: A Festschrift in Honor of Professor George Huntston Williams*, edited by George Huntston Williams, Rodney Lawrence Petersen, and Calvin Augustine Pater, pp. 307–18. Kirksville, MO: Thomas Jefferson University Press, 1999.

————. "Women in Pentecostalism." In *Encyclopedia of Women and Religion in North America*, edited by Rosemary Skinner Keller, Rosemary Radford Ruether, and Marie Cantlon, pp. 394–406. Bloomington: Indiana University Press, 2006.

Blumhofer, Edith Waldvogel and Randall Herbert Balmer. *Modern Christian Revivals*. Urbana: University of Illinois Press, 1993.

Bolt, Christine. *The Women's Movements in the United States and Britain from the 1790s to the 1920s*. Amherst: University of Massachusetts Press, 1993.

Boskin, Joseph. *Sambo: The Rise & Demise of an American Jester*. New York: Oxford University Press, 1986.

"Boy Cured by Miracle Is Taken from Meeting." *Topeka Daily Capital*, August 12, 1915. In *Maria Woodworth-Etter: The Complete Collection of Her Life Teachings*, edited by Roberts Liardon, pp. 497–9. Tulsa, OK: Albury, 2000.

Boyarin, Daniel. "Gender." In *Critical Terms for Religious Studies*, edited by Mark C. Talor, pp. 117–35. Chicago, IL: University of Chicago Press, 1998.

Boyd, Lois A. and R. Douglas Brackenridge. *Presbyterian Women in America: Two Centuries of a Quest for Status*, 2nd ed., Contributions to the Study of Religion. Westport, CT: Greenwood Press, 1996.

Boyesen, Hjalmar Hjorth. "A Mother in Israel." *New Era Illustrated Magazine*, July 1905, 74–90.

Brekus, Catherine A. *Strangers and Pilgrims: Female Preaching in America, 1740–1845*, Gender and American Culture. Chapel Hill, NC: University of North Carolina Press, 1998.

Bridgers, Lynn. *The American Religious Experience: A Concise History*. Lanham, MD: Rowman and Littlefield Publishers, 2006.

Brightman, Edgar Sheffield. *Religious Values*. New York: The Abingdon Press, 1925.

Brooks, Keith L. *Sermon Illustrations of the Bible, Topically Arranged*. Los Angeles, CA: Bible Institute of Los Angeles, 1920.

Broughton, Len G. *The Revival of a Dead Church*. Vol. 5, The Colportage Library Chicago: The Bible Institute Colportage Association, 1900.

Brown, Charles Reynolds. *The Art of Preaching.* New York: The MacMillan Company, 1922.

Brown, Elijah. *The Real Billy Sunday: The Life and Work of Rev. William Ashley Sunday, D.D., the Baseball Evangelist.* New York: Fleming H. Revell Company, 1914.

Bryce, Viscount James. *The American Commonwealth.* Vol. 2. New York: The MacMillan Company, 1910.

Burnett, Mrs. "Mrs. Burnett Outlines Woman's Sphere." *The New York Times,* September 29, 1907.

Burnstein, Daniel Eli. *Next to Godliness: Confronting Dirt and Despair in Progressive Era New York City.* Urbana: University of Illinois Press, 2006.

Burstyn, Varda. *The Rites of Men: Manhood, Politics, and the Culture of Sport.* Toronto: University of Toronto Press, 1999.

Bushnell, Katherine Caroline. *God's Word to Women: One Hundred Bible Studies on Women's Place in the Divine Economy,* 2d ed. Oakland, CA: K.C. Bushnell, 1930.

Butler, Anthea D. *Women in the Church of God in Christ: Making a Sanctified World.* Chapel Hill: University of North Carolina Press, 2007.

Butler, J. Glentworth. *The Bible-Work.* New York: The Butler Bible-Work Company, 1892.

Butler, Judith. *Gender Trouble: Feminism and the Subversion of Identity,* Thinking Gender. New York: Routledge, 1990.

Campbell, Dan. "Aimee Apparently at End of Her Kidnaping Romance." *The Evening Independent,* September 16, 1926, 1.

———. "Aimee's Captivity Traced through Various Hotels." *The Evening Independent,* October 2, 1926, 2.

Campbell, John Bunyan. *Spirit Vitapathy; a Religious Scientific System of Health and Life for Body and Soul.* Cincinnati, OH: H. Watkin, 1891.

Carter, Tomeiko Ashford. *Virginia Broughton: The Life and Writings of a Missionary.* Knoxville: University of Tennessee Press, 2010.

"Caught Evangelist in Falsehood, Is Claim of Former Boston Pastor." *The Morning Leader,* October 12, 1926, 12.

"Centenary of Trousers Rouses an Ancient Debate." *The New York Times,* January 5, 1913.

Chafetz, Janet Saltzman. *Handbook of the Sociology of Gender,* Handbook of Sociology, Social Research. New York: Springer, 2006.

Chapman, J. Wilbur. *Revival Sermons.* New York: Fleming H. Revell Company, 1911.

Chaves, Mark. *Ordaining Women: Culture and Conflict in Religious Organizations.* Cambridge, MA: Harvard University Press, 1997.

"Cheering Throngs Hail Aimee M'pherson Here: Crowd of 30,000 Showers Pastor with Flowers as She Returns; Appreciation Expressed." *Los Angeles Times,* June 27, 1926, 1–2.

Chesser, Elizabeth Macfarlane Sloan. *Woman, Marriage, and Motherhood.* New York: Funk and Wagnalls, 1913.

Chidester, David and Edward Tabor Linenthal. *American Sacred Space, Religion in North America.* Bloomington: Indiana University Press, 1995.

Church of God (Cleveland). *The Book of Doctrines: Issued in the Interest of the Church of God.* Cleveland, TN: Church of God Publishing House, 1922.

Coats, Orville. "The Ordination of Mrs. McPherson." *Moody Bible Institute Monthly* 22, no. 9 (1922): 1026–7.

Cogan, Frances B. *All-American Girl: The Ideal of Real Womanhood in Mid-Nineteenth-Century America.* Athens: University of Georgia Press, 1989.

"Cold Fails to Halt M'Pherson Crowds." *The New York Times*, February 20, 1927.

"Colleges Must Be Modern." *The New York Times*, June 4, 1909.

Collier, Elizabeth C. "My Church." *The Bridal Call Foursquare* 8, no. 3 (1924): 28–9.

Committee on the War and Religious Outlook. *Christian Unity: Its Principles and Possibilities.* New York: Association Press, 1921.

Comstock, Sarah. *Mothercraft.* New York: Hearst's International Library, 1915.

———. "Aimee Semple Mcpherson: Prima Donna of Revivalism." *Harper's Magazine*, December 1927, 11–18.

Coontz, Stephanie. *Marriage, a History: from Obedience to Intimacy or How Love Conquered Marriage.* New York: Viking, 2005.

Cooper, William H. *The Great Revivalists in American Religion, 1740–1944: The Careers and Theology of Jonathan Edwards, Charles Finney, Dwight Moody, Billy Sunday and Aimee Semple McPherson.* Jefferson, NC: McFarland and Company, 2010.

Corlett, Mrs. L. E. "Educated Motherhood." *The Iowa Year Book of Agriculture* 11 (1910): 687–94.

Cotkin, George. *Reluctant Modernism: American Thought and Culture, 1880–1900*, Twayne's American Thought and Culture Series. New York: Twayne Publishers, 1992.

Cott, Nancy F. *The Bonds of Womanhood: "Woman's Sphere" in New England, 1780–1835*, 2nd ed. New Haven, CT: Yale University Press, 1997.

"Couldn't Awaken Hynotist's Subject: Friend Cries in Vain to the Man Dead in the Morgue That His Heart Is Beating." *New York Times*, November 10, 1909.

"CPI Inflation Calculator," edited by Bureau of Labor Statistics. Washington, DC: United States Department of Labor, 2014. http://www.bls.gov/data /inflation_calculator.htm.

Crabb, Arthur. "The Superwoman." *Good Housekeeping*, May 1922, 29–30, 193–94, 97–98, 201–2, 5.

Cram, Ralph Adams. *Church Building: A Study of the Principles of Architecture in Their Relation to the Church.* Boston, MA: Small, Maynard and Company, 1901.

"Crowds Give $70,000 to Dr. Simpson's Fund." *The New York Times*, October 10, 1904.

Curtis, Heather D. *Faith in the Great Physician: Suffering and Divine Healing in American Culture, 1860–1900*, Lived Religions. Baltimore, MA: Johns Hopkins University Press, 2007.

Curwood, James Oliver and Charles Livingston Bull. *Nomads of the North: A Story of Romance and Adventure under the Open Stars*. Garden City, NY: Doubleday, 1919.

Dane, Zenas. "Useless Knowledge." *Good Housekeeping*, March 1888, 280.

"Davidson's Life Story Reads Like Fiction." *New York Times*, May 7, 1922.

Davis, Derek and Barry Hankins. *New Religious Movements and Religious Liberty in America*, 1st ed. Waco, TX: J.M. Dawson Institute of Church-State Studies, Baylor Univerisity Press, 2002.

"The Day of God's Visitation: The Lame Walk, the Blind See, the Deaf Hear." *The Latter Rain Evangel* 5, no. 11 (1913): 2–11.

"Death Comes to the Evangelist." *The Baltimore Sun*, September 28, 1944, 1–2.

DeBerg, Betty A. *Ungodly Women: Gender and the First Wave of American Fundamentalism*. Macon, GA: Mercer University Press, 2000.

"The Decoration of Trinity Church, Boston." *The American Architect and Building News* 5, no. 178 (1879): 164–5.

"Dedication to the Memory of Aimee Semple McPherson." In *I Believe in Miracles*, Vol. 5, 81 min. USA, 1973.

DeVault, Ileen A. "'Give the Boys a Trade': Gender and Job Choice." In *Work Engendered: Toward a New History of American Labor*, edited by Ava Baron, pp. 191–216. Ithaca, NY: Cornell University Press, 1991.

Diller, Theodore. "Hypnotism in a Religious Meeting." *The Medical News* 57, no. 13 (1890): 302–4.

Diner, Steven J. *A Very Different Age: Americans of the Progressive Era*, 1st ed. New York: Hill and Wang, 1998.

Dorsett, Lyle W. *Billy Sunday and the Redemption of Urban America*, Library of Religious Biography. Grand Rapids, MI: W.B. Eerdmans, 1991.

Dowie, John Alexander. "Trance Evangelist." *Leaves of Healing* 1, no. 24 (1895): 380–1.

———. "Elijah's Restoration Messages." *Leaves of Healing* 13, no. 12 (1903): 369–79.

Dowland, Seth. "Defending Manhood: Gender, Social Order and the Rise of the Christian Right in the South." Dissertation, Duke University, 2007.

"Driven Crazy by Religion; Victims of Mrs. Woodworth's Revivals in St. Lewis." *The New York Times*, April 12, 1891. In *Maria Woodworth-Etter: The Complete Collection of Her Life Teachings*, edited by Roberts Liardon. Tulsa, OK: Albury, 2000.

Drysdale, Euphemia. "Woman and the Ministry." *The Homiletic Review* 5, no. 83 (1922): 347–53.

Dye, Nancy Schrom. "Introduction." In *Gender, Class, Race, and Reform in the Progressive Era*, edited by Noralee Frankel and Nancy Schrom Dye, pp. 1–9. University of Kentucky Press, Lexington, KY, 1991.

Ebel, Jonathan H. *Faith in the Fight: Religion and the American Soldier in the Great War*. Princeton, NJ: Princeton University Press, 2010.

Elliott, Dyan. "The Eroticized Bride of Hagiography." In *The Bride of Christ Goes to Hell: Metaphor and Embodiment in the Lives of Pious Women, 200–1500*, pp. 174–233. Philadelphia, PA: University of Philadelphia Press, 2012.

Ellis, William T. *Billy Sunday, the Man and His Message*. Philadelphia, PA: The John C. Winston Company, 1914.

England, Paula. *Theory on Gender/Feminism on Theory*, Social Institutions and Social Change. New York: A. de Gruyter, 1993.

English, P. R. Hayward and Merle N. "What the Depression Is Doing to the Cause of Religious Education." *Religious Education* 27, no. 10 (1932).

Epstein, Daniel Mark. *Sister Aimee: The Life of Aimee Semple McPherson*, 1st ed. New York: Harcourt Brace Jovanovich, 1993.

Etulain, Richard W. *Western Lives: A Biographical History of the American West*. Albuquerque: University of New Mexico Press, 2004.

"Evangelist Cool as Trial Starts." *Boston Daily Globe*, September 28, 1926, 1, 4.

"Evangelist Mrs. Woodworth: Who She Is, Where She Came Frome, and What She Is Doing at Salem." *Daily Statesman*, May 29, 1892, in *Maria Woodworth-Etter: The Complete Collection of Her Life Teachings*, edited by Roberts Liardon. Tulsa, OK: Albury, 2000.

"Evangelist to End Services Tomorrow." *The Owosso Argus-Press*, March 22, 1930, 5.

"Faith-Healing, Christian Science, and Kindred Phenomena." *The Popular Science Monthly* 43, no. 2 (1893): 270–2.

"Faithful Believe She Can Cure All Ills." *The Atlanta Journal*, April 4, 1914, in *Maria Woodworth-Etter: The Complete Collection of Her Life Teachings*, edited by Roberts Liardon. Tulsa, OK: Albury, 2000.

Fanning, R. S. "The Mystery of the Ionic Volute." *Architectural Record* 40 (1916): 288.

Farrah, James. "The Work of a Pastor." *Homiletic Review: An International Monthly Magazine of Current Religious Thought, Sermonic Literature and Discussion of Practical Issues* 63 (1912): 200–1.

Fergusson, James. *History of the Modern Styles of Architecture*, Vol 1. London: J. Murray, 1902.

"Find Second Trunk in M'pherson Case." *New York Times*, November 2, 1926.

Fischer, Gayle V. *Pantaloons and Power: Nineteenth-Century Dress Reform in the United States*. Kent, OH: Kent State University Press, 2001.

Fischer, Lucy. *Designing Women: Cinema, Art Deco, and the Female Form*, Film and Culture. New York: Columbia University Press, 2003.

Fish, Thomas. "Sister Aimee's Dutch Swan Song: A Study of the Illustrated Sermon." *Journal of Religion and Theatre* 8, no. 1 (2009): 48–70.

Fishburn, Janet Forsythe. "Walter Rauschenbusch and The 'Woman Movement': A Gender Analysis." In *Gender and the Social Gospel*, edited by Wendy J. Deichmann Edwards and Carolyn De Swarte, pp. 71–86. Urbana: University of Illinois Press, 2003.

"Five in M'Pherson Case Swear Pastor in Carmel; Cheers and Hisses Greet Evangelist as Dramatic Hearing Starts; Sharp Clashes Mark Day." *Los Angeles Times*, September 28, 1926, 2.

"For More Women Pastors." *St. Joseph News-Press*, August 30, 1923, 6.

Forman, Henry James. "New Faiths, and the Men and Women Who Follow Them." *The New York Times*, December 1, 1946, BR31.

Forney, C. H. *History of the Churches of God in the United States of North America*. Harrisburg, PA: The Churches of God Publishing House, 1914.

The Foursquare Church. "Tammy Dunahoo Accepts VP Role." Last modified February 25, 2009. http://www.foursquare.org/news/article /tammy_dunahoo_accepts_vp_role.

Frankenberg, Theodore Thomas. *Billy Sunday: His Tabernacles and Sawdust Trails*. Columbus, OH: F. J. Heer Printing, 1917.

Franzen, Trisha. *Spinsters and Lesbians: Independent Womanhood in the United States*, The Cutting Edge. New York: New York University Press, 1996.

Frodsham, Stanley. "Spiritual Life Must Precede Her Cures: Alleged Divine Healer Says That Her Successes Are due to Spirit of the Lord Working through Her." *The Indianapolis Star*, September 10, 1904.

———. "Glorious Victories of God in Dallas, Texas." *Word and Witness* 9, no. 1 (1913): 1.

Fry, Jacob. *The Pastor's Guide: Or, Rules and Notes in Pastoral Theology*. Philadelphia, PA: General Council Publication House, 1915.

Gage, P. S. "American 'Boys' Find Manhood in Untamed Wilds as Members of Forest Conservation Groups." *Christian Science Monitor*, November 23, 1933.

Gallagher, Eugene V. and W. Michael Ashcraft. *Introduction to New and Alternative Religions in America*, 5 vols. Westport, CT: Greenwood Press, 2006.

Gallagher, Sally K. *Evangelical Identity and Gendered Family Life*. New Brunswick, NJ: Rutgers University Press, 2003.

Gardella, Peter. *Innocent Ecstasy: How Christianity Gave America an Ethic of Sexual Pleasure*. New York: Oxford University Press, 1985.

Garvie, Alfred E. *The Christian Preacher*, International Theological Library. Edinburgh: T. & T. Clark, 1920.

Gedge, Karin E. *Without Benefit of Clergy: Women and the Pastoral Relationship in Nineteenth-Century American Culture*, Religion in America Series. Oxford: Oxford University Press, 2003.

George, Mark K. *Israel's Tabernacle as Social Space*, Society of Biblical Literature: Ancient Israel and Its Literature. Atlanta: Society of Biblical Literature, 2009.

Gerberding, George Henry. *The Lutheran Pastor*. Philadelphia, PA: Lutheran Publication Society, 1902.

"Get Manhood in a Week." *The San Francisco Call*, February 17, 1898, 1.

Gibbes, Emily Oliver. *The Origin of Sin, and Dotted Words in the Hebrew Bible*. New York: C.T. Dillingham, 1893.

Gifford, Orrin Philip. *Honest Debtors: Sermons and Addresses*. Philadelphia, PA: The Judson Press, 1922.

Given, Percy. "Deets Pacific Bible College." *Nazarene Messenger* 12, no. 1 (1907): 10.

Godet, F. "Women's Share in the Ministry of the Word." *The Contemporary Review* 45 (1884): 48–63.

Goff, James R. and Grant Wacker. *Portraits of a Generation: Early Pentecostal Leaders*. Fayetteville: University of Arkansas Press, 2002.

Graves, Karen. *Girls' Schooling during the Progressive Era: From Female Scholar to Domesticated Citizen*, Garland Reference Library of Social Science. New York: Garland, 1998.

Green, Steven K. *The Second Disestablishment: Church and State in Nineteenth-Century America*. New York: Oxford University Press, 2010.

Grey, James M. "What about Mrs. Aimee Semple McPherson?" *Moody Bible Institute Monthly* 22, no. 3 (1921): 648–9.

Grieveson, Lee, Esther Sonnet, and Peter Stanfield. *Mob Culture: Hidden Histories of the American Gangster Film*. New Brunswick, NJ: Rutgers University Press, 2005.

H., F. "Billy Sunday." *The New Republic* 2, no. 20 (1915): 173–5.

Handy, Robert T. *The American Religious Depression, 1925–1935*, Facet Books. Historical Series, p. 9. Philadelphia, PA: Fortress Press, 1968.

Hangen, Tona J. *Redeeming the Dial: Radio, Religion and Popular Culture in America*. Chapel Hill: University of North Carolina Press, 2002.

Haldeman, Newton Marshall. *Christian Science in the Light of Holy Scripture*. New York: F. H. Revell Company, 1909.

Hall, Newton Marshall. "The Laborer and Her Hire." *The Outlook* 123, no. 4 (1919): 133–6.

Hannan, Frederick Watson. *Evangelism*. New York: The Methodist Book Concern, 1921.

Hardy, Judge Carlos S. "Carry On." *The Bridal Call Foursquare* 10, no. 2 (1926): 9, 27.

Harrell, David Edwin. *Varieties of Southern Evangelicalism*. Macon, GA: Mercer University Press, 1981.

Harris, Kristina. "Introduction." In *Turn-of-the-Century Fashion Patterns and Tailoring Techniques*, pp. i–iv. New York: Dover Publications, 2000.

Hartley, Benjamin L. *Evangelicals at a Crossroads: Revivalism and Social Reform in Boston, 1860–1910*, 1st ed., Revisiting New England: The New Regionalism. Durham, NH: University of New Hampshire Press, 2011.

Harvey, Paul. *Freedom's Coming: Religious Culture and the Shaping of the South from the Civil War through the Civil Rights Era*. Chapel Hill: University of North Carolina Press, 2005.

"Has the Day of Miracles Past?" *Framingham Daily Tribune*, August 7, 1913, in *Maria Woodworth-Etter: The Complete Collection of Her Life Teachings*, edited by Roberts Liardon. Tulsa, OK: Albury, 2000.

Hatch, Nathan O. *The Professions in American History*. Notre Dame, IN: University of Notre Dame Press, 1988.

Hatch, Nathan O. and Mark A. Noll. *The Bible in America: Essays in Cultural History*. New York: Oxford University Press, 1982.

Hays, Sharon. *The Cultural Contradictions of Motherhood*. New Haven, CT: Yale University Press, 1996.

Haywood, G. T. "Baptized into the Body." Christian Outlook: Pentecostal Assemblies of the World, circa 1925.

Hershey, Charles B. "Wiping Off Boundary Lines." *Herald of Gospel Liberty* 102, no. 14 (1910): 270.

Heuser, Herman Joseph. *The American Ecclesiastical Review: A Monthly Publication for the Clergy* 83 (1930): 139.

Hickson, James Moore. *The Healing of Christ in His Church*. New York: E.S. Gorham, 1919.

Hirsch, Emil. "A Case with a Difference." *The Advocate* 49, no. 10 (1915): 301–2.

Hirshberg, Leonard Keene. "'That Tired Feeling' Best Cured by Physical Culture." *Evening Tribune*, September 19, 1917, 4.

Holifield, E. Brooks. *God's Ambassadors: A History of the Christian Clergy in America*, Pulpit and Pew. Grand Rapids, MI: William B. Eerdmans, 2007.

Hollywood, Amy. "Performativity, Citationality, Ritualization." *History of Religions* 42, no. 2 (2002): 93–115.

Holmes, Samuel J. *The Trend of the Race: A Study of Present Tendencies in the Biological Development of Civilized Mankind*. New York: Harcourt Brace and Company, 1921.

Hoyt, Arthur Stephen. *The Work of Preaching: A Book for the Class-Room and Study*. New York: The Macmillan Company, 1917.

Humphreys, Fisher. "Altar Call." In *Encyclopedia of Religion in the South*, edited by Charles H. Lippy, Samuel S. Hill, and Charles Reagan Wilson, pp. 50–1. Macon, GA: Mercer University Press, 2005.

"Hundreds Crowd Tent of The "Divine Healer." *Fremont Evening Tribune*, September 24, 1920. In *Maria Woodworth-Etter: The Complete Collection of Her Life Teachings*, edited by Roberts Liardon. Tulsa, OK: Albury, 2000.

Hutchison, William R. *The Modernist Impulse in American Protestantism*. Durham: Duke University Press, 1992.

"Hypnotism Did It All." *New York Times*, February 15, 1907.

"Hypnotism Is Fatal: Subject's Support Gives Way and His Head Is Crushed." *Aurora Daily Express*, May 17, 1901, 1.

"Hypnotism Not a Factor." *New York Times*, April 15, 1895.

"Hypnotism Overcame Her: Begged Husband to Keep Dead Man Away as Unable to Resist His Power." *Lewiston Morning Tribune*, April 5, 1913, 1.

"A Hypnotic Revivalist Disappears: Mrs. Maria B. Woodworth Shakes the Dust of St. Louis from Her Feet." *Chicago Tribune*, April 24, 1891, 1.

"'I Am Too Tired!' Billy Sunday Cries." *New York Times*, May 30, 1917, 1.

"Indiana State News: Happenings Throughout the State during the Past Week." *Bluffton Weekly Chronicle*, September 17, 1885, 1.

Inness, Sherrie A. "'It Is Pluck, but—Is It Sense?': Athletic Student Culture in Progressive-Era Girls' College Fiction." In *The Girl's Own: Cultural Histories of the Anglo-American Girl, 1830–1915*, edited by Claudia Nelson and Lynne Vallone, pp. 216–42. Athens: University of Georgia Press, 1994.

———. *Intimate Communities: Representation and Social Transformation in Women's College Fiction, 1895–1910.* Bowling Green, OH: Bowling Green State University Popular Press, 1995.

Ireland, Hugh. "Mother." *Liahona The Elders' Journal* 14, no. 1 (1916): 713–14.

Irons, Kendra. "Madeline Southard (1877–1967) on 'Ecclesial Suffrage'." *Methodist History* 45, no. 1 (2006): 16–29.

"Is Motherhood Crime." *The Pittsburg Press*, November 14, 1913, 28.

Jacobs, Henry Eyster. *A Summary of the Christian Faith.* Philadelphia, PA: General Council Publication House, 1905.

Jacobsen, Douglas G. *Thinking in the Spirit: Theologies of the Early Pentecostal Movement.* Bloomington: Indiana University Press, 2003.

———. *A Reader in Pentecostal Theology: Voices from the First Generation.* Bloomington: Indiana University Press, 2006.

Jernigan, Charles Brougher. *Pioneer Days of the Holiness Movement in the Southwest.* Kansas City, MO: Pentecostal Nazarene Publishing House, 1919.

"Judge Issues Warning in Temple Scrap." *Lawrence Journal-World*, April 24, 1937, 1.

Kenschaft, Lori J. *Reinventing Marriage: The Love and Work of Alice Freeman Palmer and George Herbert Palmer*, Women in American History. Urbana: University of Illinois Press, 2005.

"Keyes Drops Case Against Aimee." Telegraph-Herald, January 10, 1927, 1.

"Keyes Will Listen to Miss 'X' Story; Woman Was to Get $5,000 from Aimee M'Pherson, She States." *Telegraph-Herald*, September 13, 1926, 9.

"Kidnaped Evangelist before Jury." *Warsaw Union*, July 8, 1926, 1.

Kilde, Jeanne Halgren. *When Church Became Theatre: The Transformation of Evangelical Architecture and Worship in Nineteenth-Century America.* New York: Oxford University Press, 2002.

———. "Church Architecture and the Second Great Awakening." In *Embodying the Spirit: New Perspectives on North American Revivalism*, edited by Michael James McClymond, pp. 84–108. Baltimore, MD: Johns Hopkins University Press, 2004.

Kimball, Bruce A. *The "True Professional Ideal" in America: A History.* Cambridge, MA: Blackwell, 1992.

Kimmel, Michael S. and Amy Aronson. *Men and Masculinities: A Social, Cultural, and Historical Encyclopedia*. Santa Barbara, CA: ABC-CLIO, 2004.

King, Richard. *Orientalism and Religion: Postcolonial Theory, India and 'the Mystic East'*. New York: Routledge, 1999.

Kinne, Seeley D. "God's Deeds of Mercy and Power in Chicago." *Word and Witness* 9, no. 8 (1913): 1.

Kinser, Amber E. *Motherhood and Feminism*, Seal Studies. Berkeley, CA: Seal Press, 2010.

Kitch, Carolyn L. *The Girl on the Magazine Cover: The Origins of Visual Stereotypes in American Mass Media*. Chapel Hill: University of North Carolina Press, 2001.

Kline, Wendy. *Building a Better Race: Gender, Sexuality, and Eugenics from the Turn of the Century to the Baby Boom*. Berkeley: University of California Press, 2001.

Kollin, Susan. "The Global West: Temporality, Spatial Politics, and Literary Production." In *A Companion to the Literature and Culture of the American West*, edited by Nicolas S. Witschi, pp. 514–27. Malden, MA: Wiley-Blackwell, 2011.

Kostlevy, William. *Holy Jumpers: Evangelicals and Radicals in Progressive Era America*, Religion in America Series. New York: Oxford University Press, 2010.

Kronman, Anthony T. *Max Weber*, Jurists Profiles in Legal Theory. London: E. Arnold, 1983.

Kuzma, Kevin. "The Presence of the Past," Echo Park Historical Society. Accessed June 10, 2012. http://historicechopark.org/id37.html.

Ladd, W. M. C. "George Adam Smith and Others." *The American Friend* 6, no. 42 (1899): 996–8.

LaFleur, William. "Body." In *Critical Terms for Religious Studies*, edited by Mark C. Taylor. Chicago, IL: University of Chicago Press, 1998.

Lange, A. T. "The Glory That Excelleth." *Triumphs of Faith* 29, no. 11 (1909): 250–5.

"Large Audience Hears Evangelist on Lord's Return." *The Evening Independent*, December 5, 1928, 1.

Larkin, Clarence. *Rightly Dividing the Word*. Philadelphia, PA: Fox Chase, 1921.

Lawless, Elaine. "Not So Different a Story after All: Pentecostal Women in the Pulpit." In *Women's Leadership in Marginal Religions: Explorations Outside the Mainstream*, edited by Catherine Wessinger, pp. 41–52. Urbana, IL: University of Illinois Press, 1993.

Lawrence, Amy. *Echo and Narcissus: Women's Voices in Classical Hollywood Cinema*. Berkeley: University of California Press, 1991.

"Lawyer: Televangelist Juanita Bynum Files for Divorce." *Fox News*, September 11, 2007.

Lee, Janet. *War Girls: The First Aid Nursing Yeomanry in the First World War*. New York, NY: Manchester University Press, 2005.

Leroux, Gaston. Universal Pictures Corporation, Yale University Film Collection and American Film Institute Collection. *The Phantom of the Opera*: Universal Pictures Corp., 1925.

Lightfoot, Joseph Barber. *Leaders in the Northern Church: Sermons Preached in the Diocese of Durham*. New York: Macmillan, 1890.

Lincoln, Bruce. *Authority: Construction and Corrosion*. Chicago, IL: University of Chicago Press, 1994.

Lindley, Susan Hill. *You Have Stept out of Your Place: A History of Women and Religion in America*, 1st ed. Louisville, KY: Westminster John Knox Press, 1996.

———. "Gender and the Social Gospel Novel." In *Gender and the Social Gospel*, edited by Wendy J. Deichmann Edwards and Carolyn De Swarte Gifford, pp. 185–201. Urbana: University of Illinois Press, 2003.

Lippy, Charles H. *Do Real Men Pray?: Images of the Christian Man and Male Spirituality in White Protestant America*, 1st ed. Knoxville, TN: University of Tennessee Press, 2005.

Livingston, William Pringle. *Mary Slessor of Calabar*. New York: Hodder and Stoughton, 1916.

Lohmann, Fred. "God Visiting San Antonio with Mighty Power." *Word and Witness*, February 20, 1913, 1.

Loud, Grover Cleveland. *Evangelized America*. Freeport, NY: Books for Libraries Press, 1928.

Loveland, Anne C. and Otis B. Wheeler. *From Meetinghouse to Megachurch: A Material and Cultural History*. Columbia: University of Missouri Press, 2003.

Lowe, Margaret A. *Looking Good: College Women and Body Image, 1875–1930*, Gender Relations in the American Experience. Baltimore, MD: Johns Hopkins University Press, 2003.

Lundquist, Harold L. "Sunday School Lesson." *Farmer's Advocate*, February 4, 1938, 4.

Lyman, Albert Josiah. *The Christian Pastor in the New Age*. New York: Thomas Y. Crowell, 1909.

MacCann, Richard Dyer. *Films of the 1920s*, American Movies. Lanham, MD: Scarecrow Press, 1996.

MacDonald, J. H., William Fraser McDowell, Edward B. Crawford, Charles J. Little, John Thompson, William Edwin Tilroe, and Polemus Hamilton Swift. *The Revival: A Symposium*. Cincinnati, OH: Jennings and Graham, 1905.

MacHaffie, Barbara J. "Her Story: Women in Christian Tradition." Minneapolis, MN: Fortress Press, 2003.

Mackay, William Mackintosh. *The Woman of Tact, and Other Bible Types of Modern Women*. New York: Hodder and Stoughton, 1912.

MacRobert, Iain. *The Black Roots and White Racism of Early Pentecostalism in the USA*. New York: St. Martin's Press, 1988.

"Made Whole by Faith." *Chicago Herald*, October 20, 1887.

Maguire, Jennifer Smith. *Fit for Consumption: Sociology and the Business of Fitness*. New York: Routledge, 2008.

Main, John E. *The Booze Route; a Reform Book*. Los Angeles, CA: Commercial Printing House, 1907.

"The Malcontent Woman by a Discontented Man." *The Review of Reviews* 11 (1895): 435.

"Man Sought in McPherson Case, Reappears." *The Atlanta Constitution* May 28, 1926, 5.

Mandelker, Ira L. *Religion, Society, and Utopia in Nineteenth-Century America*. Amherst: University of Massachusetts Press, 1984.

Manhar, Nurho de. "The Sepher Ha-Zohar or Book of Light." *The Word 7*, no. 1 (1907): 185–90.

"The Manhood of Men." *The Evening Missourian*, November 6, 1917, 1.

Marsden, George M. *Fundamentalism and American Culture*, 2nd ed. New York: Oxford University Press, 2006.

Marshall, Edward. "This School Teaches Women How to Be Good Mothers." *New York Times*, June 9, 1912.

Martin, Robert Francis. *Hero of the Heartland: Billy Sunday and the Transformation of American Society, 1862–1935*. Bloomington: Indiana University Press, 2002.

Marty, Martin E. *Modern American Religion*. Chicago, IL: University of Chicago Press, 1986.

"Martyr Show Given by Mrs. M'Pherson." *New York Times*, October 3, 1926.

McClymond, Michael James. *Embodying the Spirit: New Perspectives on North American Revivalism*. Baltimore, MD: Johns Hopkins University Press, 2004.

McHugh, Kathleen Anne. *American Domesticity: From How-to Manual to Hollywood Melodrama*. New York: Oxford University Press, 1999.

McIlvaine, C. P., M. Simpson, L. Beecher, A. Barnes, J. A. Broadus, and others. *Revivals: How to Promote Them*, edited by Walter P. Doe. New York: E. B. Treat, 1895.

McLoughlin, William Gerald. *Revivals, Awakenings, and Reform: An Essay on Religion and Social Change in America, 1607–1977*, Chicago History of American Religion. Chicago: University of Chicago Press, 1978.

McPherson, Aimee Semple. *Aimee: Life Story of Aimee Semple McPherson*. Los Angeles, CA: Foursquare Publications, 1979.

———. "As a Bride Adorned: Glowing Sermon on the Glorious Second Coming of Christ." *The Bridal Call 9*, no. 9 (1926): 3.

———. "Lost and Restored: Or the Dispensation of the Holy Spirit from the Ascension of the Lord Jesus to His Coming Descension." *The Bridal Call* 1, no. 2 (1918): 1–12.

———. "The Holy Spirit: Who Is He and Why to Receive Him?" *The Bridal Call 4*, no. 6 (1920): 3.

———. "When Is He Coming." *The Bridal Call 4*, no. 6 (1920): 3.

————. "This Is That." *The Bridal Call* 2, no. 11 (1920): 1.

————. "Mamoth Divine Healing Services." *The Bridal Call Foursquare* 5, no. 3 (1921): 5–10.

————. "Bringing Back the Ark." *The Bridal Call* 5, no. 2 (1921): 3–5.

————. "The Echo Park Revival Tabernacle News." *The Bridal Call* 5, no. 11 (1922): 20.

————. "Four Mountain Peaks of Glory from the Book of Ruth." *The Bridal Call* 6, no. 5 (1922).

————. *This Is That: Personal Experiences, Sermons and Writings of Aimee Semple McPherson.* Los Angeles, CA: Echo Park Evangelistic Association, 1923.

————. "Fighting His Way to Hell." *The Bridal Call Foursquare* 8, no. 3 (1924): 2–5, 29.

————. "God's David." *The Bridal Call* 8, no. 1 (1924): 8, 27–9.

————. "The Story of My Life." *The Bridal Call Foursquare* 8, no. 10 (1925): 17–19.

————. "The Vacant Chair." *The Bridal Call Foursquare* 8, no. 10 (1925): 12–14, 21.

————. "The Story of My Life: The Story So Far." *The Bridal Call Foursquare* 9, no. 8 (1926): 21–4.

————. "Rebekah at the Well." *The Bridal Call Foursquare* 15, no. 5 (1926).

————. "Satan's Master Stroke." *The Bridal Call Foursquare* 10, no. 4 (1926): 21–5.

————. "The Conquering Host." *The Bridal Call Foursquare* 10, no. 3 (1926): 5–8, 17.

————. "My Journeylog." *The Bridal Call Foursquare* 10, no. 2 (1926): 11–19.

————. "The Temple of the Word: Dome of Revelations." *The Bridal Call Foursquare* 11, no. 3 (1927).

————. "The Year of Jubilee." *The Bridal Call Foursquare* 11, no. 4 (1927): 31–2.

————. "The Need of the Hour." *The Bridal Call Foursquare* 11, no. 3 (1927): 16–17, 31.

————. "The Holy Spirit in Old Testament Types and Shadows." *The Bridal Call Foursquare* 11, no. 2 (1927): 15–17, 30.

————. "The British Isles Call Sister." *The Bridal Call Foursquare* 12, no. 7 (1928): 30.

————. "Drops from Ye Editorial Brow." *The Bridal Call Foursquare* 12, no. 7 (1928): 3.

————. "Roberta Star Semple." *The Bridal Call Foursquare* 12, no. 4 (1928): 10.

————. "There Was an Old Woman Who Lived in a Shoe." *The Bridal Call Foursquare* 12, no. 6 (1928): 25, 30.

————. "They Have Taken My Lord Away." *The Bridal Call Foursquare* 12, no. 4 (1928).

————. "Christ, Our Spiritual Gibraltar." *The Bridal Call Foursquare* 10, no. 4 (1929): 4.

————. "The Foursquare Gospel." *The Bridal Call Foursquare* 2, no. 2 (1929).

————. "Second Coming of Christ." *The Bridal Call Foursquare* 12, no. 12 (1929): 8–11.

————. "The Song of Songs: An Exposition of the Song of Solomon by Aimee Semple McPherson." *The Bridal Call Foursquare* 8, no. 7 (1929).

————. "Drops from Ye Editorial Brow." *The Bridal Call Foursquare* 15, no. 5 (1931).

————. *This Is That: Personal Experiences, Sermons, Writings of Aimee Semple McPherson.* Los Angeles: Foursquare Publications, 1979.

————. *The Personal Testimony of Aimee Semple McPherson.* Los Angeles, CA: Heritage Department of the International Church of the Foursquare Gospel, 1998.

McWilliams, Carey. "Sunlight in My Soul." In *The Aspirin Age, 1919–1941*, edited by Isabel Leighton, ix, 491 p. New York: Simon and Schuster, 1949.

Mechling, Jay. *On My Honor: Boy Scouts and the Making of American Youth.* Chicago, IL: University of Chicago Press, 2001.

"The Medical Critic and Guide." *Journal of Sociology and Humanity* 28–29 (1930): 12.

"Megachurch Pastors Put Marriage Asunder." *Deseret News*, September 1, 2007.

"Membership Doubled in Few Months." *Pittsburgh Post-Gazette*, January 18, 1927, 36.

Merrill, Leonard. "Millions in Manhood." *Los Angeles Herald*, June 1, 1905, 1.

Meyerowitz, Joanne J. *Women Adrift: Independent Wage Earners in Chicago, 1880–1930*, Women in Culture and Society. Chicago, IL: University of Chicago Press, 1988.

Miller, Dr. Page Putnam, Jill S. Topolski, and Vernon Horn. "National Historic Landmark Nomination Form," edited by Department of the Interior National Park Service. Washington, DC: National Registor of Historic Places, 1991.

Miller, Glenn T. *Piety and Profession: American Protestant Theological Education, 1870–1970.* Grand Rapids, MI: William B. Eerdmans, 2007.

Miller, J. Corson. "A Bride of Christ." *Catholic World* 112, no. 667 (1920): 85.

Miller, Robert Moats. *Harry Emerson Fosdick: Preacher, Pastor, Prophet.* New York: Oxford University Press, 1985.

Miller-Bernal, Leslie and Susan L. Poulson. *Challenged by Coeducation: Women's Colleges since the 1960s*, 1st ed. Nashville, TN: Vanderbilt University Press, 2006.

"Minors Take Part in Holy-Roller Services." *The Topeka Daily Capitol*, August 29, 1913. In *Maria Woodworth-Etter: The Complete Collection of Her Life Teachings*, edited by Roberts Liardon. Tulsa, OK: Albury, 2000.

"Miss Couzins on Law and Women." *The New York Times*, March 27, 1894.

Mobley, Kendal P. "The Ecumenical Woman's Missionary Movement: Helen Barrett Montgomery and *the Baptist*, 1920–30." In *Gender and the Social Gospel*, edited by Wendy J. Deichmann Edwards and Carolyn De Swarte Gifford, pp. 167–81. Urbana: University of Illinois Press, 2003.

Molnar, Thomas Steven. *Authority and Its Enemies*. New Brunswick, NJ: Transaction, 1995.

Montgomery, Carrie Judd. "The Work and the Workers." *Triumphs of Faith* 10, no. 1 (1890): 19–22.

———. "The Fulness of the Spirit." *Triumphs of Faith* 49, no. 9 (1929): 198–200.

Moore, Dr. A. F. "Spirituality." *Herald of Gospel Liberty* 103, no. 27–52 (1911): 1139.

"More Hypnotism on Women." *Lewiston Morning Tribune*, 1913, 2.

Morgan, David and Sally M. Promey. "Introduction." In *The Visual Culture of American Religions*, edited by David Morgan and Sally M. Promey, pp. 1–26. Berkeley: University of California Press, 2001.

Morison, Thomas D. *The Evangelical Repository*. Philadelphia, PA: W.S. Young, 1883.

"A Mother in Israel." *Baltimore Sun*, October 19, 1909, 1.

Mothercraft: A Selection of Courses of Lectures on Infant Care Delivered under the Auspices of the National Association for the Prevention of Infant Mortality. London: National League for Physical Education and Improvement, 1916.

Mountford, Roxanne. *The Gendered Pulpit: Preaching in American Protestant Spaces*, Studies in Rhetorics and Feminisms. Carbondale: Southern Illinois University Press, 2003.

"Mrs. Aimee Hutton Home." *New York Times*, August 2, 1933.

"Mrs. Aimee McPherson, Noted Evangelist, Dead." *The Milwaukee Journal*, September 28, 1944, 14.

"Mrs. Hutton's Flock Uneasy over Control." *Chicago Tribune*, June 10, 1933, 6.

"Mrs. M'Pherson, Evangelist, Faces Probe." *Beddeford Weekly Journal*, October 1, 1926, 1,7.

Muncy, Robyn. *Creating a Female Dominion in American Reform, 1890–1935*. New York: Oxford University Press, 1991.

Murphy, Kevin P. *Political Manhood: Red Bloods, Mollycoddles, and the Politics of Progressive Era Reform*. New York: Columbia University Press, 2008.

Nadis, Fred. *Wonder Shows: Performing Science, Magic, and Religion in America*. New Brunswick, NJ: Rutgers University Press, 2005.

Neely, Bishop Thomas Benjamin. *The Minister in the Itinerant System*. New York: Fleming H. Revell Company, 1914.

Nelson, Milton O. "The Church and the Critic: A Few of the Comments from the Independent Readers on the Article by Dr. Franklin H. Giddings,

'Can the Churches Be Saved?'" *The Independent* 106, no. 3784 (1921): 153–4.

Nesbitt, Paula D. *Feminization of the Clergy in America: Occupational and Organizational Perspectives.* New York: Oxford University Press, 1997.

Neve, Juergen Ludwig. "Shall Women Preach in the Congregation? An Exegetical Treatise." *Lutheran Quarterly* 23, no. 3 (1903): 1.

"The New Woman: What She Is Saying, Thinking, and Doing." *Mansfield Daily Shield*, December 9, 1904, 14–16.

"New York Letter—By 'Stylus'." *The Christian Advocate* 75, no. 6 (1900): 24.

Niblo, Fred, Louis B. Mayer, Samuel Goldwyn, Irving G. Thalberg, Carey Wilson, Bess Meredyth, June Mathis, Cedric Gibbons, Ramon Novarro, Francis X. Bushman, May McAvoy, Betty Bronson, Clare McDowell, Lew Wallace, Metro-Goldwyn-Mayer, and Turner Entertainment Co. Collection (Library of Congress). "Ben-Hur: A Tale of the Christ." 14 film reels of 14 on 7 (ca. 129 min., 11,554 ft.). Los Angeles: Metro-Goldwyn-Mayer, 1925.

Noll, Mark A. *A History of Christianity in the United States and Canada.* Grand Rapids, MI: W.B. Eerdmans, 1992.

———. *America's God: From Jonathan Edwards to Abraham Lincoln.* New York: Oxford University Press, 2002.

"Norris Acquitted in Swift Trial." *New York Times*, January 26, 1927, 1–2.

"Norris, Amid Sobs, Tells of Killing." *New York Times*, January 22, 1927, 1, 7.

Odem, Mary E. *Delinquent Daughters: Protecting and Policing Adolescent Female Sexuality in the United States, 1885–1920*, Gender and American Culture. Chapel Hill: University of North Carolina Press, 1995.

Official Proceedings of the Grand Lodge, Free and Accepted Masons. Macon, GA: Smith and Watson, 1908.

"Ordination of Rev. George Fuller." *The Pacific Unitarian* 10, no. 1 (1901): 229–30.

"Our Own Opinion." *Public Opinion: A Comprehensive Summary of the Press throughout the World on All Important Current Topics* 39 (1905): 523.

"Paralyzed Negro Becomes Athlete: Moses Foreford Takes Treatment of Mrs. Woodworth-Etter at Revival Meeting." *The Indianapolis Star*, September 28, 1904. In *Maria Woodworth-Etter: The Complete Collection of Her Life Teachings*, edited by Roberts Liardon. Tulsa, OK: Albury, 2000.

Patterson, Martha H. *Beyond the Gibson Girl: Reimagining the American New Woman, 1895–1915.* Urbana: University of Illinois Press, 2005.

Patterson, R. M. "Revival Preaching." *The Presbyterian Banner* 88, no. 36 (1902): 12.

Pattison, Harold. *For the Work of the Ministry: For the Classroom, the Study and the Street.* Philadelphia, PL: American Baptist Publication Society, 1907.

Payne, Rodger M. *The Self and the Sacred: Conversion and Autobiography in Early American Protestantism*, 1st ed. Knoxville: University of Tennessee Press, 1998.

Peck, J. O. *The Revival and the Pastor*. New York: Cranston and Curts, 1894.

Peak, Mayme. "Mrs. McPherson Wrings Sobs from Congregation." *Boston Daily Globe*, September 20, 1926, A8.

Pegues, A. W. "The Necessity of a Trained Ministry." In *The United Negro: His Problems and His Progress*, edited by Irvine Garland Penn and John Wesley Edward Bowen, pp. 118–21. Atlanta, GA: D. E. Luther Publishing, 1902.

Penrose, Charles W. "The Death of Mrs. E. H. Cannon." *Deseret News Weekly*, February 1882, 24.

"Pentecostal Resource Page." In *The Pew Forum on Religion and Public Life*. Pew Research Center, 2006. Accessed January 1, 2014. http://www.pewforum.org/2006/10/05/pentecostal-resource-page/

Perciaccante, Marianne. *Calling Down Fire: Charles Grandison Finney and Revivalism in Jefferson Country, New York, 1800–1840*. Albany: State University of New York Press, 2003.

Petit, Jeanne D. *The Men and Women We Want: Gender, Race, and the Progressive Era Literacy Test Debate*, Gender and Race in American History. Rochester, NY: University of Rochester Press, 2010.

Petrie, W. M. Flinders. *Egypt and Israel*. New York: Society for Promoting Christian Knowlegde; E. S. Gorham etc., 1911.

Phillippi, Rosa M. "Application for Admission Lighthouse of International Foursquare Evangelism." edited by LIFE Bible College, p. 2. Echo Park—Los Angeles: Angelus Temple, 1929.

"Plan Nation-Wide Eugenics Society." *New York Times*, November 16, 1913, 1.

"Pledges for Missions." *New York Times*, October 15, 1900.

"Police Check Hoodlumism. Pentacostal [Sic] Meeting at Montwait Interrupted Many Times Last Evening." *Framingham Daily Tribune*, August 7, 1913. In *Maria Woodworth-Etter: The Complete Collection of Her Life Teachings*, edited by Roberts Liardon, pp. 497–9. Tulsa, OK: Albury, 2000.

"Political Pot-Pie." *The Seattle Republican*, January 13, 1905, 8.

Poloma, Margaret M. *The Assemblies of God at the Crossroads: Charisma and Institutional Dilemmas*, 1st ed. Knoxville: University of Tennessee Press, 1989.

Poloma, Margaret M. and John Clifford Green. *The Assemblies of God: Godly Love and the Revitalization of American Pentecostalism*. New York: New York University Press, 2010.

Pond, Irving K. *The Meaning of Architecture; an Essay in Constructive Criticism*. Boston, MA: Marshall Jones Company, 1918.

Pope-Levinson, Priscilla. "Revivalism." In *Encyclopedia of Women and Religion in North America*, edited by Rosemary Skinner Keller, Rosemary

Radford Ruether, and Marie Cantlon. Bloomington: Indiana University Press, 2006.

"Preacher Slayer Ready for Trial." *New York Times*, October 31, 1926, 1.

Prelinger, Catherine M. *Episcopal Women: Gender, Spirituality, and Commitment in an American Mainline Denomination*, Religion in America Series. New York: Oxford University Press, 1992.

Press, United. "Angelus Temple Funds Tied up by Mrs. Kennedy." *Berkeley Daily Gazette*, July 30, 1927, 1.

Price, Charles. "Letters from the Foreign Field." *Golden Grain* 1, no.3 (July 1926): 21–3.

———. "Make Me a Blessing," *Golden Grain* 10, no. 11 (1936): 15–20.

Price, Charles S. "The Opening." *The Bridal Call* 6, no. 8 (1923): 15–16.

Prosser, Anna W. "Wedding Bells." *Triumphs of Faith* 10, no. 6 (1890): 1–2.

Putney, Clifford. *Muscular Christianity: Manhood and Sports in Protestant America,* 1880–1920. Cambridge, MA: Harvard University Press, 2001.

Quale, William A. "The Gospel of Mastery." *The Advance* 51, no. 2108 (1906): 424–6.

Quarberg, Licoln. "Aimee Ordered Held over for Perjury Trial." *Berkeley Daily Gazette*, September 2, 1926, 1.

Quinn, Anthony. *The Original Sin: A Self-Portrait*, 1 ed. Boston: Little, Brown and Company, 1972.

Randolph, Elizabeth. "Young People's Work." *The Sabbath Recorder* 89, no. 1 (1920): 379–80.

"Religion: Disappearance." In *Time*, 1: Time Warner, 1926.

"Religion: Fosdick." *Time*, October 13, 1924.

"Religion: McPherson V. Voliva." *Time Magazine*, September 16, 1929.

"Religion: Return." In *Time*, 1: Time Warner, 1926.

"Religion: Sisters V. Satan." In *Time*, 1: Time Warner, 1937.

"Religion: Terror's Troth." *Time Magazine*, January 10, 1938.

Riley, William Bell. *The Perennial Revival; a Plea for Evangelism*, 2nd ed. Philadelphia, PA: American Baptist Publication Society, 1916.

———. *Revival Sermons; Essentials in Effective Evangelism*. New York: Fleming H. Revell Company, 1929.

Riley, Woodbridge. "Esoteric Cults." *The Saturday Review of Literature* 5, no. 20 (1928): 455.

Roberts, Don. "Sister Aimee and Ma." *The Pittsburg Press*, September 24, 1930, 40.

Roberts, Evan, Arthur Goodrich, G. Campbell Morgan, W. T. Stead, Evan Henry Hopkins, and E. W. Moore. *The Story of the Welsh Revival as Told by Eyewitnesses: Together with a Sketch of Evan Roberts and His Message to the World*. New York: F.H. Revell, 1905.

Roberts, Gerald. *The Strenuous Life: The Cult of Manliness in the Era of Theodore Roosevelt*. East Lansing, MI: Michigan State University Press, 1977.

Robertson, Pamela. "Feminist Camp in *Gold Diggers of 1933*." In *Hollywood Musicals, the Film Reader*, edited by Steven Cohan, pp. 129–40. New York: Routledge, 2002.

Robinson, Thomas A. and Lanette R. Ruff. *Out of the Mouths of Babes: Girl Evangelists in the Flapper Era*. New York: Oxford University Press, 2011.

Roediger, David R. *Working toward Whiteness: How America's Immigrants Became White—the Strange Journey from Ellis Island to the Suburbs*. New York: Basic Books, 2005.

"Roosevelt Boomers Issue Statement." *Reading Eagle*, February 11, 1912, 1, 5.

Rotundo, E. Anthony. *American Manhood: Transformations in Masculinity from the Revolution to the Modern Era*. New York: BasicBooks, 1993.

Runyon, Damon. *Guys and Dolls*. New York: Frederick A. Stokes, 1931.

"Said to Be Religion: Strange Scenes At 'Revival Meetings' Held in Indiana." *New York Times*, January 23, 1885, 1.

Sanders, Cheryl J. "History of Women in the Pentecostal Movement." *Cyberjournal for Pentecostal-Charismatic Research*, no. 2 (1997). Accessed January 1, 2014. http://www.fullnet.net/np/archives/cyberj/sanders.html

Schlater, Angela. "Flaming Youth: Gender in 1920s Hollywood." Loyola University, 2008.

Schmidt, Leigh Eric. *Holy Fairs: Scotland and the Making of American Revivalism*, 2nd ed. Grand Rapids, MI: W.B. Eerdmans Publishing, 2001.

Scott, Joan Wallach. *Gender and the Politics of History*, Gender and Culture. New York: Columbia University Press, 1988.

"Sea Did Not Give up Dead." *The Evening Independent*, May 24, 1924, 1.

"Sees Visions of Heaven: Strange Reports from Mrs. Woodworth's Meetings." *Chicago Daily Tribune*, December 21, 1890, 1.

Selikowitsch, G. "Flats and Sharps." *The Advocate: America's Jewish Journal* 37, no. 1 (1909): 15.

Sennett, Richard. *Authority*, 1st Vintage Books ed. New York: Vintage Books, 1981.

Seymour, William. "Behold the Bridegroom Cometh." *The Apostolic Faith* 1, no. 5 (1907): 2.

———. "The Holy Ghost and His Bride." In *The Azusa Street Revival*, edited by Roberts Liardon, pp. 129–30. Shippensburg, PA: Destiny Image Publishers, 2006.

Shaw, Anna Howard and Elizabeth Garver Jordan. *The Story of a Pioneer*, National American Woman Suffrage Association Collection. New York: Harper and Brothers, 1915.

"She Will Be Tried." *St. Louis Post-Dispatch*, September 2, 1890. In *Maria Woodworth-Etter: The Complete Collection of Her Life Teachings*, edited by Roberts Liardon. Tulsa, OK: Albury, 2000.

Sheffield, Kathryn Irene. "The Creation of Female Gender Identity on Evangelical Television: Old Wine in New Bottles," PhD dissertation, Arizona State University, ProQuest LLC, 2009.

Shepson, Bill. "More Female Senior Pastors Than Ever Before." *Foursquare*, 2010.

Shuler, Robert. *"Fighting Bob" Shuler of Los Angeles*. Indianapolis, IN: Dog Ear Publishing, 2011.

Shreve, Dr. Charles A. "A Beautiful Bride." *The Bridal Call Foursquare* 14, no. 13 (1931): 6–7.

Sibley, Frank. "Aimee Arrives for Big Revival." *Daily Boston Globe*, 1931, 1–2.

Simmons, Christina. "Modern Sexuality and the Myth of Victorian Repression." In *Passion and Power: Sexuality in History*, edited by Kathy Lee Peiss, Christina Simmons, and Robert A. Padgug, pp. 157–77. Philadelphia, PA: Temple University Press, 1989.

———. *Making Marriage Modern: Women's Sexuality from the Progressive Era to World War II*, Studies in the History of Sexuality. New York: Oxford University Press, 2009.

Simon, Yves René Marie. *A General Theory of Authority*. Notre Dame, OH: University of Notre Dame Press, 1980.

Simonsen, Janet. Interview with the author. The Foursquare Heritage Center in Los Angeles, 2008.

Simpson, A. B. "A Larger Christian Life," 1 v. New York: Christian Alliance Publishing, 1889.

———. *Wholly Sanctified*, On Cover: The Alliance Colportage Series. New York: Christian Alliance Publishing, 1890.

———. *The Holy Spirit*. New York: Christian Alliance Publishing, 1895.

"Simpson Will Explain; He Is to Address the Christian Alliance Camp Meeting, Answering Charges of Misuse of Funds." *New York Times*, August 13, 1899, 1.

Sims, Frank K. "A Model Mother and a Father Who Failed." *Expositor and Current Anecdotes* 11, no. 1 (1909): 507–9.

Sinclair, Albert Thomas. *American Gypsies*. New York: The New York Public Library, 1917.

"A Slipping Sister." *The Miami News*, May 5, 1927, 6.

Smith, Angela Marie. "Monsters in the Bed: Horror-Film Eugenics of Dracula and *Frankenstein*." In *Popular Eugenics: National Efficiency and American Mass Culture in the 1930s*, edited by Susan Currell and Christina Cogdell, pp. 332–58. Athens: Ohio University Press, 2006.

Smith, Gipsy. *Real Religion; Revival Sermons Delivered during His Twentieth Visit to America*. New York: George H. Doran Company, 1922.

Smith, Jonathan Ritchie. *The Wall and the Gates*. Philadelphia, PA: The Westminster Press, 1919.

Smith, Jonathan Z. *Drudgery Divine: On the Comparison of Early Christianities and the Religions of Late Antiquity*, Jordan Lectures in Comparative Religion 14. Chicago, IL: University of Chicago Press, 1990.

Smith-Rosenberg, Carroll. *Disorderly Conduct: Visions of Gender in Victorian America*, 1st ed. New York: A.A. Knopf, 1985.

Society, American Bible. *The Holy Bible, Containing the Old and New Testaments*. New York: American Bible Society, 1901.

Solomon, Barbara Miller. *In the Company of Educated Women: A History of Women and Higher Education in America*. New Haven, CT: Yale University Press, 1985.

"South African Question." *The New York Times*, January 4, 1904.

Squires, Judith. *Gender in Political Theory*. Malden, MA: Polity Press Blackwell Publishers, 1999.

Stanley, Susie Cunningham. *Holy Boldness: Women Preachers' Autobiographies and the Sanctified Self*, 1st ed. Knoxville: University of Tennessee Press, 2002.

Stead, W. T. *Life of Mrs. Booth, the Founder of the Salvation Army*. New York: Fleming H. Revell Company, 1900.

"Steals Men's Wits Away. Male and Female Bipeds in Frenzied Prayer. They Cry, Shout and Swing Their Arms in Air Till Exhausted. Woman Evangelist Charged with Hypnotizing Her Hearers." *Boston Daily Globe*, September 1, 1890, 1.

Stephenson, Lisa P. *Dismantling the Dualisms for American Pentecostal Women in Ministry: A Feminist-Pneumatological Approach*, Global Pentecostal and Charismatic Studies. Boston: Brill, 2012.

Sterba, James P. *Controversies in Feminism*, Studies in Social, Political, and Legal Philosophy. Lanham, MD: Rowman and Littlefield, 2001.

Sternheimer, Karen. *Celebrity Culture and the American Dream: Stardom and Social Mobility*. New York: Routledge, 2011.

Stone, Lucy, Antoinette Louisa Brown Blackwell, Carol Lasser, and Marlene Merrill. *Friends and Sisters: Letters between Lucy Stone and Antoinette Brown Blackwell, 1846–93*, Women in American History. Urbana: University of Illinois Press, 1987.

Stroh, Grant. "Women as Pastors." *Moody Bible Institute Monthly* 21, no. 1 (1920): 25.

"Student of Occult Sciences Falls Unconscious after Experiments." *New York Times*, May 20, 1908, 1.

Studlar, Gaylyn. *This Mad Masquerade: Stardom and Masculinity in the Jazz Age*, Film and Culture. New York: Columbia University Press, 1996.

Sturgis, Russell. "The Revival of Cathedral Building: Great Christian Houses of Worship Which Have Been Erected in Recent Years or Are Now in Process of Construction—Their Effectiveness and Artistic Meaning." *Munsey's Magazine*, April 1907, 186–95.

Sumner, Allene. "Prison Bars Will Not Dim Ardor of Aimee McPherson's Faithful." *Milwaukee Journal*, September 25, 1926, 1.

Sunday, Billy. *Get on the Water Wagon*: William Ashley Sunday, 1915.

———. *Easter*. Film. United States, April 8, 1917.

Sunday, Billy and William T. Ellis. *"Billy" Sunday, the Man and His Message, with His Own Words Which Have Won Thousands for Christ*, Authorized ed. Philadelphia, PA: The John C. Winston Company, 1914.

"Sure She Is Dead." *Berkeley Daily Gazette*, June 4, 1926, 2.

Sutton, Matthew Avery. *Aimee Semple McPherson and the Resurrection of Christian America*. Cambridge, MA: Harvard University Press, 2007.

Swift, Donald Charles. *Religion and the American Experience: A Social and Cultural History, 1765–1997*. Armonk, NY: M.E. Sharpe, 1998.

"Swindled by an Adventuress." *The Star*, December 24, 1904.

Synan, Vinson. *The Holiness-Pentecostal Tradition: Charismatic Movements in the Twentieth Century*, 2nd ed. Grand Rapids, MI: W.B. Eerdmans Publishing Company, 1997.

Synnott, Anthony. *Re-Thinking Men: Heroes, Villains and Victims*. Burlington, VT: Ashgate, 2009.

Szasz, Ferenc Morton. *The Divided Mind of Protestant America, 1880–1930*. University: University of Alabama Press, 1982.

"Takes Manhood to Live for Christ, Billy Sunday Says." *Boston Daily Globe*, January 20, 1917.

Taves, Ann. "The Camp Meeting and the Paradoxes of Evangelical Protestant Ritual." In *Teaching Ritual*, edited by Catherine M. Bell, pp. 119–32. New York: Oxford University Press, 2007.

Taylor, Frederick E. "The Gospel for This Age." *The Bible Magazine by Bible Teachers Training School* 1, no. 7 (1913): 509–21.

Taylor, George Floyd. *The Spirit and the Bride: A Scriptural Presentation of the Operations, Manifestations, Gifts and Fruit of the Holy Spirit in His Relation to the Bride with Special Reference to the "Latter Rain" Revival*. Dunn, NC, 1907.

Taylor, H. B. "New Testament Restrictions of Women." *Western Recorder* 85, no. 27 (1910): 1–4.

"Tells How She Got "Power." *Boston Globe*, August 30, 1913, 2.

"Texas Minister Kills Man in Church; the Rev. J. Frank Norris, Fundamentalist, Shoots Fort Worth Lumberman." *New York Times*, July 18, 1926.

Thompson, Albert E. *The Life of A. B. Simpson*. Brooklyn, NY: The Christian Alliance Publishing Company, 1920.

"Thousands Wait Many Hours for Pastor's Resurrection." *The Atlanta Constitution*, May 24, 1926, 1.

Tillett, Wilbur Fisk. "Southern Womanhood." *The Century Illustrated Monthly Magazine*, November 1891, 9–16.

"Took Her Child to See Christ, She Tells Judge." *Topeka Daily Capital*, August 13, 1915. In *Maria Woodworth-Etter: The Complete Collection of Her Life Teachings*, edited by Roberts Liardon, pp. 500–501. Tulsa, OK: Albury, 2000.

"Took No Money for Healing: Mrs. Etter Gave God Credit for Cures." *Boston Daily Globe*, August 29, 1913, 1, 4.

Torrey, R. A. *Revival Addresses*. Chicago, IL: Fleming H. Revell Company, 1903.

———. *Talks to Men about the Bible and the Christ of the Bible*. New York: F. H. Revell, 1904.

"Trance Religion." *Kokomo Dispatch*, May 28, 1885.

Trawick, Henry. *Modern Revivalism.* Nashville, TN: Barbee and Smith, 1898.

"A Tribute to Aimee Semple Mcpherson from Her Elders, Workers and Members in Honor of Her Birthday." *The Bridal Call Foursquare* 12, no. 5 (1928): 5, 31.

Tucker, Cynthia Grant. *Prophetic Sisterhood: Liberal Women Ministers of the Frontier, 1880–1930,* 1st Indiana University Press ed. Bloomington: Indiana University Press, 2000.

Tucker, Ruth and Walter L. Liefeld. *Daughters of the Church: Women and Ministry from New Testament Times to the Present.* Grand Rapids, MI: Academie Books, 1987.

"Turns on Sunday: Evangelist's Former Secretary to Reveal 'Inside Workings'." *The Daily Star,* June 15, 1915, 2.

"Two Fine Specimens of Physical Manhood." *The Deseret News,* February 13, 1900.

Tyson, W. A. *The Revival.* Nashville, TN: Cokesbury Press, 1925.

"Urges Occupation for Every Woman." *New York Times,* February 28, 1915, 1.

"U.S. Religious Landscape Survey." In *Pew Forum on Religion and Public Life.* Pew Research Center, 2007.

Vallone, Lynne. "'The True Meaning of Dirt': Putting Good and Bad Girls in Their Place(S)." In *The Girl's Own: Cultural Histories of the Anglo-American Girl, 1830–1915,* edited by Claudia Nelson and Lynne Vallone, pp. 259–84. Athens: University of Georgia Press, 1994.

Van Cleave, Nathaniel M. and Ronald D. Williams. *The Vine and the Branches: A History of the International Church of the Foursquare Gospel.* Los Angeles, CA: Foursquare Publishing, 1992.

"Very Latest." *The Clinton Age,* June 22, 1888, 1.

"Victims of Hypnotism; Religious Frenzy Inspired by an Insane Revivalist." *The New York Times,* September 1, 1890, 1.

"Visions in Trances." *Warsaw Daily Times,* May 18, 1885, 4.

Wacker, Grant. *Heaven below: Early Pentecostals and American Culture.* Cambridge, MA: Harvard University Press, 2001.

Waggoner, W. E. "Noted Wichita Journalist Reviews Revival." *The Bridal Call* 6, no. 1 (1922): 17–18.

Warner, Wayne. *The Woman Evangelist: The Life and Times of Charismatic Evangelist Maria B. Woodworth-Etter,* Vol. 8, Studies in Evangelicalism. Metuchen, NJ: Scarecrow Press, 1986.

———. *Maria Woodworth-Etter: For Such a Time as This.* Alachua, FL: Bridge-Logos, 2009.

Watson, Dr. John. *Church Folks: Being Practical Studies in Congregational Life.* New York: Doubleday, Page, 1900.

Weber, Max, Hans Heinrich Gerth, and C. Wright Mills. *From Max Weber: Essays in Sociology,* Routledge Classics in Sociology. New York: Routledge, 2009.

Wendite, Charles W. "Voodoo Priestess." *Oakland Tribune*, November 30, 1889. In Wayne Warner, *The Woman Evangelist: The Life and Times of Charismatic Evangelist Maria B. Woodworth-Etter* (Metuchen, NJ: Scarecrow Press, 1986), 79.

Wentz, Richard E. *American Religious Traditions: The Shaping of Religion in the United States*. Minneapolis: Fortress, 2003.

Wessinger, Catherine. *Women's Leadership in Marginal Religions: Explorations Outside the Mainstream*. Urbana: University of Illinois Press, 1993.

———. *Religious Institutions and Women's Leadership: New Roles Inside the Mainstream*, Studies in Comparative Religion. Columbia, SC: University of South Carolina Press, 1996.

Westerkamp, Marilyn J. *Women and Religion in Early America, 1600–1850: The Puritan and Evangelical Traditions*, Christianity and Society in the Modern World. New York: Routledge, 1999.

"What Do the People of Lewiston and Auburn Think of Sunday and His Boston Campaign." *Lewiston Evening Journal*, November 25, 1916.

Whitaker, Alma. "Aimee Semple M'pherson." *The Los Angeles Times*, June 13, 1926, 1.

White, Alma. *The New Testament Church*. Denver, CO: Pillar of Fire, 1907.

———. *The New Testament Church*. Bound Brook, NJ: The Pentecostal Union, 1912.

White, James F. *Protestant Worship: Traditions in Transition*, 1st ed. Louisville, KY: Westminster John Knox Press, 1989.

"'Who Is City's Greatest Preacher?' Here's Pen Picture of Popular One." *New York Tribune*, March 10, 1919.

Wiggin, Kate Douglas, Pickford Film Corporation, and Artcraft Pictures Corporation. *Rebecca of Sunnybrook Farm*. Los Angeles: Pickford Film Corporation Released by Artcraft Pictures Corporation, 1917. Motion Picture.

Wilcox, Alanson. *A History of the Disciples of Christ*. Cincinnati, OH: The Standard Publishing Company, 1918.

Winders, James A. *Gender, Theory, and the Canon*. Madison: University of Wisconsin Press, 1991.

Winston, Diane H. *Red-Hot and Righteous: The Urban Religion of the Salvation Army*. Cambridge, MA: Harvard University Press, 1999.

"Woman and Home." *Washington Reporter*, November 11, 1892, 3.

"Woman Pastor Found, Canada Dispatch Says; Aimee Semple McPherson Reported in Alberta by Detectives." *Miami Daily News*, June 5, 1926, 1.

"Woman's Part in Life as Dr. Adler Sees It." *New York Times*, January 13, 1913, 1.

Woodruff, Wilford. "Talks to the Sisters." *Deseret News*, February 24, 1894, 285–9.

Woodworth-Etter, M. B. *Spirit-Filled Sermons*. Indianapolis, IN: Mrs. M. B. Woodworth-Etter, 1921.

Woodworth-Etter, Maria Beulah. *Trials and Triumphs of the Evangelist Mrs. M. B. Woodworth Written by Herself.* St. Louis, MO: Mrs. M. B. Woodworth, 1885.

———. *The Life, Work, and Experience of Maria Woodworth, Evangelist, Written by Herself.* St. Louis, MO: Commercial Printing Company, 1894.

———. *Life and Experience Including Sermons and Visions of Mrs. M. B. Woodworth-Etter.* St. Louis, MO: Commercial Printing, 1904.

———. *Acts of the Holy Ghost.* Dallas, TX: John P. Worley Printing, 1912.

———. *Acts of the Holy Ghost, or the Life, Work, and Experience of Mrs. M. B. Woodworth-Etter, Evangelist.* Dallas, TX: John F. Worley Printing, 1915.

———. *Signs and Wonders.* Chicago, IL: Hammond Press, 1916.

———. *Holy Ghost Sermons by Mrs. M. B. Woodworth-Etter.* Indianapolis: Mrs. M. B. Woodworth-Etter, 1918.

———. *Spirit Filled Sermons.* Indianapolis, IN: Mrs. M. B. W. Etter, 1921.

———. *Marvels and Miracles God Wrought in the Ministry for Forty-Five Years.* Indianapolis, IN: Mrs. M. B. W. Etter, 1922.

———. *Life and Testimony of Mrs. M. B. Woodworth-Etter.* Indianapolis, IN: August Feick, 1925.

———. *Signs and Wonders.* New Kensington, PA: Whitaker House, 1997.

———. "Woman's Privilege in the Gospel." In *Marvels and Miracles God Wrought in the Ministry for Forty-Five Years.* Indianapolis, IN: Mrs. M. B. W. Etter, 1922.

———. "Woodworth-Etter Campaign in Indianapolis." *The Christian Evangel* 242, no. 308 (1918): 531–32.

Woodworth-Etter, Maria Beulah, and Roberts Liardon. *Maria Woodworth-Etter: The Complete Collection of Her Life Teachings.* Tulsa, OK: Albury, 2000.

"Woodworth-Etter Goes into a Trance." *The Indianapolis Star*, October 2, 1904. In *Maria Woodworth-Etter: The Complete Collection of Her Life Teachings*, edited by Roberts Liardon, p. 423. Tulsa, OK: Albury, 2000.

Woofter, Thomas Jackson. *Studies in Citizenship*, Vol. 23. Athens: University of Georgia School of Education, 1920.

Woosley, Louisa M. *Shall Woman Preach? Or, the Question Answered.* Caneyville, KY: Cumberland Presbyterian Church, 1891.

Young, Dinsdale T. *The Crimson Book.* New York: A. C. Armstrong and Son, 1903.

Young, William Henry. *How to Preach with Power*, 3rd ed. Athens: The How Publishing, 1909.

Index

Printed and bound in the United States of America